The Art of Losing Control

A Philosopher's Search
for Ecstatic Experience

JULES EVANS

CANONGATE

This paperback edition published in 2018 by Canongate Books

First published in Great Britain in 2017 by Canongate Books Ltd,
14 High Street, Edinburgh EH1 1TE

canongate.co.uk

1

British Library Cataloguing-in-Publication Data
A catalogue record for this book is available on request from the British Library

ISBN 978 1 78211 878 7

Typeset in Bembo by Palimpsest Book Production Ltd,
Falkirk, Stirlingshire

Printed and bound in Great Britain by Clays Ltd, St Ives plc.

To my brother, Alex,

and to Frederic Myers and Thomas Traherne,
two English ecstatics who deserve still to be in print.

Contents

Introduction:
Welcome to the Festival

I was walking along the beach beside Bamburgh Castle in Northumberland. It was a clear, bright September afternoon on one of the most beautiful stretches of coast in England. Across the water was Holy Island, where St Cuthbert had worshipped standing in the sea, and his followers had created the Lindisfarne gospels, the oldest and perhaps most beautiful book in European culture.

But I wasn't thinking about any of that. I was trying to get an internet connection. I was expecting an important email. I checked my phone again. Still nothing. I was in a tetchy mood. I'd come up there for a peaceful getaway from London, but was disturbed until the early hours by a wedding party in the hotel bar, then awakened at six by sea-gulls cackling at me from the street outside. Bloody sea-gulls. Bloody wedding party. Bloody internet. Bloody beach.

And then something changed. I started to enjoy the walk, the exertion, the feel of the wind on my face, the give of the damp sand under my boots. The rhythm of walking calmed my mind. The waves washed in, nibbled at my boots, and washed out again. A Labrador ran up and wagged hello. I looked up and noticed quite how huge the sky was. It was streaked with thin white wisps, like marble, lit up by the sun setting behind the castle, and the light was reflected in the water on the sand.

It was as if the world was exploding with fiery intelligence. It filled me with an almost painful sense of its beauty. Yet this was just one moment in one corner of Earth, more or less unnoticed, except by the handful of people walking along the beach. My heart lifted with gratitude for this planet of endless free gifts.

I set off for my hotel in a completely different mood. I felt lifted beyond the narrow anxiousness of my ordinary ego, switched into a more open, appreciative and peaceful mindset. I thought about taking a photo of the sunset and sharing it on Facebook. And then I thought, 'No, there's no need to go begging for others' likes.' Just enjoy the moment without trying to convert it into social capital. But, obviously, I *did* take a photo, and I did post it on Facebook. It got ninety-one likes!

Our basic need for transcendence

In some ways, that moment was quite ordinary. It was just one of those moments that come along now and then, when our consciousness expands beyond its usual self-obsessed anxiousness into a more peaceful, absorbed and transcendent state of mind. It can happen when we're sitting on a bus, playing with our children, reading a book, walking in the park. Something catches our attention, we become rapt, our breath deepens, and life quietly shifts from a burden to a wonder. These are the little moments when we expand beyond the ego, and they're deeply regenerative.

The writer Aldous Huxley argued that all humans have a 'deep-seated urge to self-transcendence'. He wrote: 'Always and everywhere, human beings have felt the radical inadequacy of their personal existence, the misery of being their insulated selves and not something else, something wider, something in Wordsworthian phrase "far more deeply infused".'[1] The psychologist Abraham Maslow likewise thought humans have a fundamental need for 'peak experiences' in which they go beyond the self and feel connected to something bigger than them.[2] More recently, the psychologist Mihály Csíkszentmihályi wrote of how humans all seek 'flow', by which he meant moments in which we become so absorbed in something that we lose track of time and forget ourselves.[3]

The philosopher and novelist Iris Murdoch called it 'unselfing'. She wrote: 'We are anxiety-ridden animals. Our minds are continually active, fabricating an anxious, usually self-preoccupied, often falsifying veil which partially conceals our world.' But this anxious ego-consciousness can shift through focused attention, particularly when we're absorbed by something beautiful, like a painting or a landscape. Murdoch continued: 'I am looking out of my window in an anxious and resentful state of mind, oblivious of my surroundings, brooding perhaps on some damage done to my prestige. Then suddenly I observe a hovering kestrel. In a moment everything is altered. The brooding self with its hurt vanity has disappeared. There is nothing now but kestrel.'[4]

All of us need to find ways to unself. Civilisation makes great demands of us: we must control our bodies, inhibit our impulses, manage our emotions, 'prepare a face to meet the faces that you meet'. We must play our role in the great complex web of globalised capitalism. Our egos have evolved to help us survive and compete, and they do a good job at this, by spending every second of the day scanning the horizon for opportunities and threats, like a watchman on Bamburgh Castle looking out for Vikings. But the self we construct is an exhausting place to be stuck all the time. It's isolated, cut off by walls of fear and shame, besieged by worries and ambitions, and conscious of its own smallness and impending mortality. That's why we need to let go, every now and then, or we get bored, exhausted and depressed.

From flow to ecstasy

We all have our own ways to unself, during the day and throughout the week. My former housemate had a bath-time ritual – he'd light candles, play music through a little speaker, add various oils to the water, and get into the bath for up to an hour. Others might lose themselves in a book, or gardening, or going for a walk. Playing tennis is my favourite way to forget myself – I sometimes reach a moment when the normal ego-chatter dies down, my attention becomes absorbed, and life is blissfully reduced to the area of the tennis court.

And then there are the deeper forms of ego-loss that people find in deep contemplation, or psychedelics, or during incredible sex, or in close brushes with death, or through spontaneous transcendent experiences. In profound moments of ego-loss, people feel deeply connected to something greater than them – nature, the cosmos, humanity, God – to the extent they go beyond any sense of 'I' and 'you'. In mystical literature, these deeper moments of ego-loss are known as 'ecstasy', from the ancient Greek *ekstasis*, which literally means 'standing outside' the self. Today, we think of 'ecstatic' as meaning 'very, very happy', but ego-loss can also be terrifying. As psychedelic researcher Gordon Wasson wrote: 'In common parlance ecstasy is fun. But ecstasy is not fun. Your very soul is seized and shaken until it tingles. After all, who will choose to feel undiluted awe? The unknowing vulgar abuse the word; we must recapture its full and terrifying sense.'[5] These deeper experiences are rare, but many of us have experienced them – in a survey I did in 2016, I asked respondents if they'd ever had an experience where they went beyond their ordinary self and felt connected to something bigger than them (this is my working definition of ecstasy). Eighty per cent of respondents said they had – this included Christians, atheists, agnostics, and 'spiritual but not religious' people.

As Mihály Csíkszentmihályi has shown, there is a continuum between the everyday moments of light ego-loss, which he called 'flow', and the much deeper moments of ego-loss which the mystics called 'ecstasy'. He told me: 'Flow is a kind of toned-down ecstasy, something that has some of the characteristics of ecstasy – the feeling that you're losing yourself in something larger, the sense of time disappearing – but flow happens in conditions that are usually rather mundane. It can happen washing the dishes or reading a good book or having a conversation. It's a kind of experience which culminates in ecstasy.'

Healthy and toxic transcendence

Everyone seeks ways to turn off the ego's chatter and feel a sense of connection to other people and the world. However, there are better and worse ways of reaching this state. There is healthy transcendence, which improves our life and our society, and there is toxic transcendence, which damages us and our society. Any method of letting go, however innocuous, can become problematic. We could become addicted to switching off the mind with a bottle of wine every night, or junk TV, or a spliff, or Valium, or porn, or heroin, or violence. One in four people in the UK is obese, one in twelve suffers from alcohol dependency, millions of Americans are addicted to the $10 billion opiate-painkiller industry, and we're all addicted to the internet.[6] The actor Martin Sheen, a recovering alcoholic, has said that addiction is really a misdirected search for transcendence, connection and love. Aldous Huxley called it downward transcendence – we turn off the mind, but in an unhealthy way.

How we let go, then, is a question of fundamental importance for us and for our society. Do you let go in ways that are healthy or toxic? Does our society offer us good ways of losing control, or does it offer only shallow and toxic forms of transcendence? The critic Susan Sontag warned of the 'traumatic failure of modern capitalist society . . . to satisfy the appetite for exalted self-transcending moments . . . The need of human beings to transcend "the personal" is no less profound than the need to be a person, an individual. But this society serves that need poorly.'[7]

Learning to lose control

I work at the Centre for the History of the Emotions, at Queen Mary University of London. I'm fascinated by how our inner lives are shaped by our culture and history. I wrote my first book, *Philosophy for Life: And Other Dangerous Situations*, about how Greek philosophy inspired cognitive behavioural therapy, and how it still helps many people through difficult periods of life, including me. I've spent the last few years working to revive Stoic philosophy, teaching it in schools, prisons and even a rugby club. But I decided I can no longer call myself a Stoic (despite getting a Stoic tattoo on my shoulder in a moment of rashness) because it misses a lot out.

Stoicism insists the way to flourishing is via rational self-analysis and self-control. That's often true, but not always. There is something to be said for those moments when we *lose* control, when we surrender to something greater than us, even if it means going beyond critical rationality. The Stoics had little positive to say about romantic love, or intoxication, or music, dancing and the arts in general – all of which involve moments of ecstatic surrender. Their philosophy lacks rituals, myths and festivals, which have helped humans find ecstasy over the millennia. And Stoics have never been great at community. As we'll see, one of the important functions of ecstatic experience is to connect people to one another in love. Midway through my life, I decided to go beyond Stoicism and search for the ecstatic. As an introverted, cerebral, bachelor academic, I wanted to loosen up and learn to let go. I was looking for a greater connection to other people, and also perhaps to God . . . or, at least, for some form of ego-transcendence.

Over the last four years, I've ventured way beyond my comfort zone. I attended a week-long tantra festival. I put myself through a ten-day Vipassana retreat, where we meditated for ten hours a day. I joined a charismatic Christian church for a year, and learned to speak in tongues. I went on a rock and roll pilgrimage to Memphis and Nashville, and sang gospel at the church of Al Green. I taught myself lucid dreaming, debated the reality of elves with a roomful of psychedelic scientists. I even went to a 5Rhythms ecstatic dance workshop. It's been a long, strange ride. I wanted to discover how other people find ecstasy in modern Western culture, a culture in which the traditional route – Christianity – is in decline, judging by church-attendance figures. I interviewed many people about their preferred route to ego-loss, using online surveys and through conversations with experts, including the psychologist Mihály Csíkszentmihályi; the Bishop of London; the musicians Brian Eno, David Byrne and Sister Bliss; the author Philip Pullman; and the hypnotist Derren Brown.

Western culture's problem with ecstasy

I've decided that Western culture has a problematic relationship with ecstasy, and this narrows and impoverishes our experience of reality. In 1973, the anthropologist Erika Bourguignon undertook a survey of 488 societies around the world, and found that 90 per cent of them had institutionalised rituals for achieving ego-loss.[8] Western society is very unusual in its lack of such rituals and its denigration of non-rational states of mind. That's a consequence of the Enlightenment, and the shift from an enchanted to a materialist world-view.

In an enchanted world-view, ecstasy is a connection to the spirit-world. The animist cosmos teems with nature spirits, the spirits of the dead, deities and spiritual energy. The Christian cosmos is created by God and filled with benevolent and malevolent spiritual forces. The human psyche in an enchanted cosmos is 'porous', to use the philosopher Charles Taylor's phrase – our ego is a rickety old shed in a haunted forest.[9] In an ecstatic experience, the shed is filled with spirits. We may be possessed by evil spirits, but we may also be inspired by good spirits and blessed with charismatic powers of healing, creativity or prophecy. The shaman, prophet and artist are ecstatic mediators between the tribe and the spirit-world, keeping relations cordial. Otherwise the spirit-world may destroy us with madness or environmental destruction – as the god Dionysus destroys King Pentheus in Euripides' *Bacchae*. We're not really masters of ourselves in the enchanted cosmos. We're meeting-houses for spiritual forces, and we must learn to let the right ones in.

In a materialist world-view, there are no spirits or gods out there. Ecstasy is a mental delusion. The universe is a giant lava-lamp of matter, beautiful but inanimate, ruled by mechanical laws. The human body is likewise a machine, which somehow produces consciousness in the brain. Spiritual explanations of physical or psychic phenomena are ignorant and childish. In this disenchanted world-view, ourselves are 'buffered', to use Taylor's phrase: we are walled off from other people and from nature by our self-conscious rationality. We must learn to govern ourselves and control our impulses, not to placate any supernatural beings, but rather to win the approval of the Public, the new god of the humanist universe. The Public is always observing us, and we must remain polite and self-controlled at all times, lest people think we're unreliable or crazy, and we get ridiculed or ostracised or locked up. We are – or must struggle to be – masters of ourselves. Rational control is the basis of morality, and losing control is shameful.

The demonisation of ecstasy

As Western civilisation shifted to a materialist world-view, it increasingly denigrated ecstatic experiences, and privileged rationality as the only sane and reliable form of consciousness. Dreams had been a gateway for divine messages. Now they were just side-effects of physical processes. Visions had been sacred revelations. Now they were 'idols of the brain', in the words of materialist philosopher Thomas Hobbes. From the sixteenth century on, ecstasy was increasingly labelled 'enthusiasm', which came to signify a mental illness, the product of an overheated brain or an over-active imagination.[10] Enthusiasm was the 'anti-self of the Enlightenment'.[11] It was a threat to the Enlightenment ideal of the rational, autonomous, polite and industrious self. The religious enthusiast became an object of ridicule in the works of Jonathan Swift, Henry Fielding and William Hogarth. Enthusiasm was also a threat to public order. The seventeenth-century Wars of Religion showed, supposedly, how much damage religious enthusiasm could do. The *Encyclopédie* warned that 'Fanatical superstition, born of troubled imagination, overturns empires.' To protect public order, the state should be secular and rational, and religion should be banished from the public sphere, privatised, rationalised, and drained of all ecstatic fervour. The better-educated the populace, the less likely they'd fall prey to ecstasy. 'Science', wrote the philosopher Adam Smith, 'is the great antidote to the poison of enthusiasm and superstition'.[12]

Then, in the nineteenth century, as European imperialism spread around the world, Victorian anthropologists increasingly associated ecstatic states with primitive cultures, that were considered less civilised, less rational and more superstitious and childish than Westerners.[13] To give way to ecstasy was to degenerate to their primitive level. As the sociologist Barbara Ehrenreich said: 'The essence of the Western mind, and particularly the Western male upper-class mind, was its ability to resist the contagious rhythms of the drums, to wall itself up in a fortress of ego and rationality in the seductive wildness of the world.'[14] If you let the drums seduce you and gave way to ecstasy, you'd end up like Kurtz in Conrad's *Heart of Darkness* – a depraved lunatic.

At the dawn of the twentieth century, the discipline of psychiatry tried to prove that ecstasy was a physical disease of the brain. The French psychiatrist Jean-Martin Charcot claimed ecstasy was one of the stages of 'hysteria', a degeneration of the brain that affected both men and women (but mainly women). He insisted that the ecstatics of yesteryear, from St Teresa of Ávila to Joan of Arc, were actually suffering from hysteria. This medicalisation of ecstasy was part of a broader political campaign by Charcot and his colleagues to secularise medicine and replace nuns with nurses in hospitals. Charcot wasn't able to cure many of the hysteric women at his clinic, although one patient, Jane Avril, claimed to have healed herself through dancing – she went on to become a famous dancer at the Moulin Rouge in Paris. Charcot also failed to locate the physical basis of hysteria. But over the next century Western psychiatry moved in the direction he outlined.[15] Psychiatrists were – and to a large extent still are – deeply hostile to religious experience, and tend to diagnose unusual experiences, like visions, as symptoms of neurophysical pathologies, which must be suppressed with anti-depressants and anti-psychotics.

Ecstasy, then, has been demonised over the last three centuries of Western culture. It's been attributed to the nervous temperament or weak education of women, the working-class and non-white cultures.[16] Because of our cultural suspicion of ecstasy, there is a taboo around spiritual experiences. Aldous Huxley said: 'If you have these experiences, you keep your mouth shut for fear of being told to go to a psycho-analyst'[17] – or, in our day, a psychiatrist. I've experienced this taboo myself - I had a near-death experience when I was 24, which I describe in the next chapter, but never told anyone about it, even though it was a positive and healing experience. It was too far beyond the bounds of the normal. But this fear of any states of consciousness besides the rational narrows our existence and makes an enemy of reality. Peter Berger, the sociologist of religion, wrote in 1970:

> Human life has always had a day-side and a night-side, and, inev-
> itably, because of the practical requirements of man's being in the
> world, it has always been the day-side that has received the strongest
> 'accent of reality'. But the night-side, even if exorcised, was rarely
> denied. One of the most astonishing consequences of secularisation

has been just this denial . . . [This] constitutes a profound impov-
erishment . . . human life gains the greatest part of its richness from
the capacity for ecstasy.[18]

The sixties revival of ecstasy

There have been counter-movements over the last 300 years of Western
civilisation, attempts to revalidate ecstatic experiences, but on the whole
they've taken place at the popular level. There was Methodism,
Pentecostalism and other ecstatic forms of Christianity. But they were
generally working-class movements, mocked by the intelligentsia. There
was the political ecstasy of nationalist movements, from the French
Revolution to the Nazi Third Reich, but that didn't end very well. The
rapturous mob at Nuremberg associated ecstasy in intellectuals' minds
with what Gustave Le Bon called the 'madness of crowds'. There was
the Romantic Sublime, the individual feeling overwhelmed by the arts
or nature. But this was very individualistic, rather elitist, and not hugely
transformative – in the Sublime, the Romantic is always on the verge
of losing control, but never quite does (one wouldn't want to make a
scene in the gallery).

The biggest revival came in the 1960s, when there was a sudden
explosion of ecstatic practices into mass culture. The writer Marilynne
Robinson has suggested the 1960s were a Great Awakening, comparable
to the religious revivals of the eighteenth and nineteenth centuries.[19]
As Robinson notes, the ecstasy started in black churches in America,
then spread to other Christian denominations. But the ecstatic explosion was not confined to Christianity. The philosopher Charles Taylor
suggests we are 'now living in a spiritual supernova, a kind of galloping
pluralism on the spiritual plain'. Eastern contemplative practices,
including Vipassana, yoga, tantra, Transcendental Meditation and Hare
Krishna, were brought over to the West in the 1960s and attracted
huge followings. New Age spirituality flourished through Wicca, magic,
neo-shamanism, nature-worship and human potential encounter
sessions. Psychedelic drugs became widely available. The sexual revolution encouraged people to search for the ultimate orgasm at swinger

parties and leather clubs. People sought immersive experiences at art-happenings, experimental theatre and underground cinema. Rock and roll took Pentecostal ecstasy from black churches, secularised it, and brought it to white middle-class audiences. Even sport became a means to transcendence – people turned to surfing, mountain-climbing and jogging as a way to get out of their heads. There was a widespread urge to lose control, turn off the mind, find your authentic self, seek intense experiences.

We're still feeling the effects of that supernova. It permanently changed our attitude to sex, drugs, religion, pop culture, contemplation and, through all of these, ecstasy. As a result, while religious attendance is declining, ecstatic experiences have become steadily more reported in national surveys. In 1962, 22 per cent of Americans told a Gallup poll they'd had a 'religious or mystical experience'. By 2009 the figure had grown to 49 per cent. The sixties made us more open to ecstasy – and that includes atheists. Christopher Hitchens remarked shortly before his death: 'I'm a materialist . . . yet there is something beyond the material, or not entirely consistent with it, what you could call the Numinous, the Transcendent, or at its best the Ecstatic . . . It's in certain music, landscape, certain creative work; without this we really would merely be primates.'[20]

But the sixties has something of a tarnished record in many people's minds. Baby-boomers' enthusiastic search for ecstasy led to some dark places. Seekers ended up in toxic cults. Charismatic Christianity became associated with huckster mega-churches and the intolerant politics of the religious right. Eastern gurus turned out to have clay feet. The New Age embraced all kinds of nonsense, from horoscopes to crystal skulls. LSD turned out to be less benign than its prophets had predicted – people lost their minds, ended up in psychiatric institutions. The free-love revolution climaxed in an epidemic of sexually transmitted diseases. The imperative to lose control and seek your personal high threatened to undermine the social order: violent crime rose steeply from the 1960s to the 1980s, as did divorce and single-parent families. And the world was not as radically changed as sixties utopians expected. Instead, late capitalism absorbed young people's yearning for ecstatic experiences, packaged it, and sold it back to them.

As a result of the tarnished legacy of the 1960s, Western culture today has a deeply ambivalent attitude to ecstasy. We're fascinated by ecstatic experiences, but terrified of losing our minds. We're frightened of being brainwashed and ending up in a cult. We dislike the idea of religious authority: we want ecstasy, but on our own terms, preferably without dogma, hierarchies, or long-term contracts. Can we learn to lose control safely, or is it always dangerous? To answer this, I needed to look not just to history but to the new science of ecstatic experiences.

Body, mind, culture and spirit

For much of the twentieth century, the scientific study of altered states of consciousness was 'relegated to the academic dustbin'.[21] There was very little research on ecstasy, and what there was tended to treat it as pathological or primitive. But since the sixties, and particularly in the last decade, the science of altered states has become more mainstream and accepted. There's still much we don't understand about this area of human experience, but we're learning a lot, and it's transforming our model of the psyche.

You can examine ecstasy from four levels: body, mind, culture and spirit. First, we can explain ecstasy as alterations in our neural chemistry, in our brain functioning and our autonomic nervous system. We know that giving people chemicals can trigger ecstatic experiences – a dose of the hormone oxytocin makes them feel spiritually connected to other beings, while a dose of LSD radically alters brain functioning and leads to mystical feelings of ego-loss. We know some ecstatic experiences are connected to brain disorders, like migraines and temporal lobe epilepsy. Neuroscientists have attempted to locate the precise part of the brain responsible for transcendence – the 'God spot' – but most now think ecstatic experiences are too complex and various to be attributed entirely to one neural location.[22] Many of the ecstatic experiences we'll encounter are deeply embodied – they are visceral reactions involving the brain and autonomic nervous system, which regulates breathing, circulation, digestion, the genitals, and other bodily functions. However, just because ecstatic experiences affect the brain and body, that doesn't mean they are nothing but neurochemical processes.

At the next level up, we can explore ecstasy by examining how it affects people's consciousness, and asking them to describe their experience. This is the phenomenological approach taken by William James in his 1902 classic *The Varieties of Religious Experience*, by other pioneers of psychology, like Carl Jung and James's friend Frederic Myers, and by modern researchers in the field of 'transpersonal psychology'. We can measure ecstasy using psychometric scales like the Hood Mysticism Scale or the Spiritual Transcendence Scale, which ask people to what extent they agree with statements like 'I felt connected to all things'. The phenomenological approach explores how ecstasy alters people's ordinary sense of self and takes them into altered states of consciousness. Rationality, James insisted, is just one mental state in a much wider spectrum of consciousness, including dreams, epiphanies and states of deep absorption. The everyday conscious self is a small shed in the dark forest of the subliminal mind, made up of subconscious and embodied patterns of thought, emotion and behaviour. Moments of ecstasy, according to James, Myers and Jung, are moments when the ordinary ego dissolves and the larger subliminal mind comes into consciousness.

At the third level, we can explain ecstatic experiences as socio-cultural phenomena. This was the approach taken by the sociologist Émile Durkheim, by anthropologists like Victor Turner and I. M. Lewis, and by social psychologists including Jonathan Haidt.[23] We can look at how rituals trigger ecstatic experiences in groups, and bond those groups together in what Durkheim called 'collective effervescence'. We learn how to lose control from our culture – for example, the anthropologist Tanya Luhrmann studied how people in charismatic churches learn to speak in tongues.[24] Cultural history helps us examine the rituals, forms and structures through which people have dissolved their egos over time, from acid house to jihadism, from flagellants to football hooligans. Humans are constantly improvising new scripts, new ways to lose control, and these new scripts spread virally through groups like a medieval dancing plague.

There are long and bitter academic disputes between these three ways of explaining ecstasy but the three levels interact in fascinating ways. In a Pentecostal church, for example, the ritual of worship absorbs and alters people's consciousness, which triggers deep reactions in their brains and autonomic nervous systems.

And then there is the fourth level, the spiritual level of explanation. People sometimes describe their ecstatic experiences as an encounter with some Other beyond the human. This is the level at which academic science gets embarrassed and fidgety. It's easy to dismiss this level as woo-woo, because it's difficult, if not impossible, to falsify people's accounts. But before we reject people's beliefs as nonsense, it's worth reminding ourselves of what we don't know: we don't know what consciousness is, we don't know how our consciousness is connected to other beings and to matter, we don't know if there are intelligences higher than humans, we don't know if consciousness survives death. Nor am I going to try to answer any of these questions definitively.

At the spiritual level of explanation, we can follow the lead of William James: he thought there may be a spiritual dimension (or dimensions) to reality, which humans are not usually aware of, but which we some-times connect to in moments of ecstasy. But he remained agnostic, as I will throughout this book. What we can do is honestly describe our own experience, and the experience of others: did it feel to you as if you were connecting to some spiritual entity or power? And we can look at the fruits of such experiences in our lives. Did it lead to healing, inspiration and flourishing, or was it bad for you?

Ecstasy is healing, inspiring and socially connecting

Ecstasy is very often good for us. First, ecstatic experiences can be profoundly healing. Stoic philosophy and cognitive behavioural therapy (CBT) teach that the way to heal negative emotions is to use rationality to examine and change our thoughts and beliefs. However, CBT heals only 40 to 50 per cent of cases of anxiety and depression; many find it *too* rational and cerebral. There's an alternative model of the emotions and how to change them, put forward by William James,[25] and refined by neurophysiologists such as Antonio Damasio and Stephen Porges. In James' model, emotions arise not only through thoughts, but also through gut reactions in our autonomic nervous system. In James' model, you can change your emotions not just from the top-down, using rationality, but also from the bottom-up, through the body – by altering your breath, exercising, singing or dancing, listening to music, going for a walk in nature, having sex, eating, taking intoxicants, and so on. James also taught that we can heal the psyche through non-rational states of consciousness – flow states, spiritual experiences, trances, dreams, psychedelic trips – which dissolve the rigid walls of the ordinary ego and tap into the healing power of the subliminal mind. This can liberate people from ingrained psychophysical habits, like depression, fatigue or addiction. Most cultures in the world have rituals in which people find healing through ecstatic surrender. Aristotle, despite being a rationalist, recognised that such rituals have 'an orgiastic effect on the soul' through which people 'are restored as if they had undergone a curative and purifying treatment'.[26]

Second, ecstatic experiences can be inspiring – a word that has its roots in classical and Christian ideas of spirits breathing into us. Plato insisted that artistic inspiration comes from 'divine madness', and many artists and scientists say some of their greatest inventions and creations come to them through subliminal states of consciousness, and feel like a gift from 'beyond' (although they differ in their explanations of what that 'beyond' is).

Third, ecstatic experiences are connecting. Ecstasy is the experience of bursting beyond the walls of the ego and feeling a sense of love-connection to other beings. Ecstatic rituals create the feeling of *communitas*, *agape*, goodwill or tribal unity. Secular modernity shaped us into walled-off rational selves disconnected from our subliminal mind, our bodies, each other, the natural world and (perhaps) from God. It's boring and lonely to be stuck in that rickety old shed. Émile Durkheim warned that modern Western society, lacking an outlet for 'collective effervescence', risked descending into anomie, loneliness and mental illness. His prediction proved prescient: in a 2010 survey, 35 per cent of Americans over 45 said they felt lonely much of the time; two-fifths of older people in the UK said the television was their main company; 10 per cent of British people said they don't have a single close friend; one in five said they felt unloved.[27] We need outlets for more ecstatic connection in our societies, or people turn to toxic communities, like cults, gangs and networks of addiction.

Finally, moments of ecstasy can give people a sense of meaning and hope in the face of death. We feel connected to nature, to the cosmos, and perhaps to God in some form or other, and this can give us a sense of identity beyond the 'I', and the hope that perhaps something in us survives beyond death. I'm not going to try to prove the immortality of the soul, but it's certainly the case that people emerged from Greek or Christian ecstatic cults able to 'die with a better hope', in Cicero's words. Likewise, people emerge from near-death experiences less afraid of death. Several recent trials found that psychedelics dramatically reduce depression and anxiety in the terminally ill by triggering mystical experiences. A more ecstatic society may transform our attitude to death.

The dark side of ecstasy

But it ain't all roses. There are risks to ecstasy too. When you dissolve the ego, you can be flooded with repressed aspects of the psyche – what Jung called 'the shadow'. We'll examine the difficult experiences people can have through meditation, and also through psychedelics. Spontaneous spiritual experiences also have their risks: people can become grandiose, suffer ego-inflation or convince themselves that they're the Messiah.

When we're in states of deep absorption, our critical rationality is suspended and we become highly suggestible. That can be healing if you're in a safe and nurturing environment, less so if you're in a cult. As I mentioned, the spiritual supernova of the 1960s led to a proliferation of cults, from Jonestown to the Manson Family. Daesh, or ISIS, has many of the features of a charismatic death-cult. The flipside of the ecstatic sense of togetherness is a paranoid demonisation of outsiders – the world becomes neatly divided into Us versus Them. At the extreme, the sense of a cosmic battle can lead to the dark catharsis of blood-sacrifice: the demonic outsiders become the scapegoat, whose blood will purge the body politic.

But the most common risk in our culture is that we become unhealthily obsessed with the ecstatic. Modern spirituality can become all about the peaks, the rapture, the 'God-like hours'. Spirituality can become commodified into an ecstatic experience economy - this moment of transcendence was brought to you by Red Bull. The obsession with heightened experiences can lead to an unattractive spiritual entitlement: you don't get it unless you've spoken in tongues/been to Burning Man/taken magic mushrooms. And we might never put in the hard work to turn the epiphany into durable habits. Abraham Maslow warned: 'Peak emotions may come without any growth or benefit of any kind beyond the effects of pleasure. The rapture may be very profound but contentless.'[28]

The festival of ecstasy

I've imagined the book as a festival, with each chapter as a different tent or zone. Each tent explores a different way that people find ecstasy in modern Western culture. As at a festival, in some tents you'll feel at home; others might seem a bit weird, but just go with it and see what happens. Not everyone you meet will be trustworthy but I'll try to point out the dodgy geezers. I hope the book provides a map to help people find the good stuff at the festival, while avoiding the risks.

One of the most useful ideas to keep in mind, as we navigate through the festival, is sixties psychedelic guru Timothy Leary's emphasis on 'set and setting'. 'Set' means the mindset or intention one brings to an ecstatic experience. When we journey beyond the ego, we can have euphoric or terrifying experiences, and it's important to maintain equanimity and not give way to mania or panic. At the moment, Western culture is inclined to what the religious scholar Karen Armstrong calls 'unbalanced *ekstasis*' – either we're terrified of it, as a consequence of the Enlightenment, or we're manically attached to it, as charismatic Christianity and New Age spirituality can be. We need to try to greet whatever comes our way with equanimity. The other important intention to cultivate is humility and compassion. There's a real risk, when you go beyond the normal bounds of the ego, that you succumb to pride and ego-inflation. Humility, from the Latin *humus* meaning earth, helps us to 'earth' ecstasy, in Armstrong's words, to prevent it 'from becoming selfish and self-indulgent, and give it moral direction'.[29]

The second part of Leary's 'set and setting' concerns the context in which an ecstatic experience takes place. Context has a decisive effect on the outcome of ecstatic experiences, and on whether they're healthy or toxic. We'll explore many different cultural contexts for modern ecstasy, from New Age rituals to rock festivals to charismatic churches to extremist gangs. Some communities I really immersed myself in, others I skirted at the edges of. You might say this approach is typically post-modern – a sort of spiritual bungee-jumping where one dips into traditions without ever swimming in the deep end. Maybe so. But it's not my intention to convert you to any particular religion. It's up to you to choose which tent you want to stay in.

The festival begins with spontaneous spiritual experiences. Then we look at how we can actively seek these experiences and integrate them into our life. We explore the world of ecstatic Christianity, then explore how the arts and rock and roll have become alternative 'churches for the unchurched'. Next we find ecstasy through drugs, sex and contemplation, before considering the ecstasy of war and extreme sports. In the penultimate chapter we consider how ecstatic experiences connect us to nature; and finally we explore transhumanism, and the idea that technology enables us to transcend our humanity and become gods.

Remember, I'm not suggesting Western civilisation should become a permanent festival of ecstasy. That would be dangerous escapism, not to say impractical. The ecstasy of Dionysus (the Greek god of intoxication) needs to be balanced with the rational scepticism of Socrates. Without Dionysus, Socratic rationality is arid and soulless, but without Socratic reflection and practice, Dionysiac ecstasy is just a rush. It's only through repeated practice that epiphanies become habits – the Buddhist teacher Jack Kornfield wrote: 'After the ecstasy, the laundry.'[30]

In Aldous Huxley's *Island*, one character ponders: 'Which did more for morality and rational behaviour – the Bacchic orgies or *The Republic*? The *Nicomachean Ethics* or the maenads?' To which the reply is given, 'The Greeks were much too sensible to think in terms of either-or. For them it was always not-only-but-also. Not only Plato and Aristotle, but also the maenads . . . All we've done is take a leaf out of the old Greek book.'

Now it's time to enter the festival. Let's head to the Entrance Gate, to explore spontaneous spiritual experiences.

1: The Entrance Gate

In the winter of 1958, a 17-year-old American named Barbara Alexander wandered into the tiny town of Lone Pine, California. She'd spent the night in a car with two friends, hadn't slept, and had barely eaten in days. As the sun rose over the Sierra Nevada, she left her two friends sleeping in the car by the highway, and wandered through the desert and into town. She walked through the empty streets, and then suddenly:

> the world flamed into life . . . There were no visions, no prophetic voices or visits by totemic animals, just this blazing everywhere. Something poured into me and I into it. This was not the passive beatific merger with 'the All', as promised by the Eastern mystics. It was a furious encounter with a living substance that was coming at me through all things at once . . . Nothing could contain it. Everywhere, 'inside' and out, the only condition was overflow. 'Ecstasy' would be the word for this, but only if you are willing to acknowledge that ecstasy does not occupy the same spectrum as happiness or euphoria, that it participates in the anguish of loss and can resemble an outbreak of violence.[1]

The experience – or 'encounter' as she thought of it back then – didn't burst out of nowhere. For some years, Barbara had experienced moments of dissociative absorption, when something 'peeled off the visible world, taking with it all meaning, inference, association, labels and words' and she felt plunged into 'the indivisible, elemental material out of which the entire known and agreed upon world arises'. She was also a depressed, introspective and solitary teenager, with an alcoholic father, a suicidal mother, and few friends or boyfriends. She was gripped by a search for life's meaning, torn between a reductive materialism and the Romantic mysticism of Dostoevsky and Walt Whitman.

The encounter seemed a response to her searching. But who or what had she encountered? She had no religion to make sense of it – she had come back from a Baptist summer-camp contemptuous of the 'mental degenerates' she'd met there. Her confusion and sense of loss when the moment failed to reoccur led to a half-hearted suicide attempt. And then, gradually, she grew up and joined the human race: she went to college, took a PhD in cellular immunology, got married, had kids. When lab work seemed too dry for her, she became a freelance writer and campaigner for socialism and feminism. Like others in the progressive movement, she was a committed atheist, and wrote off her teenage experience as a mental disorder, possibly even an attack of schizophrenia. But she couldn't shake off the feeling she'd betrayed her younger self.

In middle age, she experienced the 'return of the repressed'. She started to write about the history of ecstasy, first about the ecstasy of war in her 1997 book *Blood Rites: Origins and History of the Passions of War*, and then the ecstasy of dancing in her 2006 book *Dancing in the Streets: A History of Collective Joy*, both of which were big inspirations for this book. Barbara Ehrenreich, as she was called by then, was engaging with her own past through the medium of third-person cultural history. And then in 2014 she took the plunge and wrote a first-person account of her own spiritual experiences, *Living with a Wild God: A Nonbeliever's Search for the Truth about Everything*. She has decided her teenage experiences really were 'encounters' with spiritual beings, but she still isn't sure who They are, what Their purpose is, whether They even care about humans. She is worried her fellow scientific atheists will think she is insane ('when good sceptics go bad' is how leading atheist Jerry

Coyne reacted) but she insists she remains committed to rational empiricism. 'I want science to look at these odder phenomena,' she told one perplexed fellow atheist in an interview, 'and not rule out the possibility of mystical experiences. We need databases. It is unexamined, the data that might be there . . . This is going to sound totally crazy to you but this is a public health issue! When people have a shattering type of experience and never say anything about it, it is time to investigate.'[2]

The science of spontaneous spiritual experiences

In fact, such a database already exists. In an unassuming building in the Welsh town of Lampeter there is a room full of cardboard boxes, and in those boxes – like the warehouse in *Raiders of the Lost Ark* – there is a collection of 6,000 accounts of people's spiritual experiences, filed and classified for scientific research. A crowd-sourced Bible stuffed with so many revelations that some remain unread to this day – who knows what divine message has slipped down the back of the filing cabinet?

The Religious Experience Research Centre (RERC) – where this archive exists – was the brainchild of Sir Alister Hardy, a distinguished biologist who devoted the last two decades of his life to studying religious and spiritual experiences. Hardy grew up in Nottinghamshire, where as a teenager he'd experienced moments of spiritual communion with the natural world:

> There was a little lane leading off the Northampton road to Park Wood as it was called, and it was a haven for the different kinds of brown butterflies. I had never seen so many all together . . . I wandered along the banks of the river, at times almost with a feeling of ecstasy . . . Somehow, I felt the presence of something that was beyond and in a way part of all things that thrilled me – the wild flowers and indeed the insects too . . . I became so overcome with the glory of the natural scene that, for a moment or two, I fell on my knees in prayer.[3]

Hardy studied zoology at Oxford, where one of his tutors was Julian Huxley, brother of Aldous. He eventually became the Linacre chair of zoology at Oxford, the leading marine biologist of his day, with students including Richard Dawkins. Hardy always considered himself a fervent Darwinian, yet he felt that the reductive materialism which usually accompanied evolutionary biology missed out something important – the spiritual aspects of human nature, and in particular humans' ubiquitous sense of being in contact with a spiritual power, presence or energy, which guides and revitalises us. In this sense, he was more of a disciple of Alfred Russel Wallace than Charles Darwin. Wallace, who discovered natural selection at the same time as Darwin, believed in a spiritual and teleological dimension to reality that is part of the evolutionary process. But he was side-lined for his embarrassing views, and evolutionary biologists stubbornly debunked the spiritual aspects of human existence. As a result, Hardy believed, Western culture had become spiritually desiccated. Christianity was intellectually incredible, but there was no new cult to help us connect to God. People still had spontaneous spiritual experiences, but they were embarrassed to talk about them in case people thought they were mad. Hardy himself never told any colleagues, or even his family, about his spiritual experiences or his interest in the topic.

Perhaps, Hardy wondered, there could be a *science* of religious experiences, a new sort of natural theology, which would build up a sufficient evidence base to prove this was a very common aspect of human nature, one that was positive, beneficial and adaptive. 'What we have to do,' he later wrote, 'is present such a weight of objective evidence in the form of written records of these subjective spiritual feelings and of their effects on the lives of the people concerned, that the intellectual world must come to see that they are in fact as real and as influential as the forces of love.'[4] The database would be the foundation for a new 'experimental faith'.

Collecting specimens

The endeavour was inspired by the example of William James, Frederic Myers and the Society for Psychical Research, which had tried to launch the scientific study of religious and paranormal experiences in the 1890s by collecting first-person accounts and searching for common features. Hardy wondered if he could continue their work in a more systematic fashion. When he turned 60, he decided to leave behind the plankton and dedicate the rest of his life to his spiritual research. He would collect specimens of religious or spiritual experience, as Darwin and Wallace had collected specimens of fossils, birds and insects. He set up the RERC at Manchester College in Oxford, then set out nets to collect the specimens, via a series of announcements in newspapers. He posed what's become known as 'the Hardy Question': 'Have you ever been aware of or influenced by a presence of power, whether you call it God or not, which is different from your everyday self?'

The specimens began to flood in, numbering around 4,000 within ten years. But how to classify them all? A good science of spiritual experiences needs a reliable taxonomy – one needs to be able to categorise and classify the specimens, like Linnaeus classifying the natural world into kingdoms, classes, orders, genera and species. Without a good taxonomy, you simply have a jumble of anomalous experiences – less like the Natural History Museum, more like a seventeenth-century cabinet of wonders. And yet religious experiences proved hard to pin down. Hardy initially tried to classify experiences according to a dozen categories (visual, auditory, sensory and so on) but the taxonomy rapidly spiralled out of control, with more and more categories being added. The 18th entry in the database is classified by the following labels: 'Visions nitrous oxide dentists movement tunnels light karma beard Paul reincarnation Jesus Christ brain'. As the decades progressed, the RERC classification system grew even more complicated. A recent entry is classified: 'Presence of Deceased Relative. Tears. Noises. Ghost. Apparition. Dreams. Guidance. Automatic Writing. Healing. Father. Voice. Hymns. Book. David Cameron.' Even the numerical classification for the online database goes haywire: it goes from one to 2,000, then jumps to three million, then back to 4,000. Many of the entries are also blank – revelations apparently so ineffable they were beyond words.

Bertrand Russell, who himself had a mystical experience shortly before the First World War, thought that one of the arguments mystics had in their favour was the apparent unanimity of their experiences. They seemed to point to a common core experience. But what conclusions can one draw if the specimens one collects are incredibly varied, from psychic experiences to UFO abductions to encounters with evil spirits to celestial visions on the dentist's chair? Is there something in the nature of ecstasy that resists rational classification?

Spiritual experiences are becoming more common

One conclusion we can draw, at least, is that such experiences are common, and apparently becoming more so. In 1978, 36 per cent of respondents to a RERC survey said they'd experienced 'a presence or power, whether you call it God or not, different from your ordinary self'. In 1987, the figure had risen to 48 per cent. In 2000, more than 75 per cent of respondents to a UK survey conducted by RERC director David Hay said they were 'aware of a spiritual dimension to their experience'. In the US, spiritual experiences are also apparently becoming more frequent – in 1962, when Gallup asked Americans if they'd 'ever had a religious or mystical experience', 22 per cent said yes. That figure rose to 33 per cent by 1994, and 49 per cent in 2009. I carried out my own online spiritual experiences survey in 2016, sending it out through my website and newsletter.[5] I asked people if they had 'ever had an experience where you went beyond your ordinary sense of self and felt connected to something bigger than you'. I received 309 responses to the survey from a cross-section of Christians, atheists, agnostics and those who describe themselves as 'spiritual but not religious' that is roughly equivalent to national demographics. A surprising 84 per cent of people said they had; 46 per cent had had less than ten such experiences in their lives, while 37 per cent had them quite often.

Spiritual experiences seem to happen all through life, but particularly in childhood and adolescence. They are slightly more common in women than in men and, interestingly, more common in 'spiritual but not religious' than in the religiously affiliated. This may be because some Christian denominations, like Baptists, are suspicious of putting too much emphasis on spiritual experiences, although this is not the case with Methodists, Pentecostalists and other charismatic Christians. Atheists are the least likely to report such experiences: 43 per cent of atheists in my survey said they'd never had a spiritual experience, although that still means the majority of atheists had had one or more. William James thought such experiences mainly happened to people on their own. In fact, 63 per cent of respondents said they'd had spiritual experiences with others.

Why are spiritual experiences becoming more common? As I argued in the introduction, I think it's a consequence of the sixties counter-culture and the explosion of interest in ecstatic experiences, which has lessened the taboo around discussing them. When David Hay undertook his first survey in 1976, 40 per cent of people said they had never told anyone about their spiritual experience, out of fear of being thought mad.[6] In my survey, 75 per cent of respondents agreed that there was still a taboo against talking about such experiences in Western society. However, 70 per cent said they had told a few other people about them. So, although it's still deemed a bit weird and taboo to talk about spiritual experiences, particularly if you claim an encounter with a spiritual being, we're becoming more prepared to admit to them.

Spiritual experiences may also be becoming more common because we increasingly *expect* to have them, due to the expansion of higher education since the 1960s. Hay's surveys found spiritual experiences occur more often to the university-educated than those who leave education at 16 or 18. This suggests the importance of education, particularly arts education, in establishing cultural expectations of epiphany. We are primed for them through our reading of Romantics, like Wordsworth, Whitman, Tolstoy, Kerouac and others.

Although the RERC database houses an initially bewildering variety of specimens, and my own survey also brought in a rich and exotic haul, one can identify three spontaneous experiences that seem to occur quite often in a similar form:

1) epiphanies of connection and oneness
2) a surrender to God when at a particularly low ebb
3) near-death experiences

7

Epiphanies of connection and oneness

One evening in the winter of 1969, the author Philip Pullman had a transcendent experience on London's Charing Cross Road. He told me:

> Somewhere in the Middle East, some Palestinian activists had hijacked a plane and it was sitting on a runway surrounded by police, soldiers, fire engines, and so forth. I saw a photo of it on the front page of the *Evening Standard*, and then I walked past a busker who was surrounded by a circle of listeners, and I saw a sort of parallel. From then on for the rest of the journey [from Charing Cross to Barnes] I kept seeing things doubled: a thing and then another thing that was very like it. I was in a state of intense intellectual excitement throughout the whole journey. I thought it was a true picture of what the universe was like: a place not of isolated units of indifference, empty of meaning, but a place where everything was connected by similarities and correspondences and echoes. I was very interested at the time in such things as Frances Yates's books about Hermeticism and Giordano Bruno. I think I was living in an imaginative world of Renaissance magic. In a way, what happened was not surprising, exactly: more the sort of thing that was only to be expected. What I think now is that my consciousness was temporarily altered (certainly not by drugs, but maybe by poetry) so that I was able to see things that are normally beyond the range of visible light, or routine everyday perception.

Pullman has rarely discussed the experience, although it left him with a conviction that the universe is 'alive, conscious and full of purpose'. He told me: 'Everything I've written, even the lightest and simplest things, has been an attempt to bear witness to the truth of that statement.' Most famously, the experience informed the world of his *Dark Materials* trilogy, in which an animist cosmos is filled with conscious particles of dust.

Many of us have also had spontaneous experiences in which we have a sudden blissful and quasi-mystical sense of the oneness of all things. When I asked people to describe their spiritual experiences, the most common word they used was 'connection', and similar words like 'unity', 'at one', 'merging', 'dissolving' – such words appeared in 37 per cent of survey respondents' descriptions. This tallies with what Dr Cheryl Hunt, editor of the *Journal for the Study of Spirituality*, told me: 'Connection is the word people use most often to describe such experiences.' Connection to what? Lots of things. People reported feeling connected to nature, to humanity, to all beings, to a loved one, to a group of people, to an animal, to the cosmos, angels, the Logos, the Holy Spirit, God, to the interdependence of all things. Atheists and theists reported similar moments of deep connection; they just interpreted them differently.

Here, for example, is one report of a connection to nature and the cosmos:

> It was in a park, recently. A windy day, and I cut through these magical woods en route, and passed a natural pond, which was absolutely alive. The wind was in such a direction that it was inspiring all kinds of amazing patterns in the pond. I was mesmerised looking at this and felt in a trance. I imagined diving into this mystery. I felt part of the pond, the wind, the patterns, my thoughts and feelings, the trees, wildlife, and was laughing out in joy.

Here's another moment of nature-connection: 'Standing on the tip of a mountain, watching the snow fall and suddenly feeling a strange sense of expansion and contraction where I became aware of an underlying "sameness" between me, the snow and the mountain.'

People also report moments of ecstatic connection in cities: 'I was in Bangkok surrounded by strange sounds and smells. Bells were ringing. It was quite hot, I was in a rickshaw. Momentarily I felt as though my own spirit had left my body and I became part of everything.' T. S. Eliot wrote in *Four Quartets* of how 'the intersection of the timeless moment/ Is England and nowhere never and always' – a particular time and place suddenly seems flooded with the eternal. The most unlikely times and places can be intersections, as in this account from the RERC database:

> Vauxhall Station on a murky November Saturday evening is not the setting one would choose for a revelation of God! ... The third-class compartment was full ... For a few seconds only (I suppose) the whole compartment was filled with light ... I felt caught up into some tremendous sense of being within a loving, triumphant and shining purpose ... A most curious but overwhelming sense possessed me and filled me with ecstasy. I felt that all was well for mankind ... All men were shining and glorious beings who in the end would enter incredible joy.[7]

In these moments, we feel we have transcended time and space. We also transcend the fretful ego and feel a love-connection between ourselves and other beings. One survey respondent writes: 'On public transport, surrounded by people I have no connection with, I suddenly get an overwhelming feeling of love for them all.' The love-connection can be with humans or non-humans – a recent moment of ecstasy for Barbara Ehrenreich came when she was kayaking in a bay and was surrounded by dolphins. The rationalist philosopher Bertrand Russell wrote of one moment of 'mystical illumination' he experienced when 'I felt that I knew the inmost thoughts of everybody that I met in the street, and though this was, no doubt, a delusion, I did in actual fact find myself in far closer touch than previously with all my friends, and many of my acquaintances.'[8] Those five minutes, he said, turned him from an imperialist into a pacifist.

Moments of surrender in life-crises

The second most common type of spontaneous spiritual experience is a moment of surrender in a life-crisis. People find themselves at a low ebb, they feel powerless and helpless, and they give up, surrender to God/the cosmos/a higher power. They then often report a sense of healing power, or grace, which enables them to continue with life and sometimes radically improves their situation. They're not so much 'peak experiences' as 'trough experiences'. Here's one such account from the RERC:

During my late 20s and early 30s I had a good deal of depression. I felt shut up in a cocoon of complete isolation and could not get in touch with anyone . . . things came to such a pass and I was so tired of fighting that I said one day, 'I can do no more. Let nature, or whatever is behind the universe, look after me now.' Within a few days I passed from a hell to a heaven. It was as if the cocoon had burst and my eyes were opened and I saw. Everything was alive and God was present in all things . . . Psychologically, and for my own peace of mind, the effect has been of the greatest importance.

Here is the dramatic moment of grace experienced by Bill Wilson, founder of Alcoholics Anonymous, when he hit rock-bottom in his struggle to give up booze:

All at once I found myself crying out, 'If there is a God, let Him show himself! I am ready to do anything, anything!' Suddenly the room lit up with a great white light. I was caught up in an ecstasy which there are no words to describe. It seemed to me in my mind's eye that I was on a mountain and that a wind not of air but of spirit was blowing. And then it burst upon me that I was a free man. Slowly the ecstasy subsided. I lay there on the bed, but now for a time I was in another world, a new world of conscious-ness . . . and I thought to myself, 'So this is the God of the preachers!' A great peace stole over me.[9]

William James, in *Varieties of Religious Experience*, noted that such moments of surrender can be profoundly healing. They're the precise opposite of the self-help attitude of Stoicism and CBT. You're not relying on your self, you're surrendering to some Other. 'Give up the feeling of responsibility,' James wrote, 'let go your hold, resign the care of your destiny to higher powers, be genuinely indifferent as to what becomes of it all, and you will find not only that you gain a perfect inward relief, but often also, in addition, the particular goods you sincerely thought you were renouncing.' But what are we surrendering to? James was ambivalent. One may be surrendering to a genuine 'higher power', or it may be a healing power in the subliminal mind, which we access via a sort of self-hypnosis. 'If the grace of God miraculously operates,' he wrote, 'it probably operates through the subliminal door.'

Either way, it works for a lot of people, as the success of Alcoholics Anonymous and other 12-step programmes shows. Several AA attendees I've spoken to say the 'surrender to a Higher Power' aspect of the programme was very helpful for them, even if they weren't sure what they were surrendering to. However, AA doesn't work for everyone: AA says 33 per cent of participants are still abstinent after a decade, while other reports suggest only 5 to 10 per cent stay sober.

Near-death experiences

Finally, the third most common type of spontaneous spiritual experience is the near-death experience. I had one of these myself, back in 2001, when I'd been suffering from post-traumatic stress disorder (PTSD) for five years, following a terrifying trip on LSD when I was 18. For 5 awful years, I had been beset by panic attacks, mood swings, depression and social phobia, which made me deeply ashamed and crippled my ability to connect to others. I felt dissociated, a stranger to myself, and had no idea if I would ever get better.

My family and I were on our annual skiing holiday in Norway, where my great-great-grandfather had built a hut in the woods. On the first morning, we decided to go down the black slope on the mountain opposite our hut. At the steepest part of the slope, I crashed through the fence on the side of the mountain, fell 30 feet or so, broke my femur and back, and knocked myself unconscious. I woke up and was bathed in a warm white light. It felt like the white light was conscious, that it was a separate being that loved me, but also that it was the deepest part of my nature, and of all our natures. It was incredibly peaceful to rest in the unconditional love of this white light, like coming home after long wandering. I felt released from all the anxiety and fear I had been carrying around for the last five years – the fear that my brain was broken and I was destined to be miserable, the need to prove myself to others. It seemed to me that there

12

is something within us far bigger than the ego, and this 'something' – this luminous loving-wisdom – can never be entirely lost, not even in death. I still don't know what it was exactly that I encountered – whether it was my soul, or God, or just a bang on the head. But I do know that this brief experience was fundamental to my recovery from PTSD. It gave me the insight that what was causing my suffering was not burned-out neural transmitters but my own beliefs, which I could change. I felt rejuvenated, reconnected to my deepest self, able to open up and trust other people. I never told anyone what had happened, because it was so beyond my normal frame of reference. But I've always felt grateful to whatever it was that I encountered, and it permanently changed my attitude to death.

The scientific study of near-death experience (NDE) began in the late-nineteenth century, and took off in the 1970s with the publication of scientist Raymond Moody's bestseller, *Life After Life*. NDE research is now a well-established academic field, with several research teams around the world.[10] Thanks to better cardiac resuscitation methods, more and more people survive cardiac arrests, and roughly five per cent of survivors report some sort of NDE. In a few cases, survivors have out-of-body experiences during surgery and are able to report many details of the operating procedure. People often report quite similar NDEs, and researchers have built up a model of typical features: an NDE is rated 'shallow' or 'deep' according to how many of these features it has (my own NDE rates a shallow four, rather gallingly). The typical characteristics include:

- an out-of-body experience, seeing the body left behind
- moving through darkness, often described as a tunnel
- going into a light
- meeting deceased relatives
- an encounter with a 'being of light' often identified as God, accompanied by feelings of peace, joy, bliss
- a life-review
- visions of celestial lands, often seen as a garden
- a barrier or border

- a decision whether to go on or go back, sometimes made by the NDE-er, sometimes made for them
- return into the body
- life-changes such as increased openness and spirituality

If NDEs are genuine journeys to another dimension, you'd expect them to be similar in all times and places, but are they? Gregory Shushan, a cultural historian at the University of Oxford, has compared contemporary NDE accounts from around the world with historical accounts of NDEs from the religious literature of India, China, Egypt and Mesopotamia, and found marked similarities – leaving the body, rising into a light, meeting spirits, a life-review, the return. We see similar accounts in classical literature (Plato's myth of Er is a famous account, as is Cicero's *Dream of Scipio*) and in Christian accounts, although medieval Christians tended to report seeing Hell populated by corrupt priests. Shushan speculates that various cultures' conception of the afterlife may have sprung from a core NDE experience, with cultural dogma then added to survivors' accounts.[11]

There are some cultural differences in people's accounts, however. Some Western accounts report meeting Jesus, particularly in evangelical Christian books, while Indian NDE-ers are more likely to meet Yama, god of death. Indians are also more likely to say they were sent back to their body not because they had a mission to complete, but because of a bureaucratic error. In general the similarities are more marked than the differences. This is one reason that evangelical Christianity, having become briefly enraptured by 'heaven-tourism' accounts, like *Heaven Is Real* and the recently debunked *The Boy Who Came Back from Heaven,* now distances itself from NDE research. In 2015, a leading evangelical bookstore stopped selling heaven-tourism books,[12] because most NDE accounts do not fit with traditional Christian accounts of the afterlife: the physical body is not resurrected, the soul goes to Heaven immediately rather than at the Last Judgment, the soul doesn't necessarily meet Jesus, and it doesn't apparently matter if you're Christian or not. And most NDE survivors come back *less* religious, less likely to identify with a particular religion and less likely to go to church.

Are NDEs epiphenomena caused by physiological processes, or glimpses of another dimension? The evidence is not decisive either way. Some researchers have tried to prove consciousness leaves the body by hiding a sign in the top corner of an operating theatre to see if any NDE survivors happen to catch a glimpse of it on their way to Heaven. None has. Sceptics have put forward materialist explanations for NDEs: they are the last fireworks show of a brain shutting down from oxygen-starvation; the tunnel is the visual processing system atrophying; the loving white light and gathered spirits of loved ones are the ego trying to console itself in the face of its annihilation. If that is the case, if the brain is capable of putting on such a vivid, coherent and consoling virtual-reality show while going offline, all I can say is 'Well played, brain.' The alternative to the brain-restricted theory of consciousness is that the mind is not confined to the brain, the brain instead acts as a sort of filter or radio-receiver, and consciousness survives and expands after the brain dies. Ecstasy, then, is a glimpse of a vaster consciousness that our sense of self emerges from and returns to. That is what Myers, James and Huxley believed. It was what I felt during my NDE. But you'd need some pretty solid evidence to overturn the brain-restricted theory of consciousness, such as strong proof of telepathy, or remembrance of past lives, or messages from beyond the grave. Myers, James and colleagues began to collect such evidence in their work for the Society for Psychical Research, which attracted some of the best minds of the day, including Marie Curie and the philosopher Henri Bergson. Unfortunately, para-psychology does not have the prestige it had in James and Myers's day. Today, it is often written off as a respectable object of enquiry by the guardians of science and it struggles to attract funding, which is a pity, considering there's plenty we don't yet understand about the nature of consciousness.[13]

The fruits and risks of spontaneous spiritual experiences

What are the fruits of spontaneous spiritual experiences? In all three cases – the moments of connection, the moments of surrender, and near-death experiences – people typically report positive benefits to their mental health. They find such moments healing, connecting and inspiring. People responding to my survey said they felt their spiritual experiences had made them feel more 'at home in the universe'; they felt more connection and empathy to other beings, and also more love for themselves. Spontaneous spiritual experiences also make people more open: they 'made me open to other ways of looking at things', they 'made me less sceptical, less quick to judge, more compassionate'. They made some people feel that we are not 'just' our brains, bodies or egos, and perhaps something in us survives after death. One of the most common emotional changes from NDEs is that people come back less afraid of death because they think death is not the end.

For some people, including me, spontaneous spiritual experiences led to a feeling of deep psychic regeneration after a time of crisis. One respondent writes: 'It allowed me to relinquish my desperate control over my negative feelings, either physical pain or mental depression or spiritual guilt. It's like my well has run dry, but the very last bit of digging uncovers the spring that refills the well of my soul.' Although such experiences are very different from the rationalism of CBT, there are parallels. We are stuck in a prison of negative ego-beliefs; liberation comes when we let go of them. In CBT, this liberation comes from the slow, rational dismantling of beliefs, a chipping away at the walls of the shed. In ecstatic experiences, people are suddenly liberated – the walls fall down and they are free. But you probably still need regular ethical practices to turn your epiphany into durable habits.

However, it is a mistake to think that spontaneous spiritual experiences are always joyful and life-enhancing. There can be aspects of spontaneous experience that are difficult to accept or integrate. First, people may encounter a spiritual presence they perceive as threatening, evil or demonic. Up to 10 per cent of NDEs involve a Hell experience – some accounts are worthy of Hieronymus Bosch. And, of course, many people's experience of hearing voices or seeing spirits is deeply intrusive and distressing, for example a voice repeatedly telling you to kill yourself. How should we view such negative experiences? I'd suggest the best way is to see them as 'shadow' aspects of our own psyche, not fundamentally real, just a projection from our subconscious that we can transform if we maintain courage, wisdom and compassion. *The Tibetan Book of the Dead* tells us: 'Be not daunted or terrified or awed. Recognise whatever appears as the reflection of your own consciousness.' Eleanor Longden, who delivered a much-watched TED talk about hearing voices, says she managed to come to terms with an intrusive, aggressive and 'grotesque' demonic presence, who plagued her for years, by recognising him as 'the unaccepted aspects of my self-image, my shadow'. By taking a more practical and compassionate approach to him, and not letting herself be bullied, Eleanor and her shadow managed to work out a more balanced and amicable relationship.[14]

Even positive spontaneous experiences can be difficult to integrate into one's life. One can find mundane reality disappointing after having had an ecstatic glimpse of God or Heaven. Some NDE survivors say they wish they hadn't come back. Personally, I have longed to have another such experience but am still searching for the door. It can also be very difficult to communicate an ecstatic experience. Other people may not understand or care. The RERC database is full of tragi-comic moments like this:

> Starting around 1967, there were several different times in the middle of the night that silvery figures appeared on my side toward the bottom of the bed ... At one time in particular I was so startled that I made a noise which awakened my husband as they vanished. When I told him that there were three humanoids standing there, he sarcastically shouted, 'Well, do me a favour: the next time they come don't wake me up.' From that time on I never mentioned anything of the sort to him.

One also often finds competing interpretations between the experiencer, who thinks their encounter is spiritual, and a psychiatrist, who thinks it is indicative of schizophrenia. Western psychiatry has, thankfully, become better in the last two decades at overcoming its strong historical aversion to spiritual experiences, and less hasty to label them as physical pathologies requiring medication. Instead, psychiatrists are realising that 'out-of-the-ordinary experiences', like hearing voices, seeing

17

a spirit or sensing a presence, are quite common in the general population. Myers and his colleagues at the Society for Psychical Research first pointed this out in a national survey of 1882, where they found around 10 per cent of the population reported having had 'a vivid impression of seeing, or being touched, or hearing a voice . . . not due to any external cause'. More recent surveys have also put the prevalence of 'hallucinations' in the general population at around 10 per cent – much higher than the one per cent diagnosed with schizophrenia.[15] Sensing a presence is particularly common among the bereaved: 50 to 90 per cent of bereaved people sense the presence of their loved one following their death. Crucially, for most people, sensing a presence is not distressing, not correlated with mental pathology, and has never required medication or hospitalisation. On the contrary, it's more often found to be comforting and associated with improved mental health. Cognitive scientists now suggest that *all* of our experiences of reality are, in a sense, 'controlled hallucinations' – our minds improvise a version of reality based on the flood of raw data from our brains and senses.[16] How we interpret incoming data depends in large part on our culture.

But some people's spiritual experiences really do seem pathological. This is all too apparent as one reads through the RERC database. Although Hardy intended it to prove the spiritual nature of man to 'the intellectual world', it sometimes seems a catalogue of human folly. Hardy actually had to start a whole category, 'File Z', for reports that seemed to be sent straight from the asylum. Respondents leap to conclusions, seizing on the flimsiest evidence as certain proof of divine communication. Some think they can control the weather, travel through time, or alter geopolitical events with their mind. They lose a sane sense of their ego's boundaries. They also ramble on for pages and pages - sometimes even the heroic patience of Hardy's secretary wears thin as she transcribes the accounts:

> The Revelations started in 1968 and got stronger. At first I was told with a Voice in My Head. Then 1969 The Vioce [*sic*] said Get Pen & Paper. The Vioce [*sic*] which said I AM The Lord The Lord of Hosts they call Me. If you asked for The Sun I would not give

it you, then went on to tell me why. Then said You have heard the
saying a bad Apple in a barrel of Good ones will turn all bad unless
taken out. (This goes on in a disjointed and illogical manner for
3 pages, which have not been put on to computer disk.)

One would expect this mixture of the sublime and the pathological
in spiritual experiences, according to the James–Myers–Jung theory of
the psyche. The subliminal mind, wrote Myers, 'is a rubbish-heap as
well as a treasure-house'.[17] Spiritual experiences, by their theory, are
liminal moments when the border between the conscious ego and the
subliminal mind becomes porous, and the contents of the subliminal
mind burst through. It can reveal pearls of wisdom, healing and power.
But it can also reveal a lot of nonsense. We need to find a middle
ground between the uncritical embrace of such experiences as perfect
revelations, and the complete rejection of them as mental pathology.

What to do in a spiritual emergency

In 1971, the 23-year-old David Lukoff dropped out of Harvard's doctoral
programme in social anthropology and hitchhiked his away across the
USA. In San Francisco he dropped acid for the first time. Four days
later, he woke up in the middle of the night, went into the bathroom
in the friend's flat where he was crashing and looked in the mirror.
He saw his right hand was in the classic *mudra* position. He immediately
realised he was the reincarnation of the Buddha. And Jesus. He also
realised his mission: to create a new Holy Book to redeem the human
race. For the next week, he wrote in a rapture, barely sleeping, channelling the spirits of the Buddha, Locke, Hobbes, Rousseau, Jung, R.
D. Laing and Bob Dylan. When he'd finished his 47-page revelation, he
made several copies, then handed them out on a street corner in Berkeley.
To his surprise, his new religion failed to take off. Over the next two
months, his messianic certainty began to fade. He was still sure he'd
written a work of genius, but as he read more widely and realised how
unoriginal many of his insights were, this certainty also began to fade.
He became ill, insomniac and depressed. Luckily for him, all this time

he was supported by friends and family, who kept him fed, gave him somewhere to sleep and didn't hospitalise him or insist he was crazy. Gradually, he began to recognise the positive aspects of his experience. He became interested in other people who'd gone through temporary psychoses with a strong religious or spiritual component. He came across the term 'spiritual emergency', introduced by transpersonal psychologists Stanislav and Christina Grof in 1978.[18] He took a doctorate in psychology and worked at UCLA and elsewhere, particularly with psychotic patients also convinced they were God or the Messiah, to whom he found it quite easy to relate.

In 1989, Lukoff managed to get a new diagnosis introduced in the *Diagnostic and Statistical Manual*, volume IV, the handbook for clinical psychiatry and psychology in Western culture, called 'religious or spiritual problem'. This distinguished temporary spiritual psychosis, such as he had experienced, from the classic diagnosis of schizophrenia. A religious or spiritual problem was temporary, not a biological brain disorder, but could involve psychotic features, such as ego-inflation, hyper-meaning detection and disordered conduct. It might have positive aspects, like a greater sense of meaning and motivation.

Supportive communities

The challenge for a person having an 'out-of-the-ordinary experience', and for their loved ones, peers, psychologist or psychiatrist, is to integrate the experience and recognise its positive aspects, while guarding against the negative, like paranoia or ego-inflation, and then to find a positive calling that connects the person back into society. Lukoff says: 'I was lucky in having a supportive peer group and family. Otherwise, I'd probably have ended up hospitalised with a lifelong diagnosis of schizophrenia, with all the stigma and medication that goes with that.' A 2012 study by Charles Heriot-Maitland et al. found that while out-of-the-ordinary experiences like hearing voices or sensing a spirit happen in roughly 10 per cent of the population, those who are hospitalised for such experiences tend to have a worse outcome than those who aren't.[19] The crucial factor for determining if such an experience is problematic, they decided, was whether people found a community that helped them to a positive interpretation for their experiences. Most psychiatric hospitals are the precise opposite of such places: you are locked up and told your voices are the product of a crippling lifelong biological disease, that they're meaningless and should be ignored, and that your diagnosis means you're likely to be on the scrapheap of society for the rest of your life.

Of course, there are risks on the other side too: spiritual or religious communities may impose their own equally dogmatic interpretation on your experience, declaring it to be the Holy Spirit, or a demon, or a past life, or an alchemical symbol from the collective unconscious. One friend of mine, suffering from drug-induced psychosis, was told by a psychic healer that he was suffering karmic retribution for his previous life as a Nazi war criminal. This was not helpful. The best support networks seem to be more grassroots communities, which share authority horizontally and have a pragmatic, flexible and sympathetic response to the variety of people's interpretations of their experiences.

A good example is the Hearing Voices Network, which was launched in 1987 and has revolutionised Western psychology's attitude to voice-hearing. It was launched by two Dutch psychiatrists – Marius Romme and Sandra Escher – and by a voice-hearer called Patsy Gage. While in treatment, Gage read Julian Jaynes's *The Origin of Consciousness in the Breakdown of the Bicameral Mind*, which argues that voice-hearing used to be a much more ubiquitous phenomenon earlier in the development of the human brain – look how often people in ancient Greek culture heard the gods talking to them, from Galen to Socrates. Gage declared to Romme: 'I'm not schizophrenic, I'm ancient Greek!'[20] Together, they helped to create groups where voice-hearers could meet to discuss their experiences, explore meanings, and provide support for each other. There are now several hundred Hearing Voices groups around the world, and they've been a life-saver for Eleanor Longden and many others. What I like about them is they're pragmatic in their metaphysics. Many people in the group think their voices or experiences are encounters with spiritual beings; others think they are aspects of the self. The groups support and help you, give you a social connection and a social role, no matter what your metaphysics. It helps people to find a more balanced and equal relationship with their voices – they learn that they don't have to take their pronouncements as the Absolute Word of God.

As for Hardy's grand vision, in some ways it could be said to have been a failure. The RERC constantly ran out of money, and was moved from Oxford to Lampeter in 2000, where the database slumbers, its warehouse of revelations more or less ignored. And yet, in other ways, Hardy's vision has become mainstream. People in Western societies report more and more spiritual experiences, and the attitude of mainstream psychology and psychiatry to such experiences has shifted considerably in the last two decades. While the number of church attendees continues to decline across Western societies, the number of 'spiritual but not religious' rises.[21] Spiritual experience could be said to be at the centre of the West's new democratic spirituality – we rely more on our own personal experiences than on traditional institutions, authority figures or sacred texts.

The risk of this cultural shift, however, is that our post-religious spirituality becomes *all* about experiences, descending into a sort of consumerist thrill-seeking. Philip Pullman warns: 'Seeking this sort of thing doesn't work. Seeking it is far too self-centred. Things like my experience are by-products, not goals. To make them the aim of your life is an act of monumental and self-deceiving egotism.' Hardy's database is full of comments like 'That moment was worth more than all the rest of my life put together.' Is that a healthy attitude to the spiritual life? Imagine a marriage where you thought all the value existed in one date.

We need to integrate these moments into our everyday reality. But how? Hardy, like James, Myers and Jung, was wary of collective ecstasy. Their preferred spirituality was highly individualistic. Yet surely communities have an important role in helping us to make sense of ecstatic experiences, supporting us in the disciplines and practices we need to integrate them, and directing us outwards to serve our fellow beings.

It was with this in mind that I decided to join a charismatic Christian community. Let's head to the Revival Tent to meet them.

2: The Revival Tent

I'm standing on a stage in a packed church, in front of 500 believers, next to the most famous Christian preacher in Britain, Nicky Gumbel. 'So, Jules,' he says, 'what difference has Jesus made to your life?'

What am I going to tell the audience, I wonder? And how did I end up here?

It all started in 2012. When I finished my last book, *Philosophy for Life*, I'd become aware of the limits of Stoic philosophy: it was too rational, too individualistic; it left out important things like the arts, myth, ritual, sex, dancing and ecstatic experiences. I was searching for deeper community. I was a Stoic, single-dweller, bachelor, freelance writer – I was about as individualist as you could get. Philosophy clubs like the School of Life or my own London Philosophy Club were fun, but not the sort of loving community I imagined churches might provide. I was dating a Christian woman, and was impressed by how she and her Christian friends cared for one another. They seemed more open to ecstatic experiences than philosophers. One of my girlfriend's mates, Jack, was a curate at Holy Trinity Brompton (HTB), home of the famous Alpha Course. Jack asked me if I fancied doing the course. I'd rejected Christianity when I was 16, never read the Bible and tended to think Christians were weird. But why not? If nothing else, it would be interesting research. 'Careful you don't get brainwashed,' a friend told me, as I set off for HTB one Wednesday evening in January 2013.

There is a kind of self-consciousness the average English person now feels about going to church, more than if one went to a yoga session or Vipassana retreat. As the sceptic psychologist Richard Wiseman put it: 'Being a Christian used to be shorthand for being good. Now it's shorthand for being odd.' In 2013, the UK became a post-Christian nation, with the majority now subscribing to no religion. There's been a cataclysmic decline in church attendance since the 1960s, particularly in the last decade – only 750,000 people go to church on Sundays, less than 2 per cent of the population. The Anglican Church appears to be heading for extinction in England (although it's booming in Africa). But you wouldn't guess that if you visited HTB.[1]

As I approached the church in South Kensington, I joined a long line of people queuing to sign up for the Alpha Course, mainly well-dressed people in their 20s and 30s. There was a mixture of nationalities and ethnicities. HTB is particularly popular with new arrivals to the UK, and with single people – it's been nicknamed Hunt the Bride. We were registered by a team of young volunteers, radiating positivity and wholesomeness, and divided into 40 or so groups. The groups of ten to 15 people sat in circles around the church, eating the free lasagne and introducing themselves. I was in a group with Nicky Gumbel, who is vicar at HTB. Nicky is a 60-something Old Etonian ex-barrister, grey-haired, charming, not the most obvious vessel for ecstasy – although he's full of enthusiasm and says 'amazing' a lot, like everyone else in the church. He and his wife Pippa are good-looking, in love, and have charming children and grandchildren – they're like the ideal mother and father of the extended HTB family.

When he speaks to you, Nicky fixes you with a sort of Aslan focus, as if he sees your potential role in the Great War. It's flattering, you feel eager to sign up. He often mentions HTB's vision: 'the re-evangelisation of the nations, the revitalisation of the Church, and the transformation of society'. It seems a doomed mission in a country where church congregations are flat-lining, yet the success of HTB has been cited by everyone from historian Simon Schama to former *Economist* editor John

Micklethwait as evidence that 'God is back'.[2] To date, the Alpha course has been taken by more than 29 million people in 169 countries. Hundreds of thousands have watched the Alpha videos, which feature a shirtless Bear Grylls (a member of HTB's extended congregation). Nicky's Bible app, Bible In One Year, has been downloaded more than a million times. In London, HTB attracts a Sunday congregation of 4,000 people, across ten services and four sites, and it has played an important role in making London the one English diocese in which the Church is growing. HTB curates have ventured forth like missionaries and opened at least 30 'church plants' from Birmingham to Brighton. 'Whenever people see a church unused or turned into a block of luxury flats, it's like the empty palace of a long-forgotten king,' Nicky says. 'But when you see a church that's full, people know the King lives!' HTB's influence spreads far and wide – Justin Welby, Archbishop of Canterbury, came from the HTB congregation; Tony Blair spoke at HTB's leadership conference; David Cameron praised Alpha in his special Easter message; various celebrities have done Alpha, from Will Young to Geri Halliwell. When you're in the warm cocoon of HTB, you really start to believe revival is possible.

Upon this rock I will build my church

After we've introduced ourselves and eaten our lasagne, the band on the stage starts to play. We rise for a couple of hymns, singing the words as they appear on the video screens. It's at this point that I realise something has changed in the Church of England. Gone are the Victorian hymns and the wheezy organs; they've been replaced by rock bands and Coldplay-esque anthems. On Sundays, the congregation sings, arms aloft, or sways with their eyes closed beneath the twinkling lights. Initially, I found this very cheesy, sacrilege even – how dare Christians steal rock and roll? Later I learned how much rock and roll had stolen from the Church, how it's always been a two-way stealing process. Besides, why *shouldn't* people wave their hands in the air while worshipping God? We think that's normal if we're at a Bruce Springsteen concert, but if people behave like that for God, we think they're getting carried away. I actually grew to like it, the feeling of 500 people all singing the same song, the feeling of surrendering and being carried on a wave of music. I'd loved being in a choir at school, and I realised how much I missed collective singing. But, sometimes, the sugariness of the songs got a bit cloying. They're all love songs for Jesus. 'There's nothing I want more/You're all that I adore'; 'Everything I've lost/I have found in you'; 'Your love never fails, it never gives up, it never runs out on me'; 'Come and have your way.' And they're all sung in an American accent, so you don't actually worship God, you worship Gaaahd.

After the singing, Nicky bounded on stage to welcome us to Alpha and assure us HTB is not a cult and we won't be harassed if we decide to leave. He clearly recognises how alienated most young British people are from the Church, and he was eager to show that it's not weird. Alpha talks are filled with reassuring references to pop culture – Russell Brand and Freddie Mercury are quoted, and we're told Elton John, Madonna and Jennifer Lopez all wear crosses. The theology is straightforward: Christ died for us and was resurrected, and His sacrifice liberated us from sin and death and gave us new life. We can have a personal relationship with Jesus by letting the Holy Spirit into our hearts. The great intellectual challenges Christianity faced over the last 250 years – evolution, Biblical criticism – are brushed aside. 'Science tells us how, but it doesn't tell us why,' said Nicky. Besides, there is a difference between 'head knowledge' and 'heart knowledge'. The most important thing is not conceptual logic, but relationships – our relationship with God, our relationship with each other. Personal feelings and personal testimonies are key. Even in the Alpha session on 'how to read the Bible', the speaker spent most of the talk telling his own story.[3]

The power of small groups

The Alpha course runs for 10 sessions. Each Wednesday evening, after the worship and the 20-minute Alpha talks, we'd go into our 'small groups' to discuss the ideas we'd heard. In our group, Nicky, Pippa and Jack sat back and let the rest of us discuss the topic among ourselves, even when we raged against God and Christians. Gradually, over the ten sessions, people expended all their rage and cynicism, and started to open up about their own lives, their setbacks, their longing for God and community. It was a profoundly cathartic and bonding experience to meet regularly with the same group of strangers – people of different ages, nationalities and races – and be honest and vulnerable about what matters to you. Every Wednesday evening we could take off our masks, be real, and feel accepted and cared for. I hadn't done that sort of thing since my early 20s, when I'd been in an anxiety support group, and I'd missed it. Bit by bit, Nicky and Jack introduced us to various Christian practices, teaching us how to pray and encouraging us to pray for each other. 'Does anyone have someone they'd like us to pray for?' asked Jack.

One lady, Sarah, spoke first. 'I was in Spain on holiday last week and I saw a really mangy-looking cat, with one eye. It looked so unhappy. We could . . . pray for that?'

'Jules,' said Jack, eyes twinkling, 'would you like to go first?'

So the first time I ever prayed out loud was for this anonymous cat. 'Lord . . . there's a cat in Spain, with one eye. Help this cat, O Lord.' Praying aloud felt ridiculous at first. I even resented being prayed for. 'How would you feel if someone prayed for you, Jules?' Pippa Gumbel asked me. 'Patronised,' I replied. But, again, I grew to like praying for each other, with a hand on each other's shoulder. Belonging to a small group, meeting once a week to hear each other's problems, wish each other well, and wish the world well – what could be more normal and therapeutic? The sociologist Robert Putnam thinks this community of care is the reason people in religious communities typically report higher life satisfaction than the non-religious.[4]

Alpha directly addresses a basic problem most of us have: we don't always feel loved. We feel there is something about us that is unworthy of love and will make people reject us. We feel small and alone and we know we're going to die and be forgotten. So we try various strategies to feel more loved and significant. We try to please our parents, but we don't always understand each other. We try to win love through achievements and status, but success doesn't make us loved, just admired, envied, even disliked. We seek love through the internet, staring at our phones in the hope of likes and interactions, however casual. We seek love through sex, through substances, through therapy. But even in therapy we know it's not really unconditional, that at the end of the hour we have to pay and leave. No one talks about our need to be loved because if we did we might have to admit that we feel lonely and needy, and that is pathetic in our individualistic and success-oriented culture. What if there was a God and He loved us? What if the creator of the universe had a special concern for us, even at our worst? What if that love was free? We could let go of our fear, our shame, our inhibitions, our sense that we're not well and have to hide it to avoid others' rejection. We could stop trying to prove our importance to the world. We could relax and expand in God's love, like a sponge in a warm bath. This is what Alpha tries to teach: the Jesus cure. God's love will cure you of your shame, your addictions, your hang-ups, your desperate striving for the world's approval. Your Alpha group will love and accept you. The wider community of HTB will love you too, particularly if you're a 'seeker'. You are the prodigal son (or fatted calf), whose return to God is cele-brated by the saints and angels. You will never be higher status than as a seeker on the Alpha course.

In week seven, all the groups went on the 'Alpha weekend', staying in a hotel on the coast in West Sussex. Nicky said we would learn how to invite the Holy Spirit into our hearts. The Holy Spirit doesn't enter unless you invite him. 'The Lord is a gentleman,' another pastor explained, meaning that, unlike Zeus, Jesus doesn't rape you – although the word 'rapture' comes from the Latin *raptus,* meaning 'abduction' or 'rape'. Nicky explained that the Church had sometimes been suspicious of 'manifestations of the Holy Spirit', but they actually have a central role in the Bible, as in the Pentecost episode in the Acts of the Apostles. The Holy Spirit can grant all of us the charismatic power the apostles possessed. To get the fires burning, Nicky said we would pray the oldest prayer in Christianity: Come, Holy Spirit. 'You might feel a warmth in your chest,' he said, 'or a tingling, or your palms might feel a bit sweaty . . . Come, Holy Spirit . . . Come . . . Thank you, Lord . . . Thank you . . . Even now, the Holy Spirit is here, at work in some of you.' I could hear some people gently sobbing around me. One woman behind me started quietly singing in tongues, like a Mediterranean baby-talk. I opened my eyes and Nicky appeared by my elbow. 'Can I pray for you, Jules?' he asked. I was flattered. 'Lord, we ask that you fill Jules with your Holy Spirit, and reveal Your *amazing* plan for his life.' I opened my eyes and Nicky smiled at me eagerly. 'How was it?'

A brief history of charismatic Christianity

It's remarkable that the Church of England should have become so ecstatic, considering it was established back in the Reformation as a prophylactic *against* ecstasy. The Bishop of London, Richard Chartres, tells me that during the Reformation there was a 'fear of the irrational, a fear of the ungovernable spirit'. This is unsurprising, given some Protestants were using the Holy Spirit as a justification to start revolutions. Luther dubbed such ecstatic revolutionaries 'enthusiasts', and insisted that it was heretical to claim special gifts or revelations from the Holy Spirit. The Church of England was, from its birth, suspicious of ecstasy – the Holy Spirit was 'edited out' of Thomas Cranmer's 1540 prayer book, according to the Bishop of London. Monasteries and nunneries, which provided a cultural framework for ecstatic voyages, were dissolved by the state and their assets seized. In the second half of the seventeenth century, after the English Civil War and the Thirty Years War, the secular nation-state emerged triumphant and 'enthusiasm' was deemed a medical illness and threat to public order. Christianity was rationalised: all claims to personal revelation were subject to reason. God became distant, a blind watchmaker or Deist Supreme Ruler, and Christianity became a matter of agreeing with a handful of propositions.

There was always going to be a reaction to this repression of ecstasy. Christianity, suggests the Bishop of London, 'exists as a massive symphony, where the truth is given by the interplay of the various parts. If you omit any part of it, then there is a reaction and exaggeration of the missing element.' Ecstasy came back into Anglicanism with a vengeance in the mid-eighteenth century. To be precise, it came back on 24 May 1738, at 8.45 p.m., in Aldersgate Street in London. A pious young

Christian called John Wesley felt his heart 'strangely warmed' after attending a gathering of ecstatic Protestants called the Moravians. His brother, Charles, had likewise experienced a 'baptism of the Holy Spirit' three days before. The Wesleys spread their new vision throughout the Anglican Church, although it later split from Anglicanism and became known as 'Methodism'. At its heart is the idea that Christians can encounter the Holy Spirit today, and this baptism of the Spirit gives us the assurance that we are saved. Methodists became famous – or infamous – for their highly emotional services, their theatrical sermons, their wonderful hymns (many of them written by Charles Wesley) and their strenuous evangelism, particularly to the working class. They would organise 'love-feasts', where hundreds or even thousands of people would gather for open-air services and 'camp meetings', which could go on for hours or days. Attendees wept, fainted, shook, groaned, danced, laughed and leaped for joy as the Holy Spirit descended upon them and they committed their life to Jesus.

The Holy Spirit spread across the world, and is still spreading, through spectacular revivals. There was the Welsh Methodist revival of the 1730s–50s, in which 'old men and women leaped around like roe deer'.[5] There was the First Great Awakening of American Christianity in the 1730s and 1740s, and the Second Awakening of the early-nineteenth century; there was the Welsh revival of 1904, and the Azusa Street revival of 1905, which kickstarted Pentecostalism. Since the 1980s, Pentecostal churches have experienced extraordinary growth in the developing world, as people in Latin America, Africa and Asia move to the city and look to the Holy Spirit for life-guidance. Around 35,000 convert to Pentecostalism every day – think of that, 24.3 intense personal surrenders to the Holy Spirit every minute.

Ecstatic revivals tended to follow a similar script: someone had an ecstatic experience, it spread, and the religiosity of their community abruptly went through the roof, with people flocking to all-day all-night services, where they burst into prophecy or song as the Spirit came upon them. Sometimes charismatic preachers stirred the crowds to heights of emotion, but equally often the congregation themselves took charge, including working-class men, women, black people, people whose voices were not always heard in less ecstatic times. The Spirit was no respecter of order or hierarchy. Like wildfire, the revival would spread to a nearby community, and again people would be swept up in religious excitement, a sense that they were living in extraordinary times, perhaps even End Times, when great miracles were possible, when bodies were healed, sins cleansed, souls saved, churches revived.

Gifts of the Spirit

Sceptics, including many Christians, observed these revivals with a mixture of amusement and horror, as a regression to primitive irrationalism, like the flagellant craze or dancing manias of the Middle Ages. No wonder, critics sneered, revival ecstasy was so common among women, the working class, ethnic minorities – these groups were naturally more unstable, emotional and credulous. But in some ways, Methodism and its later descendants could be seen as a *product* of the sceptical Enlightenment, as well as a reaction to it – it was an 'experimental religion', as John Wesley put it, in which God's existence and personal love for you was 'proven' by the intense physical and emotional experience of ecstasy, as well as in dreams, healing, prophecy and other 'gifts of the Holy Spirit'. Mainstream Protestantism and Catholicism had, since the Reformation, insisted such gifts of the Spirit had ceased after the first generation of Christians (a doctrine known as 'cessationism'). But the Wesleys helped to popularise a new form of 'charismatic Christianity', which insisted the Holy Spirit was still handing out the free gifts (*charis* in Greek means 'grace', 'favour' or 'gift'). Like good Enlightenment scientists, churches kept statistical records of how many people made 'commitments to follow Jesus' as statistical proof of God's power and love. In total, around a hundred thousand supposedly made 'commitments' in the Welsh revival of 1904, a tenth of the population, although it's not clear how many were Christians already, or how many remained Christian once the collective ecstasy had subsided.

Revivals tended to take place in nonconformist Protestant congregations – Methodist, Mormon, Baptist, Pentecostalist, Shaker, Seventh-day Adventist and so forth. Mainstream middle-class Catholic and Anglican churches stoically resisted invasion by the Holy Spirit.[6] But in the 1960s that changed. Baby-boomers sought spiritual experiences of all kinds and some of them stumbled across Christianity – specifically the charismatic Christianity found in Methodism and Pentecostalism. One charismatic young hippie called Lonnie Frisbee, who would later be rejected by the Church for being gay, encountered Jesus while tripping on LSD. Lonnie started zapping the Holy Spirit to other hippies, who became known as 'Jesus Freaks'. They gathered at Calvary Chapel in southern California, and later at a network of Californian churches known as the Vineyard, run by John Wimber. The Jesus Freaks took the Holy Roller ecstasy of Pentecostalism and connected it to white middle-class congregations. They also adopted the rock and roll services of Pentecostalism – indeed, Vineyard attracted several rock converts, including Bob Dylan.

In the 1980s, John Wimber preached at HTB in London. Nicky Gumbel – then an uptight barrister in a three-piece suit – got zapped by the Holy Spirit, and reportedly had to be carried cataleptic through the church windows. 'God is giving that man the ability to tell people about Jesus,' Wimber said, as Nicky was carried out.

HTB caught fire again in the early 1990s, via a spectacular revival in Canada called the Toronto Blessing. A press report from that time reads: 'Nicky Gumbel prays that the Holy Spirit will come upon the congregation. Soon a woman begins laughing. Others gradually join her with hearty belly laughs. A young worshipper falls on the floor, hands twitching. Another falls, then another and another. Within half an hour there are bodies everywhere as supplicants sob, shake, roar like lions, and strangest of all laugh uncontrollably.'[7] But that was back in 1994. Since then, it has been quieter at HTB, although Alpha has kept on growing all over the world. I asked Nicky if he missed those tempestuous days: 'I see it as like the ocean – there are always waves, but sometimes it's more gentle and peaceful, and sometimes there are huge waves. What matters ultimately is the fruit, and whether people's lives become more loving, gentle and peaceful.' But I still felt that charismatic Christians, including Nicky, longed for another big wave to revive our secular culture and sweep us back into church. 'More, Lord, more!' I heard pastors pray eagerly. 'Give us *immeasurably more.*'

Jesus as detergent

'How was that?' Nicky asked me eagerly.

'I felt . . . er . . . peaceful.'

In fact, nothing spectacular happened on the Alpha weekend. The speaking in tongues sounded a bit silly to me. During the service, a lady came up and asked if she could pray for me. She'd had a vision: 'You have a masculine exterior, but a floral heart.' As in I'm gay? Well, it was a kind gesture. The weekend was epic. We all felt high. After inviting in the Holy Spirit, we watched England play rugby, drank beer and danced at a disco. Our small group danced in a circle to Beyoncé's 'Crazy In Love'. We were like a little family, in which I felt accepted and cherished.

When we were back at HTB, I said I wasn't entirely sure about the whole Christian thing, but I was prepared to give it a go. Perhaps faith was like a relationship: you always had doubts but you discovered love through commitment. I was on board with the God of love, the grace of the Holy Spirit and the lovely community. I was less sure about the biblical infallibility, original sin, the Virgin Birth, the Devil, the sinfulness of homosexuality, the apocalypse, the entire Old Testament, the divinity of Jesus, or Christianity's claim to be the only way to God. But I could 'sit with that', as HTB-ers put it.

In April, a month after Alpha had finished, I received an email from Nicky saying how much he'd enjoyed reading *Philosophy for Life*, and would I come to speak at HTB about my experience of Alpha? In my egotism, I envisaged the two of us sitting on stage as equals leisurely discussing Greek philosophy and Christianity. I envisaged a whole new audience for my books. I agreed and turned up one Sunday before the main service. There was Nicky. 'Ah, Jules, *amazing*, thanks so much for coming. So, basically, there'll be about five of you. You'll each be on stage for maybe a minute. Think of it like an advert for detergent. Before, dirty shirt. Then Jesus. Now, clean shirt. Okay?' I had a sudden sense of horror. I had misread the occasion. I watched from the wings as the other four converts told their incredible testimonies to the 500-strong congregation, each one received with whoops and cheers.

'Next is Jules. Jules is a *philosopher*, he's written a great book. So, Jules, what was your life like before you met Jesus?'

'It was . . . er . . . okay, I guess.'

'And how did you meet Jesus?'

'Well, I had a sort of near-death experience when I was 21 . . . and that led me to Greek philosophy.' There was an uneasy shifting in the seats. 'But it seemed to me that Greek philosophy left some stuff out . . . so I did Alpha and . . . it was great!' A smattering of half-hearted applause.

'And how has Jesus changed your life?'

'Oh, a lot.' I limped off stage, to the least enthusiastic applause you'll ever hear at HTB. And then I had to do it at two more services. I felt annoyed with Nicky for commodifying my story and turning it into an advert for Alpha (although, to be fair, that was obviously the point of the invitation). Perhaps he feels he is a general at war, fighting against the extinction of the Church, and everything and everyone is a weapon in that war. But I didn't much like being weaponised.

For a few months I drifted in a sort of limbo, struggling to believe in Christianity but finding secular culture equally unsatisfying. I briefly played the drums in the Sunday Assembly, a humanist church somewhat modelled on charismatic Christianity, which offers a sort of 'charismatic humanism', with a rock band playing singalong covers of Bon Jovi and Queen, personal testimonies, gags and a high-energy 'celebration of life'. It's rapidly spreading all over the world. I loved the project and the people but missed the 'surrender to God' bit when I was feeling wretched. One evening, at a Christian folk charity fundraiser, I stood on the side-lines muttering to a friend, 'How could I ever fit in with . . . *this*?'

'Have you read a book called *The Grace Outpouring*?' my friend asked. 'It's about a place in Pembrokeshire called Ffald y Brenin. It's a "thin place", close to God. Extraordinary things happen there. Why don't you go?'

A man on fire

Ffald y Brenin is a small retreat in the hills near the Pembroke coast, run by Roy and Daphne Godwin. Since the mid-1990s, strange things

have been happening there – miraculous healing, conversions, proph-
ecies. I drove down for their summer conference, a three-day event in
a nearby church. I arrived in time for dinner in the church hall. All
the other attendees were over 55. I sat down at a table, feeling a little
self-conscious, and asked one of the old ladies what I could expect
from the conference. 'You can expect to be invaded by God!' she said
testily.

After dinner we all drove to a nearby church. Roy Godwin took the
mike. He's a small man, with a tanned balding head, glasses, bad teeth
and a quiet voice brimming with certainty. He spoke of the 1904 Welsh
revival, of how the first drops of a new revival were starting to be felt.
'But we want more. Come on, Lord. Bring it on. We want another
revival.' He told stories of all the miracles that took place at Ffald y
Brenin – skin conditions vanished, cancer was 'rebuked', legs were
extended (one of charismatic Christians' favourite miracles is healing
people who have one leg shorter than the other). 'We now *expect* instant
healings,' he said. 'This is real.' He clearly had a very powerful expectation of the supernatural. Indeed, the air was thick with this
expectation. The pensioners had come to call God down, like a dove
from above. And sure enough God turned up. The pensioners laughed
and twitched and groaned and even screamed as the Holy Spirit came
upon them. My God, I thought. This is the worst holiday ever. I retreated
to my hotel room in the nearby town of Newport to research the
history of revivals and go for long walks along the coast.

But by the third day, the atmosphere of the place started to work
on me. The other attendees were so friendly, their faith and hope so
strong. I walked around Ffald y Brenin, this beautiful little hobbit house
overlooking a valley, and felt the energy of the place. By Saturday
evening, as the music engulfed me, a thought came into my head that
I wanted to serve God rather than my own worldly ambitions. It was
a commitment, I guess, an intention. Suddenly, I felt my chest fill with
a powerful energy that pushed my head back, further, further, until it
almost hurt my neck muscles. It took a real effort to push it forward,
then another wave would sweep it back. It was as if painful pleasure
was bursting from my chest, so powerful it literally took my breath

away. A part of my brain was watching and thinking, *This is weird*, but I told that part of me that my ancestors had been Quakers – quaking was in my genes. This went on for three-quarters of an hour, as wave after wave of painful bliss hit me. At one point, Roy asked us to close our eyes, then raise our hands if we wanted to renew our commitment to Jesus. At the very back of the church, I raised my hand. The person next to me hugged me and wept. Then we sat down. I shakily went to the toilet to drink some water. I looked at my eyes in the mirror, my pupils were dilated and my stomach was churning slightly. Just like on E, I thought. Some sort of autonomic reaction. I offered some water to the guy next to me in the pew, like in a rave when you want to share your joy and your possessions with the people around you. *Eunoia*, the Greeks call it. Goodwill.

At the end of the final service, my legs still trembling – indeed, everyone was twitching, like there was a loose wire in the floorboards – I went to thank Roy and Daphne. I hadn't spoken to them or introduced myself for the whole three days. Roy turned to me immediately and said: 'God says that you can stand on the outside analysing, but He's here, waiting for you.'

Then one of the volunteers came up, someone I hadn't met, and said: 'In that last session, I had a vision of you, with books flying off you.'

I drove all the way back to London, down the M4, my heart on fire.

Trying to fit into church

I announced my conversion to Christianity on my blog. Several of my newsletter subscribers unsubscribed immediately, assuming I'd lost the plot and become a homophobic fundamentalist. Academic colleagues also wondered if I had gone native. I told my publishers I intended to write a Christian book next. They were horrified. Didn't they get it? Revival was coming! Meanwhile, in Christian Land, the story went round about the atheist philosopher who'd suddenly found God (in fact, I was never an atheist, but stories tend to get exaggerated on the Christian telegraph). A Christian friend assured me I had 'a mission from God'. For a few months, I was high, convinced by my experience and jubilant about my part in the coming revival. But emotional highs die down, if they're not backed up by good reasons and a strong community. The community bit was hard. The Alpha course wants to emphasise the normality of the Church. But, on the inside, you realise how different it is. As the sociologist Linda Woodhead has written, Anglican Christianity has become a subculture, a separate world from secular culture. As it's shrunk, it's become more ecstatic, and the moral barriers to membership have become higher.

The biggest barrier is sexuality. While secular culture embraces Tinder, YouPorn, bisexuality, polyamory, S&M and transgender dysphoria, charismatic Christianity insists on patriarchy, hetero-normativity, and no sex before marriage. Nicky Gumbel has said that, when he marries couples, he can always tell at the altar if they'd managed to resist having sex (presumably by the drooling). No sex before marriage is fine if you're getting married in your early 20s, but HTB is full of single people in their 30s, 40s, 50s. That's a long time to remain celibate if you're not a monk or nun. Porn is also often condemned in sermons. When you mix this sexual puritanism with spiritual ecstasy, and throw in a lot of attractive single men and women, you end up with a messy blend of the spiritual and the erotic – I remember praying for one attractive woman, and her whispering sweet prayers for me, and I wondered if this was basically a weird sex game that we've dragged God into? 'You know what they say – flirt to convert!' another girl said to me, with a coy wink.

At times I longed for the simplicity and honesty of Tinder. It's even worse, of course, if you're an evangelical who fancies your own sex. That's considered a 'lifestyle choice', which some evangelicals believe can be overcome through prayer or exorcism. Nicky says he wants HTB to be a church 'famous for love', but it's better known by its critics for condemning homosexuality. There are signs the church is finally changing: gay couples are now welcomed on HTB's marriage course, which is a major shift for such a prominent charismatic church.

I particularly resented the idea, taught to me at a theology college connected to HTB, that the Bible is an infallible book.[8] Why must I agree with everything St Paul writes? I asked. Because all Scripture is 'God-breathed', I was told. Who says so? St Paul (assuming he actually wrote 2 Timothy – scholars are still arguing about which letters are genuinely by him). Rather than accept judgements that now seem inhumane, because they're in a sacred book that's never wrong, can't we just say that Paul was an inspired human, like Socrates or the Buddha, but on some matters we now disagree? After all, the Bible disagrees with itself, copies are filled with errors, inconsistencies and forgeries, and very few Biblical scholars think all the books of the New Testament were genuinely written by the apostles.[9] The Biblical canon was set three centuries after Christ, and before that Christians believed a wide variety of different things regarding who Jesus was, what happened in His life, and how we should follow Him. Even Jesus's teachings are not perfect. Some of them are sublime – the Kingdom of Heaven is within, like buried treasure; God's love is waiting to find us and lift us out of our prisons; we must overcome pride, go beyond the ego, surrender to love, and humbly serve the outcasts of society. But Jesus was also clearly a man of His culture, i.e, first-century Jewish apocalypticism. Accept God's merciful love, *or else*. To me, it seems that He and his apostles expected the End Times any day, when evil would be utterly vanquished, the dead would rise out of their graves, and a New Jerusalem would appear. They were wrong.

Devils and miracles

Despite the apparent failure of Christ's apocalyptic predictions, contemporary charismatics continue to embrace the world-view described in Acts, in which the kingdom of Heaven is breaking out, God will answer all our prayers, and Christians have supernatural gifts of healing and prophecy. How do they sustain this belief in such a cruel and imperfect world? One way is by believing also in the Devil. In the Alpha session after the Holy Spirit weekend, a polite lady in a pearl necklace told us that, if we became Christian, we immediately became a target for Satan. The Devil is powerful, and out to attack us (but we shouldn't get too morbid about it). This was a grim message amid

HTB's cheery cosmopolitanism, like *Four Weddings and a Funeral* veering into *Rosemary's Baby*. Some charismatics think we're in the middle of a cosmic battle between God and 'the Enemy'. This is the oldest story in the book, from the Narnia chronicles to *The Lord of the Rings*. 'God is on the move!' they say, quoting C. S. Lewis.

It may very well be that there are malevolent non-human intelligences out there – why should everything in the spiritual ecosystem wish us well? But the risk of a starkly divided apocalyptic world-view is that you start to see anyone who opposes you as demonic. And that's dangerous in a multicultural society. We were told Islamist terrorism is demonic. I heard charismatics say the 'gay lobby' is demonic. Some suggested Hinduism is demonic. Others saw the EU as demonic (that's why so many voted for Brexit). The New Age is *definitely* demonic. Some other denominations thought HTB itself was demonic. Once you start looking, you can see little pointy horns jutting out everywhere.

The other way charismatics maintain their belief in an omnipotent, loving and interventionist God is by surrounding themselves with people who share that belief. It's hard to have faith when you live in a culture that barely mentions God, but it's easier if you immerse yourself in a subculture that still believes in the supernatural. Charismatic Christians mainly socialise with other charismatic Christians, and they constantly talk about the amazing things God's doing in their life. Within the subculture, there's a strong confirmation bias. Any anecdote of an answered prayer or healing miracle is greeted with whoops of 'Come on!' and 'Praise Jesus!' There was this lady who had cancer, and she prayed, and the doctor couldn't believe what he saw. *Hallelujah!* And the eight million who die of cancer each year – are they proof of God's hate or indifference?

I asked Nicky Gumbel about this confirmation bias. He replied: 'We used to have a newspaper called *Alpha News*. People used to say, "This is just full of good news stories of healing and conversions. What about the bad news stories?" My predecessor would say, "Let the Devil publish the bad news. Who's telling the good news?"'

Christianity as yet hasn't gone down the route of mindfulness, trying to prove that prayer works through randomised controlled trials, although there is a lot of evidence that belonging to a religious community is good for your health. My colleague at Queen Mary University of London, the psychiatrist Simon Dein, has studied religious healing among Pentecostals. He notes: 'There's no doubt prayer can be psychologically healing, but it can't cure cancer.'[10] I don't think one can easily separate the psychological from the physical: prayer, like self-hypnosis, can strengthen the psycho-immune system, which helps in the recovery from illness and injury. In any case, I never fully understood the focus on miraculous healing in charismatic churches – we're all going to die in the end, aren't we? It seemed to reduce God to a physiotherapist. But it is faithful to the gospels: Jesus made physical healings a central part of his mission.

Is religious experience just hypnosis?

I wondered if my experience in Wales was some sort of subliminal state I'd gone into through social contagion. I went to meet the hypnotist Derren Brown to ask him what he thought, and interviewed him in his extraordinary house filled with optical illusions, stuffed animals, and a fish-tank inhabited by conger eels. We chatted while a jealous parakeet buzzed around my head. Brown was a teenage Pentecostalist, but lost his faith when he was an undergraduate and became interested in hypnotism. He's now famous for using hypnotism to brainwash audiences in his shows. I asked him if he thought charismatic churches used a form of hypnotism to induce ecstasy in their congregations: 'Yes, I do. But it's complicated. It's difficult to pin down what hypnosis is.'

The two competing theories of hypnosis are the 'altered state theory', which suggests hypnosis transports us into some non-rational, subliminal altered state of consciousness, and the 'role-theory', where people just go along with the role-play to conform with social expectations. I'd suggest they're both right. Context and cultural expectation matter. The anthropologist Tanya Luhrmann has shown the extent to which charismatic Christians learn to lose control.[11] At Alpha, we were taught how to open ourselves to the Holy Spirit, even how to speak in tongues. We also learned by imitating the ecstatic behaviour of others. But cultural expectations and role-play can also trigger powerful neurophysical states, which feel involuntary and automatic. You become deeply absorbed in a script, you become highly suggestible to commands from a high-status figure, and you lose control. Initially you're just going along with a game, but suddenly it feels *really real*. You're not being 'brainwashed', exactly. Rather, you're finding a context in which you have permission to let go. That surrender can happen in a range of contexts, not just religious ones – it may happen at the doctor's, at an alternative healer's, at a rock concert, at the theatre, at a stage-hypnotist's show.

And it's not always bad for you: it can be healing and connecting. Indeed, Derren Brown's latest show, *Miracle*, tries to recreate the world of Pentecostal faith-healing, in a tongue-in-cheek sceptical way. He gets audience members with physical complaints to come on stage, then 'heals' them with the Holy Spirit, while acting like a flamboyant revivalist preacher. It's pretty offensive to Christians, but the weird thing is, it works. Brown tells me: 'Not only does the healing work, but I've also "slain" people, so they fall down.' I witnessed this when I saw Brown's show – it was very strange to see sceptical Londoners abruptly pass out, then queue up to testify to how much better they felt. After the show, Twitter was full of testimonies – 'It was incredible! Thanks for healing my feet'; 'Thank you for healing my back'; 'My legs started to buckle and I wet myself.' When the show was screened a few months later, the papers were full of similar miracle stories: 'Girl who suffered knee problems for 10 years claims Brown miraculously healed her in 10 seconds,' said *The Sun*. 'Derren Brown has god-like powers,' declared the girl in question. It shows that just because a person can produce ecstatic experiences in others, it doesn't mean they're blessed with spiritual gifts. Such experiences seem more triggered by a person's expectations than by the spiritual powers of the guru.[12] But the response to *Miracle* also shows how healing ecstatic experiences can be - they unlock subliminal healing and give people the faith to believe a new narrative.

A few weeks after the show, I met Nicky Gumbel and asked him if some religious experiences are really 'just' hypnosis. On the Alpha course, when he told us 'You may be feeling dizzy, or have sweaty palms or a warmth in your chest', wasn't that just hypnotic suggestion?

He said: 'Someone once said the same thing to me on the Alpha course. So the next Alpha weekend, I didn't say anything about what people might feel, and there were very powerful manifestations of the Holy Spirit, and someone came up to me afterwards and said, "Why didn't you warn us?" So what I try to say now is "These things don't need to happen, but if they do, that's okay, it's not wrong or weird." The point I try to emphasise is, that's not what matters.' He suggested there are three possibilities about religious experiences: either it's demonic, or psychological, or God. Or it could be a combination, particularly of the last two. 'What matters,' Nicky insisted, 'is the fruit. If it leads to a ministry for Alpha in the prisons, I think that was God. If it leads to people coming off heroin, that was probably God. And if it was just psychological, maybe we need more of the psychological. When John Wimber came here, and a lot of friends of mine said, "What he's doing is a well-known form of hypnosis", I repeated this to my predecessor, and he replied, "Not well-enough known."'

This is remarkably close to William James's view of the matter: it may be God, it may be hypnosis, what matters is the fruit. Even secular psychologists arrived at similar conclusions. The psychiatrist Jean-Martin Charcot initially pathologised religious experience, but his last essay on 'the faith cure' looked at Lourdes as a 'system of mass suggestion', which he admitted was often very healing.[13] Religious healing may just be the well-proven placebo effect – but what 'the placebo effect' means is people's expectations, beliefs and faith can have an extraordinary impact on the body, which can be triggered by ritual and role-play. So do we need the mass placebo of religious ritual to bring us healing, love and transcendence?

Set and setting

I know many of my atheist and agnostic friends were worried I'd joined a cult when I got into HTB. But I'd suggest it's our secular individualist culture that's weird in *not* providing 'controlled spaces to lose control' – places and rituals where people can come together to love each other, support each other, pray for each other, and dissolve their egos safely. That lack is unique in the history of *Homo sapiens*. Of course, there are risks in such places – one can lose one's mind, get exploited by a guru, or end up turning against outsiders. In the Introduction I suggested that Timothy Leary's idea of 'set and setting' are a good way to assess the risks of different contexts for ecstasy.

If we think about the 'mindset' of Anglican churches, in many ways they look a lot safer and more pro-social than other forms of contemporary ecstasy. Charismatic Christians engage with the Holy Spirit not for the thrill of it, not just to get high, but out of a sense of love of God, love of each other, and desire to help humanity. They're fairly humble in their mindset: they're so focused on worshipping Jesus that they avoid the risk of trying to be gods themselves. And the ecstasy is outward-looking; it's channelled towards trying to improve society. Although charismatic Christians sometimes think the best way to improve society is by converting other people to Christianity, they've helped in other ways: a group of young HTB lawyers campaigned to pass the Modern Slavery Act (which gives police more powers against human traffickers), just as Methodists and Quakers worked to abolish slavery in the nineteenth century.

The main risk with the mindset of charismatic Christianity is that it can be over-attached to ecstasy. This is a risk in the whole of Christian culture, all the way back to the early church (St Paul warns against getting over-attached to charismatic gifts in 1 Corinthians). Christian ecstasy is a visitation from the Holy Spirit, proof of God's love for you, an influx of charismatic power. It could bring healing, or children, or career opportunities. It could be proof you're saved and going to Heaven. It could even be a sign of the coming Rapture. How could one *not* get attached to ecstasy with all these marvellous interpretations? Particularly when your community seizes on your experience and grants you status because of it. The flip-side of over-attachment to ecstasy is that people who don't go into trance states wonder why God's not into them. And people like me, who have experienced ecstatic moments, end up feeling confused and depressed when the ecstasy departs. We can easily end up chasing it.

The setting of Anglicanism

In terms of the 'setting' of charismatic Christianity, there are, of course, risks to churches as a place of collective trance. As Derren Brown notes, Pentecostal preachers are highly adept at hypnotising their congregations into giving them money. *Forbes* magazine estimates the combined worth of five Nigerian Pentecostal pastors at $200 million. Two American Pentecostal pastors attracted ridicule recently when they explained they needed private jets so they could spend more time with God.[14] Church leaders may use their hypnotic influence to increase, then abuse, their power. This is a big problem in some of the Pentecostal 'house churches' now booming around the world, where priests have unchecked power. I interviewed one woman who described how she had suffered 'spiritual abuse' for 14 years in a London Pentecostal church, under a tyrannical pastor and his wife. She told me: 'The mind control was very extreme. They'd say the Lord had given them power to come into our houses in the spirit, meaning their spirits would leave their bodies and watch what we were doing in the privacy of our homes.' Many Pentecostal churches are also profoundly patriarchal and homophobic.

The Anglican Church seems relatively protected against these risks. Its priests are as poor as church mice, they have to report to superiors and, unlike Catholic priests, they can get married, which is a good, though not sure-fire, protection against sexual abuse. Anglicans have a healthy sense of priests' fallibility (as Denis Thatcher once said to his priest before a sermon, 'Padre, most of us know what the Sermon on the Mount is. Twelve minutes is your lot'). HTB has resisted becoming a cultish mega-church partly because Nicky insisted on remaining within the Anglican communion rather than splitting off into an ecstatic sect, like the Quakers or Methodists. He's avoided the lure of becoming a guru, despite his global fame. He still cycles to church and is nicknamed Humble Gumbel. HTB is not a cult: it doesn't try to prevent people leaving; it doesn't try to get all your money; it is open to criticism. I'm grateful to Nicky and his church for being so kind and welcoming to me, and still feel love for the community.

However, HTB's methods for soul-farming can feel somewhat

industrial. It runs three Alpha courses a year: each convert feels uniquely loved, until the next batch moves on to the conveyor belt. It's a dubious sales technique to ask people if they want to make a 'personal commitment to Jesus' in the middle of highly emotional services – that's like asking someone to marry you when they're high in Las Vegas. Like Vegas marriages, some Alpha conversions don't last – mine didn't, and the divorce was painful. The little family of our Alpha group didn't last either. We kept meeting for a few months, but I don't think any of us still go to HTB (most now go to smaller local churches).

Perhaps I looked to church for the wrong things – I was more hungry for community than for God. Communities and religions are man-made, imperfect. If you make an idol of church, you're bound to be disappointed.

I don't feel I can call myself a traditional Christian any more, because I decided I didn't believe Jesus's death saved humanity or that the only way to God is through Him. People have ecstatic experiences in many different cultural contexts; they don't always lead to Jesus, but they can still be good for us. I struggle to believe the bold hypothesis put forward by Jesus: that there's an omnipotent personal God who loves us and all we have to do for grace is ask for it (Matthew 7:7; John 14:13). My near-death experience felt like grace, but I've also seen awful suffering in people's lives, where they have begged God for help, and it hasn't obviously arrived. So I'm agnostic. Sometimes people seem to access help from beyond, but it's not reliable, predictable or knowable.

I do still consider myself an Anglican, though, by which I mean that the culture of Anglicanism is deep in my psyche, deep in my imagination, and I find it a source of transcendence and meaning, even if I think a lot of it is made up. The theologian David Ford compares Christianity to jazz improvisation.[15] This makes sense to me. Throughout Christian history, visionaries have taken up the standard songs and stories of the Bible, and improvised new versions, according to their experience and the needs of the time. St Francis improvised a new song of poverty and love of nature; medieval nuns improvised a new song of erotic mysticism; African-Americans improvised a new song of liberation from slavery. Even atheists, like Philip Pullman, Richard Dawkins, and the good people of Sunday Assembly, seem to me to be part of the same collective improvisation. This is my culture, these are my songs, they're deep in my imaginative memory, far deeper than Tibetan Buddhism or Peruvian shamanism. We don't need to reject other cultures, because Christianity has *always* merged with them, from Greek philosophy to pagan animism. But we can still use the stories, myths and rituals of Christianity as a 'setting' to guide our consciousness beyond the ego towards the Unnameable. We will keep improvising new forms for ecstasy but, as Charles Mingus put it to Timothy Leary, 'You can't improvise on nothing, man; you've gotta improvise on something.'[16]

But if Christianity is a form of creative improvisation and imaginative role-play, can we not look to culture and the arts instead? Do we still need Christianity, now that we have Shakespeare, Michelangelo, Tolstoy, *Star Wars*? We'll explore whether the arts can be a substitute for Christianity, an alternative avenue to ecstasy, as we venture into the Ecstatic Cinema.

3: The Ecstatic Cinema

When I was suffering from post-traumatic stress disorder in my early twenties, I had a recurring nightmare. I was in a car with some friends heading to a music festival. We heard on the radio that a madman had escaped from a nearby psychiatric institution. The traffic started to slow on the motorway, and we realised this was because people were leaving their cars and running away in terror from the escaped lunatic. The motorway was deadlocked with abandoned cars. My friends also ran away, but for some reason I walked forward. The motorway turned into a foggy country lane at night. I saw a figure stumble out of the fog in front of me. It was a man in a shabby overcoat, clutching his side as if he was wounded. I saw with horror that this was the escaped lunatic, and in his hand he was holding a gun. I turned to try to run away, as the lunatic raised the gun and aimed it at me. I always woke up just as the gun went off.

After I'd had this nightmare for several weeks, the story shifted. This time I was sitting in the passenger seat of a lorry, hurtling down a motorway. I looked to my left, and there was the escaped madman, filthy, laughing and drunk. The lorry careered off the motorway, smashed through the barrier on the side of the road, and teetered halfway off a cliff. Just before it fell, I managed to pull myself and the madman free of the wreckage.

At the time, these nightmares were terrifying, but in retrospect, they seem to contain a wisdom beyond my conscious rationality. They were communicating to me in metaphors and symbols, revealing the wounds in my psyche, and pointing the way to healing. The escaped madman, I think, was a metaphor for the repressed trauma in my psyche, which I had locked up and refused to confront. The trauma was now bursting out and forcing me to confront it. The second dream told me that my fate was intertwined with the madman. I needed to find a way to accept and integrate the wounded parts of me, or I risked self-destruction.

The imagination as a ladder to the subliminal mind

Dreams are humans' most common ecstatic experience. Every night, we leave our normal identity and slip into another world. Yet unlike most cultures around the world, Western science has broadly rejected the idea that dreams have anything meaningful or useful to tell us. 'The sleep of reason produces monsters,' according to Goya's famous etching. The psychoanalyst Sigmund Freud was unusual among scientists in his insistence that dreams contain insight – they are 'the royal road to the unconscious'. But the Freudian unconscious that dreams revealed was a savage jungle ruled by primitive urges towards sex and aggression. Most dreams were simply rehashes of *Oedipus Rex*. There could be no unification with this savage unconscious: civilisation requires us to keep it suppressed, and remain divided and somewhat-unhappy creatures.

Freud's disciple, Carl Jung, took a more optimistic view of the subconscious. He thought of the psyche as a self-regulating organism that naturally seeks wholeness and flourishing. If the psyche gets out of balance, our subliminal mind sends messages to try to correct it, in the form of dreams. Most dreams are not very significant, but occasionally, in times of crisis, the subliminal mind sends 'big dreams', which are unusually vivid and numinous, and help us adapt to change, particularly to break-ups, illness, bereavement, and the prospect of death.[1] Dreams communicate with the conscious ego through the imagination, via symbols, myths, stories and archetypes that can guide us to health and wholeness if we learn to speak their language.

One of Jung's dream-archetypes was called 'the shadow', which means those parts of the psyche that we have repressed or hidden away. We all construct a mask to fit in with civilisation and hide aspects of us which we think might be ugly, shameful or unacceptable. If too great a gap arises between our mask and our shadow, Jung believed, we can become depressed, dissociated or even psychotic. Jung suggested that the shadow often appears in dreams as a wild animal, a beggar, an outcast or monster. We want to run away or exterminate it, but this just makes an enemy of our dissociated self. Jung insisted that to move towards wholeness and maturity we need to confront the shadow, recognise it as a part of us, take pity on it and accept it. Then the monster is magically transformed into an ally.[2]

The arts and catharsis

The arts, according to Jung, enable us to communicate with our subliminal mind via the dream-language of symbols, metaphors and myths.[3] Because the arts bypass rationality and communicate with the subliminal mind, they can be tremendously healing and cathartic, sometimes more so than rational philosophy. They transport us beyond the shed of our ego-construction and help us confront what lies beyond.

I had first-hand experience of this when I was recovering from post-traumatic stress disorder (PTSD). I happened to pick up a play by Sophocles called *Oedipus at Colonus*. It takes place after *Oedipus Rex*, when Oedipus has been thrown out of Thebes and condemned to wander in the wilderness, a blind, homeless, hated vagabond. He is the shadow of Athenian civilisation – the nightmare worst-case scenario. Yet the play suggests that, through his endurance of the worst that life can throw at him, Oedipus gains a spiritual power that his shallow, image-obsessed civilisation has lost. He ends up in Athens and begs to be taken in as a refugee. The King of Athens, Theseus, has the courage and compassion to take pity on Oedipus, to see beyond appearances and recognise the outcast's integrity. Theseus's sympathetic attitude leads to a magical transformation: Oedipus goes from an outcast into a god, who brings blessings to Athens. The play implies that Freud was wrong and Jung was right: we can confront our shadow, accept and heal it, and transform it from a threat to an ally.

I found this play incredibly healing, even though I'd never studied classical civilisation or read a classical tragedy. Through the subliminal language of myth and symbol, it helped me to take pity on my shadow, to accept the dissociated and rejected parts of my psyche, which appeared in my own dreams as a vagabond figure, like Oedipus. I, too, felt like an outcast – I struggled to communicate with other people, and felt broken, ashamed and humiliated. Yet the example of Oedipus gave me strength to endure, to accept my wounded inner self, and to find healing and transformation.

Can the arts be a substitute for religion?

One of the reasons Christianity became a mass religion while Greek philosophy stayed a niche pursuit is that Christianity communicates not just through ethical wisdom but through the subliminal language of symbols, metaphors and myths. The ethical injunction 'forgive your enemies' is not nearly as powerful as the story of the suffering Christ. Christianity gives people a semiotic web of symbols – wine, bread, lambs, buried treasure, the virgin mother, the final battle, and so on – which are repeated over and over until they sink deep into the subliminal mind.

Yet might not the arts perform this function as well as religion? Could not the plays of Sophocles be as cathartic and ecstatic as the Gospels, even if we don't believe they are literally true? Today, many Western artists and intellectuals insist the arts can replace religion as our main avenue to transcendence. The idea is perhaps best expressed by the musician, artist and cultural theorist Brian Eno, whom I went to interview in his studio in London. He suggested that the arts give us the experience of ecstatic surrender, without requiring that we sign up to any dogma. He told me: 'I belonged to a gospel choir in Brooklyn. I was the only white person in the choir and the only atheist. But the rest of the choir made me feel very welcome, and they didn't try too hard to convert me. I think I was having the same experience as them when we were singing, but without the same structure of belief. I hope that's what the artist does – creates rich experiences of surrender, without the superstructure of beliefs.'

But surrender to what, if not God? To the world that the artist has conjured up. Like religion, the arts are a form of imaginative play, a let's-pretend game in which the artist skilfully weaves an imaginative world and the audience are transported into it. Both religion and the arts have their roots in the childhood play of 'let's pretend'. Eno has written: 'Imagining is possibly the central human trick . . . We can imagine worlds that don't exist. We can play out whole scenarios in our head in imagination.'[4] He calls this 'world-building' and suggests that the arts immerse us in alternative worlds. They let us play with alternative identities – we can step out of our usual ego-patterns, see the world through someone else's eyes, 'find out what it would be like to be otherwise'. We can be temporarily liberated from the status quo. We can see the world anew. And we can do this without hurting ourselves. Culture, Eno suggested, 'is a place where you can take psychological risks without incurring physical penalties'. Just like dreams.

Cult and culture

To consider whether the arts can replace religion as our main route to ecstasy, we need to understand how closely they used to be connected. Before the Enlightenment, religion and the arts – cult and culture – were closely intertwined. In pre-modern cultures, the shaman combined the roles of priest and performer. Using what anthropologist Mircea Eliade called the 'techniques of ecstasy',[5] the shaman wove a dream-world through verse, song, rhythm, gesture, light, costume, painting, dance and performance. These techniques altered the shaman's consciousness, taking them into subliminal states where they feel in contact with the spirit world. And they altered the consciousness of the audience, casting a spell on them and transporting them into the spirit-world the shaman has conjured up. Immersion into the collective dream-world was healing, socially connecting and adaptive – paleo-anthropologists suggest imagining alternative realities together gave *Homo sapiens* an evolutionary advantage over Neanderthals, who apparently had less capacity to share altered states through symbolic language.[6]

Jumping ahead to Greece in around 400 BC, the priest and the artist were no longer the same person: they split into separate cultural roles. The two great events of Athenian culture were the cult of Eleusis, and the Grand Dionysiac Festival, at which new comedies and tragedies were performed every year. These two poles of Athenian life – cult and culture – were quite similar. Plato suggested that both the priest and the artist went into a 'divine madness' where they channelled the inspiration of the gods (Sophocles was alleged to have communed with Aesculapius, god of healing), then transported their audiences into that ecstatic state. Both ecstatic cults and theatre gave the audience catharsis, according to Aristotle: they helped people release the tension of civilisation. But there are important differences between cult and culture. The cult of Eleusis was sacred, secret and always the same. The ritual remained more or less the same for centuries. The Grand Dionysiac Festival, by contrast, was public (it was even open to foreigners), transgressive, shocking and funny. And it was always new: where the priest strove for repetition, the playwright strove for originality. The plays of the festival often reflected on the old cults – indeed, the plays of Aristophanes, Euripides, Sophocles and Aeschylus trod a fine line and were sometimes accused of blasphemy. But the old cult *needed* the new plays, to reconnect the cult to a new audience, to keep the old myths fresh and alive, to sing the song anew. And maybe culture needed cult too, to give the artists something to riff off ('you gotta improvise on something', as Mingus said).

In Christian medieval culture, there was also a parallel between the prophet and the artist. Both got their inspiration from ecstatic states like dreams, visions and voices. You only have to step into St Peter's, or Notre Dame, or Durham Cathedral, to see how central the arts are to Christian worship – an icon, altarpiece, stained-glass window or oratorio are ways of altering reality and opening a portal to the divine. Imagination was also an important part of Christian contemplation – the medieval author of *Meditations on the Life of Christ* suggested meditators 'give authority to the imagination' when they visualise scenes from Christ's life, to make the Bible part of their inner life.[7] In medieval mystery

52

plays, entire towns took part in the imaginative enactment of the Passion or the Final Judgment, in an exuberant, riotous improvisation. The arts transport people into the imaginative world of the Bible, and adapt its messages for contemporary eras. But there's a creative tension between cult and culture – maybe artists will take the innovation too far, make stuff up, be too flashy or irreverent, or start claiming a personal revelation beyond the confines of ecclesiastical authority. Maybe they will insist their beautiful creations are proof not of the glory of God but of the genius of the artist.

The Reformation and the liberation of the arts

In the sixteenth century, the Reformation cut some of the links between cult and culture. Puritans carried out violent campaigns in churches against the visual arts, smashing statues and stained-glass windows, burning paintings, destroying murals and altar-pieces. They attacked the magical power of the arts: objects or ceremonies have no power in themselves, and to think they do is idolatry. Protestants attacked the devotional practice of 'imaginative meditation' – how dare people embellish the Bible with their flights of fancy? Puritans closed down the street performances of mystery plays: they were too carnival-esque, too irreverent, people kept making stuff up or mixing in pagan material, like the Lord of Misrule or the Green Man. Protestants insisted on a sharp divide between the literal truth of the Bible, and the made-up products of human imagination.

This sharp divide was taken up by the Enlightenment. Science reveals the literal truth. The arts are the product not of visionary imagination but of fancy. They give us pretty stories, metaphors, images, which are pleasing but not reliable, and certainly not 'magic'. If you put too much faith in imagination, you're deluded or even mad. The Reformation undermined many of the imaginative practices by which ordinary people had achieved ecstatic states. But it also led to the liberation of the arts, which offered people new technologies, new avenues to ecstatic experience beyond the confines of the Church.

No sooner had the Puritans closed down the beloved street

performances of mystery plays than the first theatre-houses opened in London, offering people a new, secular, site of collective dreaming. Aldous Huxley, lecturing on Elizabethan drama as 'visionary spectacle', noted that 'The adjective which is often applied to it is "transporting" – it transports you, takes you out of this world, and puts you in the Otherworld.'[8] This new space rapidly attained its prophet in William Shakespeare, who self-consciously explored theatre as a form of magic, in which actors and audience conjure up a dream-world together.

Shakespeare's comedies are ecstatic dreams in which traditional ego-structures are transgressed. Characters swap partners, genders, status, sexualities, even species. There's a Puckish mischief to it all – the ego is not as stable as we think, and theatre lets us play at alternative identities. The tragedies, of course, are closer to a nightmare, exploring the darker shadow side of human identity – what it's like to be betrayed, abandoned, murdered, thrown out of your home and left to howl in the wilderness. His tragedies help us face these nightmares, and endure them together.

Sir Jonathan Bate, the leading living scholar of Shakespeare, suggests the Bard was self-consciously exploring the idea of theatre as a replacement for the Catholic rituals that the Reformation swept away. Bate has said:

> [Shakespeare] was aware that the old rituals of Roman Catholicism had been under attack. He's almost beginning to think that the ritualised play of the theatre can be a substitute for some of those old rituals of Catholicism. He loves a performance – the Catholic mass was a performance, but it was banned. The religion of theatre is taking over from the religion he inherited.[9]

Yet consider how different the religion of theatre is from a traditional cult. What are the ethics of the religion of Shakespeare? One hears every possible ethical philosophy expressed. When we go beyond the ego, what spirit or God do we encounter? 'Who's there?' asks the first line in *Hamlet*. There's a radical ambiguity in Shakespeare's plays. Sometimes we encounter mischievous spirits, as in *A Midsummer Night's Dream* or *The*

Tempest, sometimes Christian providence, as in *Hamlet*; sometimes there is only darkness and cosmic evil, as in *Macbeth* or *King Lear*. We find his plays so endlessly fascinating precisely because it is not immediately obvious what they mean – they are rich with multiple possible meanings. How refreshing, compared to the grim literalism of Puritanism.

Shakespeare's theatre offers magical rituals and mythology for a sceptical age. The novelist A. S. Byatt suggests that sceptical moderns 'need a religious world full of mythology, but they don't want to be told what is right'.[10] Theatre can transport us to virtual worlds where we encounter various spiritual presences, if we have what Coleridge called the 'temporary half-faith' to go with the play.[11] I agree with Jonathan Bate that Shakespeare's last romances seem to move back to the Catholicism of his youth – *The Winter's Tale* and *The Tempest* are rich in ideas of penitence, mercy, prayer, indulgence, ritual, redemption and healing. But there's an ever-present ambiguity here too – Paulina in *The Winter's Tale* says, 'If powers divine/Behold our human action'. That 'if' says it all – imagine a priest praying, 'God, if there is a God . . .'

Shakespeare addresses the ambiguity of ecstasy directly, in *A Midsummer Night's Dream*, in which Theseus and Hippolyta consider the lovers' accounts of their collective immersion in Fairy-land. Theseus writes off the lovers' crazy stories:

> I never may believe
> These antique fables, nor these fairy toys . . .
> Such tricks hath strong imagination,
> That if it would but apprehend some joy,
> It comprehends some bringer of that joy;
> Or in the night, imagining some fear,
> How easy is a bush supposed a bear!

Theseus's speech is a reductionist account of ecstatic experience straight out of the mouth of Richard Dawkins. Ecstasy is a 'trick' or delusion of overwrought imagination. It's caused by what evolutionary psychologists now call 'hyperactive agency detection' – we imagine spirits behind natural processes. Hippolyta rejoins:

But all the story of the night told over,
And all their minds transfigured so together,
More witnesseth than fancy's images
And grows to something of great constancy,
But, howsoever, strange and admirable.

In five lines, Hippolyta encapsulates William James's pragmatic attitude to ecstatic experiences, 300 years before *Varieties*. There may or may not be spirits out there, but either way, our imagination of the ideal can grow 'to something of strange constancy' in our lives through our acts, habits and sacrifices. In fact, she goes further than James because she understands the importance of community in making the ideal real – 'their minds transfigured so *together*'.

Five centuries later, and theatre is still capable of giving us moments of ecstatic transport. In a 1961 survey on ecstatic experiences by the journalist Marghanita Laski, several respondents said watching a production of Shakespeare was the most ecstatic moment of their life.[12] The American journalist Ron Rosenbaum was one of the lucky few to see Peter Brook's 1970 production of *Dream*:

> To say it was 'electrifying' does not capture the effect; it was more like being struck by lightning. I felt 'transported' in the literal sense of being physically as well as metaphysically lifted from the muddy vesture of the earth to some higher realm.[13]

Poetry as a 'door into the dark'

At the same time as theatre was establishing itself as a new space for collective dreaming, poetry was also taking on a new and important role as a quasi-secular avenue to ecstatic experience. Christian mystics from King David to St John of the Cross had used poetry as the language of ecstatic inspiration. When God speaks, He speaks in verse. Metaphor is the ladder between man and God – the Kingdom of Heaven is like an acorn, like a mustard-seed, like buried treasure, and so on. The monk-poet or nun-poetess reads the Book of Nature and mystically interprets its signs and symbols. By the Middle Ages, secular poets had established a role for themselves outside the Church. They claimed similar ecstatic inspiration to the clergy – they wrote dream-poems or vision-poems, like Langland's *Piers Plowman*, Chaucer's *Parlement of Foules*, or Dante's extraordinary *Divine Comedy*. But secular poets were more daring, playful and transgressive than their cloistered counterparts, more willing to draw attention to their own creative skill, more prepared to go beyond dogma and mix in aspects of paganism and magic. The ecstasy they celebrate in their verse might not even be Christian ecstasy. In John Donne's poem 'The Ecstasy', it is sexual love, not the Holy Spirit, which takes the poet beyond the self.

More often than not, however, poets in the sixteenth and seventeenth centuries worked within the Christian tradition, taking up the vacancy created by the dissolution of the monasteries. Previously, monks and nuns had produced devotional literature, creating 'affective scripts' of imaginative meditation to guide lay-people's emotional and ecstatic experiences. In post-Reformation Britain, that role was taken up by poets, who became, as it were, 'mystics-without-portfolio'. As Louis Martz argued in *The Poetry of Meditation*,[14] the dissolution of monasteries leads to the great seventeenth-century flowering of English 'metaphysical poets' – Donne, Marvell, Vaughan, Crashaw, Herbert, Traherne and, later, Milton – who create new 'affective scripts' to guide the reader's imagination on ecstatic journeys, as in Vaughan's 'The Search':

> all night have I
> Spent in a roving Extasie
> to find my Saviour; I have been
> As far as *Bethlem*, and have seen
> His Inne, and Cradle; Being there
> I met the *Wise-men*, askt them where
> He might be found, or what starre can
> Now point him out, grown up a Man?
> To *Egypt* hence I fled . . . [and so on]

By the late eighteenth and early nineteenth centuries, many European intellectuals had lost their faith in Christianity, and embraced rationalism and materialism. Imagination lost the visionary status it had enjoyed in medieval and Renaissance culture, and ecstasy became increasingly pathologised. However, Romantic poets fought a rearguard action, and tried to re-validate ecstatic experiences and rebuild an animist theory of the universe, even if that universe was no longer explicitly Christian. They seized on Plato's idea of the ecstatic inspiration of the poet. Wordsworth's *Prelude* is a hymn to the poet's inspiration through dreams, visions and trance states. Yet, as in Shakespeare's theatre, it is not always clear what spiritual reality we will encounter when we follow the Romantic poet beyond the ego. We could meet nature-spirits, or Nature, or the Sublime, or a pantheistic God, or we could meet an evil demonic force, like Coleridge's Christabel, or Keats's Belle Dame Sans Merci. Romantic poetry is 'spilled religion', as the poet T. E. Hulme put it,[15] a spirituality for agnostics: it transports us beyond the ego and beyond materialism, and connects us to a . . . Something Or Other. That encounter with a Something More can be a very powerful experience, even if we're not sure what the Something is. We need Keats's 'negative capability' to surrender to the mystery 'without any irritable reaching after fact and reason'.

The poet Malcolm Guite recounts being dragged to see Keats's Hampstead home by an improving aunt when he was a 16-year-old atheist. He read the words of 'Ode to a Nightingale', which are written on the walls of Keats's bedroom, 'and had a kind of epiphany. When I read Keats's Ode, I suddenly felt there was mystery again.' That moment led him to become an agnostic, then a Christian, and then a poet-priest. He thinks poetry has an important role to play in a culture that has become overly reliant on one way of knowing – scientific empiricism – and ignored another: the imaginative, intuitive knowing of poetry, which has its own 'poetic logic'. It uses rhythm, rhyme, metaphor, allusion, paradox and other techniques to transport our consciousness and connect us to a spiritual truth beyond the rational and conceptual. Poetry, he says, can be what Seamus Heaney calls 'a door into the dark' – a window beyond the here-and-now, connecting us to a spiritual dimension. Poets, Rainer Maria Rilke wrote, are 'bees of the invisible' – it is 'within the power of the creative artist to build a bridge between two worlds'.[16]

The novel as virtual-reality technology

The novel is a technology capable of profoundly altering our consciousness. We get lost in the world of a good book. The neuroscientist Norman Holland, author of *Literature and the Brain,* wrote: 'We gain a special trance-like state of mind in which we become unaware of our bodies and environment. We are transported.' As the writer Katie Oldham put it, we 'stare at marked slices of tree for hours on end, hallucinating wildly'.[17] Psychologists at Washington University found that, when readers read, 'they mentally simulate each new situation' using neurons that 'closely mirror those involved . . . in similar real-world activities'.[18] To read deeply is to be immersed in a virtual reality that we help co-create – listen to Enlightenment *philosophe* Denis Diderot's description of reading Samuel Richardson's novels:

> How many times have I caught myself, as happens with children being taken to the theatre for the first time, shouting out: Don't believe him, he's deceiving you . . . If you go there it'll be the end of you. My heart was in a state of permanent agitation. In the space of a few hours I had been through a host of situations which the longest life can scarcely provide in its whole course.[19]

Novels let us step into another's consciousness and see through their eyes. That could be someone of another gender, another race (as in *Uncle Tom's Cabin*), another class (as in *Les Misérables* or *Hard Times*), another species (*Watership Down*), or even another world, as in the novels of C. S. Lewis, J. R. R. Tolkien, and every fantasy and science-fiction writer since.[20] The great novels of the nineteenth and twentieth centuries gave us windows into moments of heightened consciousness. In the novels of Tolstoy, Dostoevsky, Virginia Woolf, Marilynne Robinson and others, pearls of epiphany are crafted with exquisite skill then threaded along the string of the plot – indeed, Joyce planned at one point to write a 'book of epiphanies'.[21] For secular readers, great literature can be a replacement for the Good Book, a source of consolation and transcendence. A friend of mine, Casper ter Kuile, who is training to be a minister for non-religious people, presents a popular podcast that reads Harry Potter as if it were a sacred text, using the medieval technique of *lectio divina*, or 'spiritual reading', to contemplate the stories' ethical wisdom for us today.

Art as ecstatic portal

In paganism and Christianity, art is a portal to divine reality. Sacred objects are set apart, holy; they possess the awful power to connect us to saints, angels, God, or the Devil. You don't just look at an icon, it also looks into you.[22] Works of art are windows through which the divine comes to meet us, as in Fra Angelico's mural of the Annunciation. Protestant iconoclasm challenged this magic, as did the invention of the printing press and photography: how can a painting have magical power when we can reproduce endless copies of it? Yet we still think it does. The psychologist Jesse Prinz tried out a thought-experiment: he told people to imagine the *Mona Lisa* was destroyed in a fire 'but that there happened to be a perfect copy that even experts couldn't tell from the original'. He asked if people would rather see the ashes of the original *Mona Lisa* or a perfect duplicate. 80 per cent of respondents chose the ashes: 'Apparently we disvalue copies and attribute almost magical significance to originals.'[23]

Nietzsche suggested, 'Art raises its head where religions decline.'[24] Sure enough, in the nineteenth and twentieth centuries, as Christian faith began to decline in the West, intellectuals turned to painting and sculpture to fill the void. The German painter Gerhard Richter wrote in 1964: 'The Church is no longer adequate as a means of affording experience of the transcendental . . . and so art has been transformed from a means into the sole provider of religion.'[25] This faith in art was developed, surprisingly enough, by a theologian called Paul Tillich. He served as a chaplain in the German Army in the First World War.

Surrounded by the horror of trench warfare, Tillich found consolation by gazing on a print of Botticelli's *Madonna with Singing Angels*. After the war he went on a pilgrimage to see the original in the Kaiser-Friedrich Museum in Berlin. He wrote:

> Gazing up at it, I felt a state approaching ecstasy . . . It shone through the colours of the paint as the light of day shines through the stained-glass windows of a medieval church. As I stood there, bathed in the beauty its painter had envisioned so long ago, something of the divine source of all things came through to me. I turned away shaken. That moment has affected my whole life . . . [26]

Art brings us revelations – 'an ecstatic experience of the ground of being that shakes, transforms or heals', Tillich wrote. The shock of art is spiritual but also profoundly physical. Somehow the symbolic logic of the arts connects to our consciousness and body at a deep pre-rational level, bringing us hope and healing. Tillich came to believe that the arts had a world-saving role in modern post-Christian culture in that they could connect us to the 'ground of being' that exists beneath our everyday ego-shells of habit. If art has a religious function, that does not mean it should offer us the sentimental kitsch one finds in the tourist shops around the Vatican. Rather, art should confront us with the true horror of our historical situation – Tillich thought Picasso's *Guernica* was a prime example of what he called 'ecstatic art'.

When art is raised into a religion, then the art gallery and museum become temples. The paintings of Mark Rothko seem to epitomise this sacerdotal function of modern art, either in New York's Museum of Modern Art (MOMA), the Tate Modern in London, or in the Rothko Chapel in Houston. We stand in front of his paintings to seek God, or the absence of God, or a 'God who has withdrawn', as Tillich put it. And the experience often reduces people to tears. Rothko declared: 'I'm interested only in expressing basic human emotions – tragedy, ecstasy, doom and so on . . . The people who weep before my pictures are having the same religious experiences I had when I painted them.'[27] Perhaps we go into the Rothko Room at the Tate with the expectation of such an experience. But we may also have the experience of being surprised by a painting or sculpture in a gallery, mugged by it, so that we suddenly feel shaken, possessed, moved to tears. For the art historian James Elkins, coming across Bellini's *St Francis in the Desert* in the Frick Museum was a moment of tears and wonder. For Jeanette Winterson, it was an unnamed painting she walked past in a gallery in Amsterdam 'that had more power to stop me than I had power to walk on'.[28]

In 2010, the performance artist Marina Abramović explored this idea of 'gallery-encounter as ecstatic experience', in her work *The Artist is Present*. Abramović, whose great-uncle is an Orthodox saint, has something of the self-flagellating saint about her too. She said in an interview with *Whitewall* magazine: 'I'm interested in everything to do with aestheticism, high spirituality experiences and ecstasy. In performance, when you push your limit to a certain point and overcome the pain, you reach a state of ecstasy which is very similar to religious and spiritual ecstasy.' In an HBO documentary, she comments: 'The moment you go through the door of pain you enter into another state of mind . . . You suddenly become, like . . . holy, I can't explain. And that other state of mind is exactly what the public is feeling . . . you create a charismatic space . . . a direct energy between the audience and the performer . . .'[29]

During the performance of *The Artist is Present*, Abramović sat on a chair in a room at MOMA for 736 hours, during which audience members could come and sit opposite her for however long they wanted, staring at her as she stared back: 1,545 people came to sit with her. And many of them cried. Many spoke of a deep sense of connection with Abramović. She succeeded in making herself into a living icon, whom you approach with reverence and the knowledge that she looks into you, feels your pain and accepts you (or appears to, anyway). Abramović found one way to make art sacred in the age of mechanical reproduction: you create a unique immersive moment that can't be reproduced. It was magical, but also mechanical – psychologists have found that staring into another person's eyes releases the 'love hormone' oxytocin, synchronises your brains, and often triggers hallucinations.[30] Whether through magic or mechanics, Abramović succeeded in creating 'a charismatic space' in MOMA. People slept on the pavement outside the museum to be sure of an audience. One man sat with her 21 times, then had '21' tattooed on his arm. A support group was set up for those who had sat with her, to help them come to terms with the experience. For four months, Abramović transformed MOMA into a site of popular religious fervour.

Cinema and virtual reality as a cave of dreams

Finally, cinema since its inception has been concerned with how to transport audiences into dream-worlds. This twentieth-century technology of ecstasy is entirely new, but it's also in some ways reminiscent of humanity's oldest artistic technology for consciousness-alteration: the torch-lit cave-painting, as Werner Herzog explored in his documentary *Cave of Forgotten Dreams*. Cinema is a form of collective dreaming, a path to what Herzog calls 'ecstatic truth'. In some ways, it reminds me of Peter Weir's trance-like film *Picnic at Hanging Rock*, about a group of Australian schoolgirls who disappear into a mysterious cave. Cinema is this cave, a numinous place where our ordinary egos dissolve and we're transported to other worlds – Oz, Middle Earth, the Magic Kingdom, the Zone.

The great directors discovered cinematic techniques for altering the consciousness of the audience. Sergei Eisenstein, Charlie Chaplin, Luis Buñuel, Alfred Hitchcock, Federico Fellini, Andrei Tarkovsky, Jonathan Glazer, Christopher Nolan, Andrea Arnold and many other directors sought to re-create the experience of dreams, trance-states, epiphanies and ecstasies in their films.[31] Cinema, in David Lynch's words, 'allows the subconscious to speak'.[32]

The two greatest masters of trance, for me, are Lynch and Stanley Kubrick. Both are virtuosi at creating Otherworlds – the world of *Twin Peaks*, or the Escher-esque dream-palace of the Overlook Hotel in *The Shining* – which draw us in and hold us rapt. The worlds that lure us in and hold us are completely faithful to their own weird rules. They're drawn with great detail and complexity, yet brim with uneasy ambiguity. Our minds return again and again to certain unexplained details . . . What do the numbers signify in *The Shining*? Who is the dancing dwarf in *Twin Peaks*? Why the strange patterns on the carpets in the Black Lodge and the Overlook Hotel? Both Lynch and Kubrick manage to hypnotise us through a non-verbal language of sound, music and image.[33] Both take us beyond the shed of ordinary ego-consciousness to meet the mysterious presences moving in the dark forest. Who or what do we encounter there? In *2001: A Space Odyssey*, we meet extra-terrestrial intelligences, who take the place of God, as they do in other sci-fi movies, like *Close Encounters of the Third Kind*, *Contact* or *Interstellar*. Many people, from Tom Hanks to Leo DiCaprio, say that watching *2001* for the first time was a spiritual experience (at one early screening an audience member, probably on acid, shouted, 'This is God!' and had to be dragged from the theatre).[34] In *Twin Peaks* and *The Shining*, by contrast, we encounter demonic spirits. As Freud noted in his essay 'The Uncanny', the function of horror in modern culture is to recon-nect us to our animist past and show us the haunted forest beyond the secular ego. That's also the function of animation, like the films of Disney, Marvel, Pixar and Studio Ghibli: they take us back to an enchanted world where toys live, broomsticks dance, where the forest teems with spirits.[35]

In the last half-century, computer-game designers have created virtual worlds in which we can lose ourselves for weeks. Game designers quickly figured out that Otherworld-play is much more fun when it's communal, as in open-world games like Grand Theft Auto V or Minecraft. The next frontier is virtual and augmented reality, which will give experiences so gut-wrenchingly immersive, so brimming with presence, they may blur our categories of the real and the imaginary, taking us back to the world of medieval magic and mysticism where they were more intertwined. Augmented-reality games blur the boundary between the real and the enchanted – playing Pokémon Go, the streets and parks are filled with animist creatures. Virtual reality (VR), more than previous artistic technologies, can radically affect our body-awareness, altering our sense of self and even triggering out-of-body experiences. VR studios aim to engineer transcendence – new VR products include a pilgrimage to Mecca, a recreation of the Passion, and a trip to the afterlife to meet 3D-generations of deceased loved ones. We are moving, says futurist Kevin Kelly, towards the internet of shared experiences.[36] As in *A Midsummer Night's Dream*, our minds will be 'transfigured so together'.

The ecstasy of creative inspiration

Artists, then, conjure up dream-worlds that mesmerise and transport us. But is this a conscious skill, or a subliminal gift? Frederic Myers was one of the first psychologists to consider creative inspiration. He suggested that 'genius' is an unusual capacity (probably genetic) to access the creative power of the subliminal mind, combined with the conscious skill to sort out the gold from the dross. He gave the example of Charles Dickens, who would sometimes hear or see his characters rise up before him like ghosts (indeed, he once crossed the road when he saw a character approaching). In a survey by the Hearing the Voice project at Durham University, 70 per cent of contemporary novelists said they heard their characters' voices speak to them. Creativity is, partly, a shamanic capacity to open to the voices and images of the subliminal mind.[37] The artist, wrote E. M. Forster, 'lets down as it were a bucket into his subconscious, and draws up something which is normally beyond his reach'.

Like shamans, artists use techniques of ecstasy to access the subconscious. Many directors, including Fellini, Tarkovsky and Kurosawa, incorporated material from their dreams in their films. David Lynch uses Transcendental Meditation to open his mind and 'catch the big fish' swimming in his subliminal thinking; Ted Hughes would literally go fishing to transport himself into a 'slightly mesmerised' state of 'expectant attention' in which ideas and images arose from his subconscious,[38] while Alfred, Lord Tennyson would repeat his own name as a mantra to entrance himself. Others, like William Wordsworth or Jean-Jacques Rousseau, would go for a long walk in the country to get into a contemplative reverie where subliminal creativity is unlocked. Coleridge, De Quincey, Baudelaire and Rimbaud used drugs as a way of dreaming while awake. W. B. Yeats, Gertrude Stein and others used automatic writing as a means of tapping subliminal creativity.

If you're trying to access the subliminal mind, it's important you temporarily switch off your inner censor, which might be horrified by the darkness of some of the material that comes up. Friedrich Schiller once said: 'In the case of the creative mind, it seems to me, the intellect has withdrawn its watchers from the gates, and the ideas rush in pell-mell, and only then does it review and inspect the multitude.'[39] But, of course, simply being open to the subliminal mind is no guarantee of artistic quality – the RERC database is full of divinely inspired poems that are God-awful. One also needs the conscious skill to be able to sort the treasure from the rubbish.

Is inspiration a gift from beyond?

In the enchanted world of the past, creative inspiration was seen as supernatural, a gift from the Muses, spirits, or God. Modern artists also speak of creative inspiration in supernatural terms, but Mihály Csíkszentmihályi, who has studied the psychology of creative inspira-tion, tells me, 'Mostly [artists] are talking metaphorically or allegorically. I don't think I've met anyone who actually believes [in the supernat-ural].' If that's true, he can't have been looking very hard. Many of the greatest artists of the last three centuries *really did* believe creative inspiration is supernatural. Ted Hughes wrote that the poetic self lives 'its own life separate from and for the most part hidden from the poet's ordinary personality . . . [it is] not under his control . . . and it's super-natural'. The Polish poet Czesław Miłosz wrote: 'Frankly, all my life I have been in the power of a daemonion, and how the poems dictated by him came into being I do not quite understand.'[40] Keats also wrote of communicating with 'my demon Poesy'. Artists may feel they are communicating with a spirit or angel of some kind, as Blake often did, as Rilke does in his *Duino Elegies*, or that they're channelling the voices of their culture, as T. S. Eliot does in *The Wasteland*. They may feel they're channelling the spirit of a dead writer who inspires them, as Keats felt he was channelling Shakespeare, as Pico Iyer felt he was channelling Graham Greene when writing about him. Iyer is not entirely sure if this was a genuine spirit-visitation or it just felt like that.[41] Most artists ultimately don't care, as long as the inspiration keeps coming.

Brian Eno is impatient with supernatural explanations of creativity: 'I'm anti-mystical. Mysticism isn't an explanation. It's a way of getting rid of a problem. You don't know what's happening, so you call it God. I'm interested in the mechanism.' But he still emphasises the creative importance of going beyond the ego. He has an optimism that when you get the ego out of the way and surrender control, interesting and creative things will emerge. Eno's equally impatient with too much of a Myersian focus on individual genius. He prefers the term 'scenius', to describe the cultural ecosystem out of which creativity arises – the patrons, the collaborators, the rivals, the audience, the technology. But you can combine genius with scenius – David Bowie had a Myers-esque genius for delving into his subliminal mind, but he also had incredible collaborators, like Eno.

The arts as collective dreaming

Can the arts, then, really be a substitute for religion? That is more or less the role they have fulfilled in Western civilisation over the last four centuries. The arts have given us a set of technologies that take us beyond ordinary ego-consciousness and transport us into dream-worlds in ways that are profoundly enjoyable, healing, inspiring and socially connecting.

The arts heal our psyches in many different ways, but first by taking us beyond the anxious ego and giving us a blissful absorption into something beautiful. The arts guide our emotional responses to change, suffering, evil and death. They're like a secular liturgy, giving us words when we have no words. When Wordsworth died in 1850, Matthew Arnold lamented, 'Who, ah, who will make us feel?' Artists connect us to feelings we didn't even know we had, buried deep below our ego defences, and that can be profoundly healing – one thinks of John Stuart Mill struggling with a nervous breakdown, then reading Wordsworth's poems, and coming to feel that 'there was real, permanent happiness in tranquil contemplation'. Most importantly, the arts – like dreams – help us to confront and connect with our shadows, without being overwhelmed by them. The arts can teach us to take pity on our shadows, to feel compassion for the broken and wounded aspects of ourselves, as well as for the broken and wounded parts of our society. We no longer feel we are uniquely messed up: we realise *everyone* is messed up, many others have gone through crises as bad as ours, and worse. That gives us a cathartic release from the prison of shame and fear. The artist dreams stories, myths and symbols that help their society step outside its usual ego-constructions, and confront what is repressed, ignored or unsaid. In a sceptical age, the arts give us 'half-faith' in an enchanted world, a world of transcendent love and hope, even if we're not sure if it's real or just a story.

The limits of the arts as religious substitute

Turning the arts into a religious substitute has its risks. First, the cult of the artist-genius puts a heavy burden on the artist to improvise new myths for their society. That's a lot of pressure, particularly when you're operating outside a religious context, when you're just relying on your own creative genius to save the world. What if your inspiration dries up? The cult of the artist-genius can descend into an idolatry of the maestro (the cult of Wagner, for example), which is unhealthy both for the audience and the artist. Or it can descend into an idolatry of objects – the contemplative seeking transcendence degenerates into the obsessive collector, the 'art-addict', as Peggy Guggenheim called herself. Another risk of the arts as religion-substitute is that we seek the experience of ecstasy or transcendence without any ethical foundations. This is what Eno wanted to find: the experience of religious surrender, without the doctrine. That can end up in the morally bankrupt aestheticism of Dorian Gray, the thrill-seeking dandy invented by Oscar Wilde, who seeks moments of aesthetic ecstasy without any regard for morality. A work of art may also possess us in a *negative* sense – Victorians were sent into a moral panic about the decadent works of Walter Pater, Wilde and Wagner, which they thought would mesmerise young people to the ruin of their morality and health.

Great art offers us a window to transcendence but, unlike contemplative traditions, it doesn't really show us how to get *through* that window, what practices we can use each day to transform the psyche permanently. Rilke stands in front of a statue and feels it says to him, 'You must change your life.' To which Rilke could have responded, 'Sure, but *how* exactly?' Artists, unlike mystics, are, on the whole, in it for the money and status, so art-as-religion can give us commodified consumer packages of transcendence that are actually somewhat tacky. I recently made a secular pilgrimage to the Guggenheim museum in Bilbao, only to discover it had been given over to the balloon kitsch of Jeff Koons, displayed with Koons's sacerdotal pronouncements underneath: 'It's all about transcendence, about having greater experiences than the ones you had before, about creating a vaster life.' Sure it is, Jeff. Culture, we recall, is unlike cult in that it strives for originality, transgression and shock. But we're a civilisation that has lost its central cult, and now relies mainly on culture for its transcendence – which means that, particularly in the last century of modernism and post-modernism, all we have is a culture of transgression, sensation and shock, without any cult to riff off. How many Piss Christs or elephant-dung Madonnas can the art world produce before we admit that we're beyond shocking because there's no longer anything sacred to transgress?

The arts can give us healing dreams where we confront the shadow and are helped to grow. But most of the time, novels or films give us wish-fulfilment dreams that are pure escapism, easy-to-consume ego-fantasies where the heroes are invincible, the bad guys are demonic, and the lovers always live happily ever after. The virtual-reality market will likewise largely supply consoling fantasies that we can escape into as the world burns. Philosopher Roger Scruton may hold up high culture as a substitute for the Church,[42] but that avenue of transcendence is only really open to the tuxedoed elite. Christianity and paganism offered avenues to transcendence for *everyone*, the intellectual and the masses. At their best, they offered communities where people could feel they were loved and cared for. Do the arts provide that sort of community? I don't know . . . Perhaps they do. One could point to book clubs, book festivals, fan-fiction communities, or the cosplay fan-clubs of Trekkies, Jedis and Marvel maniacs, who dress up like their heroes much as C. S. Lewis suggests we should dress up like Christ.

There is one form of art that, more than any other, avoided elitism and offered a form of mass ecstasy over the last 50 years: rock and roll. Let's stretch our legs, get off the comfy sofas of the Ecstatic Cinema, and go to the Rock and Roll Main Stage, where the Reverend Al Green is just about to sing.

4: Rock and Roll Main Stage

It's not hard to find the Reverend Al Green's church in Memphis – it's right next to the enormous road sign, saying, 'Full Gospel Tabernacle Church featuring the Bishop Al Green'. When you go inside, there's a life-size cardboard cut-out of Al Green, and the service sheet has two more photos of him. There's a painting of him on the church wall, and on the stage a big armchair embroidered with 'Bishop Al Green'. And yet the great man is nowhere to be seen when my friend Joe and I arrive, one Sunday morning, feeling self-conscious and white as we tiptoe into the church. There are a few pews of smartly dressed black people at the front of the church, but at least half of the congregation look like fellow tourists – they're sitting at the back, white, dressed in T-shirts and khaki pants, not clapping but nodding enthusiastically. The music is fantastic: a six-piece band with Al Green's son on organ, and a gospel choir belting out the hymns.

And then the Reverend Al Green appears on stage, midway through a number, smiling genially as he shuffles to his throne. He's 70, greying and rather plump, but he looks well enough. Forty years ago, the man considered to have perhaps the greatest voice in soul music threw it all in when he woke up one morning on tour to hear a strange noise that turned out to be himself speaking in tongues. That was when he stopped being the womanising 'Prince of Love' and became the Reverend Al Green (now Bishop). That was pretty much the end of his music career, as far as the world was concerned – he's put out a few gospel albums since but nothing like the hits of the 1970s. But so what? He's happy and at peace with his God.

Except Al Green does not seem that happy. He takes the microphone for his sermon, and right from the get-go, his tone is angry and bitter. 'You know . . . people come to this church, and it's all about Al. Al Al Al Al Al Al Al Al. But it's not all about Al. I can't save you. It's about *Jesus*.' The Reverend gazes around the congregation. He doesn't like what he sees. 'You know, this country is heading for *damnation* . . .' He lets the word linger in the air. There is an uncomfortable shifting in the seats from the white pews. 'We got a White House that approves of sodomy . . . Homosexuality is an *abomination* . . .' He puts on a mincing voice and mimes a floppy wrist. '"It's our lifestyle and we're proud of it." No! It's a sin! Ain't no gays here, I hope. Ain't no gays in our choir!' And so it goes on. A collective realisation sinks into the audience: Al Green is a dick.

Many of the white soul pilgrims get up and leave, but that just seems to spur the Reverend on. 'Don't worry about them – they just want to hear me sing "Hound Dog". Well, this is my church! I paid for it, I can say what I want! Let me see your hands up. Do you believe in God?' Good question. Maybe we're not sure. Maybe we just wanted to hear you sing, Al. You had a golden chance to bring in non-believers and spread the message of God's love. When Elvis Costello was once asked if he'd ever had a religious experience, he replied: 'No, but I have heard Al Green.' Instead of Love and Happiness, though, you gave us Hate and Bitterness. We preferred you when you were a sinner. Now the Reverend is railing at his own congregation. 'We did a Bible class. Nobody came. Why did nobody come?' Probably because you're an angry egomaniac, and that's why, after 40 years, you still have such a tiny regular congregation. But then, having vented his spleen and driven out most of the white soul pilgrims, Al seems relieved and nods to the band. They start on a rolling gospel number, and he sings. And the voice is still there, soaring and twisting, like a kite in the wind. You feel it, along your arms, in the back of your neck, deep in your guts. And for a second, he seems like a vessel for

God's love. Then he starts on the hate-speech again, and Joe and I get up to leave.

We head across town to Graceland. It's easier to pay homage to your heroes when they're dead.

Soul-icon valley

I visited Al Green's church as part of a three-week musical pilgrimage through the Deep South. I wanted to understand how that poor corner of America was the scene of the most intense cultural innovation of the fifties and sixties. It was the Soul-icon valley of its day, producing rock and roll, soul, blues, jazz and country. In Nashville, I visited the converted church of the Ryman Auditorium to hear the *Grand Ole Opry*, America's oldest radio show and the home of country music. I went to Studio B and heard the ghostly voice of Elvis recording 'Are You Lonesome Tonight?'. I drove down Music Highway to Memphis, and visited tiny Sun Studio, where in 1958 Elvis, Johnny Cash, Jerry Lee Lewis and Carl Perkins once held an impromptu jam. I went to Stax Studios, a small family-run business that turned out some of the greatest soul hits. I visited Beale Street and B. B. King's soul-food restaurant. I stood next to weeping acolytes at Elvis's grave in Graceland.

I carried on down Highway 61 and over the bayou to New Orleans, a city whose *raison d'être* seems to be losing the self through music, magic and fancy dress. I drank a lot, I got fat on dry ribs, po' boys and hot chicken, and I listened to some of the greatest live music I've ever heard. As I drove around, I listened to a playlist of Memphis, Nashville and New Orleans hits, and grooved off B. B. King growling: 'Everybody wanna know, why I sing the blues.' And I thought, *That's a very good question, B. B. In fact, why do humans sing at all? Why is music so important to us?*

Evolutionary psychologists have come up with various answers – Steven Pinker famously declared music was like cheesecake, ultimately pointless, an evolutionary side-effect or spandrel of other more functional aspects of consciousness. Others have suggested the 'function' of music is sexual display and courtship, language learning, maternal bonding, collective identity, or well-being and emotional healing. The answer is probably that music does all these things for us.[1] Certainly one of its functions is sexual courtship and display – a 2011 study found that 92 per cent of songs in the Billboard 100 in 2009 'contained one or more reproductive messages'.[2] Another function is celebrating your civic identity – think of 'Georgia On My Mind' or 'Sweet Home Chicago'. Music helps tribes assert their solidarity before battle – Liverpool supporters belt out 'You'll Never Walk Alone' before matches. Songs also serve as places of ethical and social reflection – from sexual ethics ('If lovin' you is wrong, I don't wanna be right' is about the ethics of adultery for example) to social-justice songs like the Staple Sisters' 'Respect Yourself'. In a time of rapid social change, songs help us synchronise, move in time together. But one of the biggest reasons why people sing and dance, it seems to me, is our need for ecstatic release and cathartic healing. The Deep South gave Western culture an incredible technology for ego-loss – rock and roll – at a time when we desperately needed it.

Only when I'm dancing do I feel this free

You can find ecstatic rituals involving music all over the world and all through history, going back to shamanic religion. Here's a description of a shamanic ritual in the early twentieth century in the far east of Russia by the anthropologist Sergei Shirokogorov:

> The rhythmic music and singing, and later the dancing of the shaman, gradually involve every participant more and more as a collective action. When the audience repeats the refrains together with the assistants, only those who are defective fail to join the chorus. [It leads to a state of] mass susceptibility to the suggestion, hallucinations, and unconscious acts produced in a state of mass ecstasy.[3]

In the classical cult of Cybele, devotees put themselves into a trance by jerking their head backwards and forwards. A similar head-banging technique was used by eighteenth-century Methodists – one observer wrote: 'I have seen their heads fly back and forth so quickly that the hair of females would be made to crack like a carriage whip' – and it's still used by heavy metal fans today. The Sufi dervish put themselves into a state of *fana,* or annihilation of the self, by whirling around to music. In the *zikr* of Chechen Sufism, devotees walk slowly in a circle, chanting Islamic prayers, then speed up faster and faster until they are dissolved into a blur. They repeat this for hours until the sweat is pouring off them. In the words of eleventh-century Sufi philosopher Al-Ghazali, 'Music and dancing . . . renders man beside himself with ecstasy.'[4]

Such rituals of music and dancing have long been thought to bring healing. Aristotle suggested the ecstatic dance of the Dionysiac rituals brought catharsis, helping people purge the nervous tension produced by civilisation. Ecstatic dance rituals have been particularly popular with women, as a way to work off the oppression of patriarchal systems. In Sudan and Ethiopia, a wife may be possessed by a spirit, and suddenly become wild, rude and disobedient. The cure is not to lock her up or sedate her with drugs. No, the husband must pay for a *zar* exorcism ritual, which is basically a long and expensive dance party to which he is not invited. This may help the wife to dance off the bad spirit and return to domestic harmony, although she may decide to run off and join the *zar* priestesses permanently.[5] Dance rituals can be a way for an entire community to try to exorcise evil spirits. In Sri Lanka, the *yak tovil* is an all-night dance-exorcism ceremony. In the nineteenth-century ghost-dance cult, Native Americans danced in a vain attempt to expel the evil spirits of white invaders. In cultures around the world, carnival is a way for communities to let go of customary structures of control and hierarchy. Masks and costumes are an important part of this liberation, and cross-dressing frequently plays a role, from Dionysus the cross-dressing Greek god of intoxication to the transsexual followers of Cybele and the transvestite *Bissu* priests of Indonesia.[6]

The clampdown

Ecstatic dance cults have often been repressed by governments for encouraging oppressed groups (the poor, women, slaves) to lose control.

In ancient Rome, the Bacchanalia – a riotous worship of Dionysus – was opposed by the Senate in 186 BC because it encouraged disobedience in women. Yet most cultures have found some place for people to lose themselves in ritual dance. In the Old Testament, David's aristocratic wife Michal may have disapproved of him dancing semi-nude in front of the Ark, but Jewish worship still incorporated ecstatic circle dancing, particularly among the Hasidim. The early Christian Church retained the Jewish custom (indeed, the word 'carol' comes from the Latin *corolla*, for ring). Epiphanius, fourth-century bishop of Salamis, wrote: 'Leap wildly, ye Heavens; sing Hymns, ye Angels; ye who dwell in Zion, dance ring dances.'

Yet there was also a wariness among Christian bishops that dance could encourage sensuality – Basileios, fourth-century Bishop of Caesarea, condemned Christian women who 'dance with lustful eyes and loud laughter; as if seized by a kind of frenzy they excite the lust of youth'.[7] By the end of the thirteenth century, the clergy succeeded in banning dancing in churches, but there was still a place for it in the streets at carnival time. But that, too, gradually disappeared from European cities. The historians Peter Stallybrass and Allen White wrote: 'In the long-term history from the seventeenth to the twentieth century . . . there were literally thousands of acts of legislation introduced which attempted to eliminate carnival and popular festivity from European life.' Apparently, losing yourself to dance was contrary to the ethos of Puritanism and of industrial capitalism, in which self-control is the basis of personal and public morality. Of course, people still found ways to lose themselves, but ecstatic dance lost its place in the mainstream of European religion and culture.

From Pentecostalism to rock and roll

One of the few places where ritualised ecstatic dance survived after the Enlightenment was in dissenter Protestant sects such as Methodists, Baptists and Shakers. African-American congregations developed a form of Christian worship that combined the music and hymns of Protestant churches with the rhythm and dancing of African spirit-possession rituals. In the early decades of the twentieth century, Pentecostal churches developed a highly expressive form of musical worship, using electric guitars, organs, drums, tambourines and choirs. The preacher worked the congregation into an ecstasy using call-and-response patterns repeated over and over into a hypnotic chant, building up to a great 'shout' or scream designed to push the congregation over into a frenzy (this was known as 'house-wrecking'). One by one, the congregation would 'get happy' – the Pentecostal term for achieving a trance state, subsequently celebrated by Pharrell Williams – and express the Holy Spirit through shaking, jumping, clapping, whirling and fainting.

Rock and roll, blues and soul adapted this ecstatic script and brought it to the mainstream of Western culture, giving us access to what music writer Peter Guralnick calls 'secular ecstasy'.[8] As Mahalia Jackson said: 'I believe the blues and jazz and even the rock and roll stuff got their beat from the Sanctified church.' James Brown spoke of learning how to get down at a Pentecostal church: 'There was a lot of singing and hand-clapping and usually an organ or tambourines, and then the preacher would really get down. I liked that even more than the music. I had been to a revival service and had seen a preacher who really had a lot of fire. He was just screaming and yelling and stamping his foot and then he dropped to his knees. The people got into it with him, answering him and shouting and clapping time. After that, when I went to church . . . I watched the preachers real close. Then I'd go home and imitate them because I wanted to preach . . . It's the same spirit I feel when I'm on stage today. I feel it when I sing. I make people happy, and they feel it.'[9]

Tina Turner (real name Anna Mae Bullock) likewise learned how to lose it in a Pentecostal church in Oak Ridge, Tennessee, when she was five. Her sister, Alline, recalls: 'You'd get the Holy Ghost in those services, and you'd dance around faster and faster, and the music got louder and louder. One time Ann's underpants fell down around her ankles, she was dancing so hard. But she didn't let up.' B. B. King remembers seeing the Reverend Archie Fair perform at the Church of God in Christ at Kilmichael, Mississippi: 'He says one thing and the congregation says it back, back and forth, until we're rocking together in a rhythm that won't stop. His voice is low and rough and his guitar is high and sweet; they seem to sing to each other, conversing in some heavenly language that I need to learn. The choir joins in, and the congregation joins the choir, and I'm right in the middle of a universe filled with nothing but pure spirit.'

Elvis Presley, although brought up a Baptist, was also deeply influenced by Southern Pentecostalism. One of his backing singers, Darlene Love, recalls the strange ecstatic states he would go into: 'We would be in the middle of a rehearsal and all of a sudden there would be this glaze in his eyes and he would put up his hands and stop everything. You could never tell when these spells would come on. It was almost like some inner seizure, and his only relief would be a dose of gospel songs.' Elvis took the shaking and jittering that Pentecostalists went into when the Holy Spirit hit them and turned it into his trademark hip-shaking dance. He celebrated and sexualised Pentecostal ecstasy in songs like 'All Shook Up'. So did Ray Charles – his early R&B hit 'I Got A Woman' was based on the gospel tune 'It Must Be Jesus'. His next hit, 'Hallelujah I Love Her So' offered a similar cocktail of the sacred and profane. The Isley Brothers' 'Shout' is pure Pentecostalism turned into a party anthem. Jerry Lee Lewis took Pentecostal symbolism – body-shaking, tongues of fire – and used it to express sexual delirium. (Lewis himself thought 'Great Balls Of Fire' was demonic, and had to be cajoled into recording it by producer Sam Phillips. 'You can save souls!' Phillips shouted at him from the recording desk.)

The fire of rock and roll was lit in the Deep South, then spread throughout the world, through radio, cinema, TV and live concerts. Rock and roll became a church for the unchurched, a way for agnostic teenagers to find ecstasy. In the words of musician Dave Grohl, drummer in Nirvana and front-man in the Foo Fighters: 'Music became my religion, the record store my church, the rock stars my saints, and their songs my hymns.'[10] That's true for a lot of us. Some philosophers – Allan Bloom, Theodore Adorno, Roger Scruton – blame pop music for destroying Western culture.[11] But I'd suggest the exact opposite: it *saved* us from an over-rational Enlightenment culture that was in danger of losing touch with its body and its soul. It gave us a shared means to trance states, a shared avenue to ecstasy. David Byrne, front-man of Talking Heads and a keen anthropologist of ecstasy, tells me that Afro-American and Afro-Cuban music 'changed not just Western culture but the whole world's culture. To be convinced and seduced by ecstasy is to be won over to a new way of looking at the world and oneself. The groove is found almost everywhere around the globe now – it's a species of globalisation, but one of joy and integration of body and spirit.'

How does music heal us?

Little Richard, a bisexual make-up-wearing rocker, who later became a Seventh-Day Adventist preacher, at one point insisted that rock and roll had a similar healing power to the Holy Spirit:

> I believe my music is the healin' music. Just like Oral Roberts says he's a divine healer, I believe my music can make the blind see, the lame walk, the deaf and dumb hear and talk, because it inspires and uplifts people. I've had old women tell me I made them feel they were nineteen years old. It uplifts the soul, you see everybody's movin', they're happy, it regenerates the heart and makes the liver quiver, the bladder spatter, the knees freeze.[12]

He later recanted his sacrilegious words, but few would doubt that he was right: music does give us a sense of healing and spiritual joy. How exactly? One way is by absorbing our attention through what anthropologist Judith Becker calls 'deep listening'. Music sets up patterns of expectation which we get pleasure in noticing and predicting. And the best music disrupts those patterns, or introduces complexity into them, producing a surge of pleasant surprise, which absorbs our attention further.[13] In James Brown's 'Don't Tell It', one of his funkiest songs, the groove is both repetitive but also subtly different on each revolution. In Ravel's 'Bolero', the motif is repeated over and over, with more instruments playing it each time, just as a house track builds levels of complexity on a bass foundation.

Music is also one of humans' preferred means of emotional regulation.[14] Melodies and harmonies can soothe us, taking us back to our childhood when we were being rocked and sung to by our mothers, or rouse us with warlike rhythms. Recent research suggests singing or playing a wind instrument modulates the vagus nerve at the back of our necks, which plays an important role in mood-regulation.[15] Singing and dancing can reduce rumination and self-consciousness, enabling people to get out of their heads and into the groove. Strenuous dancing may stimulate the autonomic nervous system until it switches from the sympathetic nervous system, which is used for fight-and-flight, into the parasympathetic nervous system, used for relaxation and healing. This gives us the calm, cathartic feeling we get after a really good dance.[16]

Personally, I've found music to be hugely healing when I'm stuck in my anxious ego. I've played the drums in several amateur bands (the Nervous Wrecks, Lunatic Fringe – you can tell I wasn't well when I named them), and noticed that the more depressed and introverted I felt, the better I played. I'd drum wildly, like Animal the Muppet, and after an hour or so I reached a point where I was no longer locked into myself: I felt liberated. I could feel the endorphins rippling through my brain, as if the world was flooding back into colour. Music helped reconnect me to the people around me – research suggests that singing together synchronises people's breath and even their heartbeat.[17] Singing and dancing in sync helps us dissolve our separate selves and shift into what social psychologist Jonathan Haidt calls 'the hive mind',[18] which is why we love synchronised dance routines in pop videos or musicals. If I think about the happiest moments of my life, at least three of them involve dancing at friends' weddings, surrounded by people I love.

Permission to lose control

Because it's so powerful, people have warned throughout history that music can overwhelm and harm us. In the eighteenth century, people worried that the glass harmonica would make women hysterical. In the late nineteenth century, critics warned that listening to Wagner could turn you gay.[19] In the 1950s and 1960s, guardians of the Establishment feared teenagers were being brainwashed by rock and roll. Beatlemania was compared to a Bacchic frenzy, to the hysteria of a medieval dancing plague. In 1956, the *Daily Mail* carried a cover story warning of an epidemic of 'rock and roll babies'. Rock, the paper warned, is 'sexy music. It can make the blood race. It has something of the African tom-tom and voodoo dance.' White kids were going black, was the *Mail*'s subtext – and white women might end up breeding with black men. In the same year, the Bishop of Woolwich wrote to *The Times* declaring that the 'hypnotic rhythm and the wild gestures have a maddening effect on a rhythm-loving age group and the result is the relaxing of all self-control'. But the screaming, sobbing, urinating teenagers hadn't completely lost control, of course. Like fainting Pentecostalists, they were following a new cultural script: they had finally found a place in Enlightenment culture where they could surrender executive control, allow their ego to dissolve, and get lost in music.

The sociologist Émile Durkheim wondered, in 1905, how a post-Christian civilisation would get 'collective effervescence' – the communal ecstasy we need to bond with each other. He thought nationalism and the worship of the state or leader could be an alternative religion (instead of worshipping Jesus, we can worship Putin or Trump). But thankfully, instead of Fascist rallies, God gave rock and roll to us. Instead of worshipping the Führer, we worshipped the King, Queen, Prince, Madonna. Through singing, dancing, and a quasi-religious worship of the band, we feel reconnected to the strangers we live among. And unlike ethnic nationalism, the ecstatic community is multi-racial – rock and soul were always more than just black music. So much of rock and soul was written by Jews like Leiber and Stoller or Carole King, played by mixed-race bands like Booker T and the MGs, and sung by white kids, like Elvis, the Stones and the Beatles. White kids danced to black acts, and danced next to black kids, or even (gasp!) with them.

The rock star as shaman

For me, the greatest connection to an audience and a band I ever felt was seeing Bruce Springsteen and the E-Street Band play in London in 2014. The Boss, 65 years old, played for three hours, working the band and the audience into a state of rapture that they expressed in a low chant of 'Bruuuuuce'. He roused the audience like a Pentecostal preacher:

'Tonight I want to go to that river to sanctification where all life's graces and blessings can fall down upon you like rain, but you've got to work at it . . . And tonight I want to throw a rock and roll exorcism! A rock and roll baptism! And a rock and roll bar mitzvah! That's right, we're gonna do it all tonight.'

'You're the shaman, a little bit, leading the congregation,' Springsteen told the *New Yorker*. 'You're a conduit.' Rock stars, like other highly creative individuals, have a shamanic capacity for controlled dissociation, a capacity – which Frederic Myers called 'genius' – to enter into subliminal states in order to tap their creative and healing power. Like shamans, rockers' dissociative capacity sometimes comes from a sort of crack in their ego – that's how the light gets in, as Leonard Cohen noted. Their openness to the subliminal mind might mean they see visions, as David Bowie did (in 'Oh You Pretty Things' he describes a vision in which he saw a hand reaching down from the sky). They might hear voices, as Lady Gaga did, or have an unusual ability to trance out, as John Lennon did. In his final interview, with *Playboy* magazine, Lennon said: 'When I looked at myself in the mirror or when I was 12, 13, I used to literally trance out into alpha. I didn't know what it was called then. I found out years later there is a name for those conditions. But I would find myself seeing hallucinatory images of my face changing and becoming cosmic and complete.' The crack in their ego can destroy artists, but the best learn to control their dissociative capacity, they learn the art of losing control, how to descend into the underworld, like Orpheus, and come back in one piece.

Like shamans or mediums, many pop stars use alter-egos to step out of their ordinary egos and unlock subliminal aspects of their psyche – Bowie had Ziggy Stardust, the Pierrot and the Thin White Duke; Beyoncé had Sasha Fierce; Marshall Mathers has Eminem; Lady Gaga has a male alter-ego, Jo Calderone; Prince had a female alter-ego, Camille; Snoop Dogg even has a white alter-ego, Todd. Their masks, costumes and gestures help the artists get into a trance, and get the audience into a trance too. The very witchy Beyoncé has said: 'I've created an alter-ego; things I do performing that I would never do normally ... I have out-of-body experiences [on stage]. If I cut my leg, if I fall, I don't even feel it. I'm so fearless, I'm not aware of my face or body.'[20] These created personae or masks are liberating for their audience, enabling them to step outside their habitual ego-schema and play at being someone else, play at another sexuality or even another gender – Stuart Maconie writes that seeing the sexually ambiguous Bowie on *Top of the Pops*, his arm draped around Mick Ronson, 'was a moment of epiphany and of revelation for a whole generation'.[21]

Putting on flamboyant alter-egos is hugely cathartic for the performer, particularly if they're cripplingly shy, as so many great front-men and -women are, from Bowie to Prince to Jimi Hendrix to Kate Bush to Amy Winehouse. David Byrne tells me: 'How is music cathartic for me? In so many ways. When I was younger and more socially uncomfortable music was my outlet – my way of communicating and announcing my existence.' Byrne crafted roles for himself, like the Pentecostal preacher he performed in 'Once In A Lifetime'. Later, as he grew in confidence, he 'began to sense that rhythmic and repetitive music could do something more than just be an outlet for my unspoken unheard self – it could gradually change that self ... and it seemed to be most effective in music rooted in something that had been repressed or cast aside by Western culture. I found myself more open to trance-rooted music – from dance or funk grooves to the Pentecostal Church, Vodun, gamelan, salsa, samba ... This music swallowed the individual whole. And it was in that loss of identity that the ecstasy lay. Some kinds of music are a machine for making that happen - and happen reliably.'

Like the shaman, witch or Pentecostal preacher, the rock star becomes proficient in techniques of ecstasy, ways to free themselves and their audience of their inhibitions. They may use gesture and dance – Tina Turner learned her famous spinning dance in the Pentecostal Church, and Mick Jagger learned it from her. They may use ritual and performance – James Brown's ritual of falling to his knees and being led off stage was also stolen from the Pentecostal Church. They may use costumes, lights, smoke, mirrors, explosions. They may use verse and incantation, although, in fact, many of my favourite ecstatic moments in pop music are non-verbal. Just as the shaman screams and the preacher shouts, the rocker wails. Think of Little Richard's high-pitched 'hoooo', or Al Green's pained falsetto at the end of 'Tired Of Being Alone', or Morrissey wailing like a banshee at the end of 'What Difference Does It Make?', or that incredible moment at the beginning of Arcade Fire's 'Wake Up' when the band and audience sing out in wordless yearning for transcendence.

By calling them shamans, I'm not suggesting rockers are totally unconscious ecstatics, unaware of how they create. There's some of that. But they are also *consciously* experimenting, innovating, seeing what gets a reaction in their audience. Both Sun and Stax Studios had record stores at the front, so the musicians and producers could *see* what got the kids going. As Gary Lachman – bassist in Blondie, now an expert on the occult – suggests, pop musicians are like magicians, consciously trying out technologies to alter audiences' consciousness: gestures, lights, video, costumes, sound effects. Many of the ecstatic technologies they innovate come about by accident. A guitar amplifier fell off the roof of Ike Turner's car as he was driving to Sun Studio to record in 1951. The damaged amp gave the guitar a distorted, dirty sound, but producer Sam Phillips liked it, so the band cut 'Rocket 88', the first ever rock and roll record. In 1966, the Thomas Organ Company was developing a new amplifier. A technician accidentally came across an oscillator effect, which he thought might work for wind instruments. Someone suggested they use it as a guitar pedal instead. They called it the wah-wah pedal, and the next year Jimi Hendrix seized on it as a new ecstatic technology for his 'electric church'.

God is a DJ

The music that meant most to me as a teenager – trance and techno – emerged from a similar accidental innovation. The Roland synthesiser company made a machine called the TB-303 as a bass accompaniment for guitarists practising alone. The machine was a flop, and Roland quickly stopped making them. But then a handful of experimenting musicians in Detroit realised you could make really awesome squelchy bass lines on the 303, using the knobs to modulate the sound up and down in a way that seemed to drive people on LSD and MDMA wild. They called the strange music they made 'acid house'. For many people, including me, house, techno, trance and drum & bass became a sort of pop-up religion, a church for the unchurched. One such acolyte was Sister Bliss, who went on to play in the band Faithless. She tells me: 'The drugs, the lights, the music and the sense of the illicit turned raves into communal ecstatic experiences where one could forget the self. There was a palpable energy, like I imagine you would get in the middle of a religious service with the laying-on of hands and talking in tongues. People lost themselves in the music in a really primal, tribal way. They probably felt more connected to other people than ever before. A lot of people aren't so comfortable in the social world or in their own skins. House music was a really embracing place. It broke down barriers of class, race, gender. And it came out of a tough political era. Very disillusioned people were seeking some kind of community.'

In some ways, acid house had the hallmarks of a religious revival or even a medieval millenarian movement. There was a sense in the late 1980s that a new Age of Love might be dawning – E (or Adam, as it was originally known) would free us from neo-liberal capitalism and take us back to a prelapsarian utopia, a return to the innocence of childhood. Ravers sucked lollipops and babies' dummies, and danced to house remixes of childhood TV theme-songs. Certain clubs inspired particular religious fervour, like Danny Rampling's Shroom in London. Matthew Collin writes: 'One Shroomer gave away all his possessions and the following weekend was seen running naked down the Portobello Road. Others came to believe that there were supernatural forces of Good and Evil battling for the soul of the City . . . A few, lost in Shroom, convinced themselves that Danny Rampling was some kind of Messiah: the master of the dance, the orchestrator of emotions.'[22] At the Paradise Garage in New York, meanwhile, 'people seemed to transcend human limits', wrote journalist Frank Owen. 'Men crawled around on their hands and knees howling like dogs, while others gyrated and leapt as if they could fly.'[23]

Like rock and roll, acid house rapidly provoked a moral panic – parents worried their kids were losing their minds and ruining their careers in Dionysiac ecstasy. In 1994, the British government banned outdoor dancing to repetitive beats – one of the more remarkable pieces of anti-ecstatic legislation. But by that point dance music had gone mainstream in super-clubs, like Creamfields and Fabric, and in legal festivals, like Glastonbury or Tribal Gathering, where 'superstar DJs' like Sasha were worshipped as gods. For my friends and I, clubbing was a high point of our lives, in terms of taking us to massively altered states. I remember wandering around Club UK when I was 17, so high on LSD I couldn't remember my name. I arrived in a cavern where semi-naked sweating bodies spasmed to thumps and bleeps. I wasn't in London any more, this was some alien planet. My self was reduced to an autonomic nervous system, jacked in to the beat. Eventually I came down a bit, remembered who and where I was, and found my friends. We embraced, shared our worldly goods, assured each other we were friends for life. Then the pills wore off and the lights came on, and we crept, basilisk-eyed and shivering, into the day.

Sister Bliss, meanwhile, fondly remembers Faithless playing the Glastonbury Pyramid stage in 2002: 'It was like tantric energy – there was this huge crowd giving you love, and you give it back to them. You're seeing the most beautiful part of people, people who have pain and troubles in everyday life, but for a moment they're feeling unadulterated joy. That's God-like. It's beyond ego. I've never had a religious experience, but I imagine that's as close to religion as it bloody gets.' Glastonbury and other festivals like Woodstock or Burning Man offered post-Christian versions of eighteenth-century Methodist 'love feasts', where thousands of worshippers would come together in camps for three days of singing, dancing and collective trancing (indeed Michael Eavis, founder of Glastonbury, is a Methodist). Methodists thought their worship could call down God, make of their camp a holy *shekinah*, a temporary Zion. Likewise, ravers hope to turn their festival sites into

what Sufi philosopher Hakim Bey calls temporary autonomous zones
– spaces of collective dreaming.

The God that failed?

Rock and roll, soul, psychedelic, punk, disco, heavy metal, New Wave,
hip-hop, rave, indie, grime . . . The last 50 years have turned out so
many new musical forms, each of them like their own new cult. Festivals,
raves and gigs offer pop-up, bricolage rituals that grant emotional healing,
connection and joy. It's offered us a 'reason to believe', as Springsteen
put it, even if we're not sure what we believe in. You could see how
much pop means to people when David Bowie died in January 2016.
His death came on the same day that the Anglican Church voted against
same-sex marriage. Few cared what the homophobic Church thought
– pop music was our church, and we had just lost one of its leading
prophets.

And yet is rock really a substitute for religion? In some ways, the
rise of the new cult in the 1950s caught everyone by surprise, from the
establishment to the performers themselves. Suddenly, teen musicians
seemed to wield the most cultural power. They were, in Timothy Leary's
words, 'the poet-philosophers of the new religion'. They were not so
much 'unacknowledged prophets' as unprepared. You can see this in the
Scorsese documentary *No Direction Home*, in Bob Dylan's obvious
discomfort at being seized on by the press as the 'voice of the generation'. Dylan reflects: 'For some reason, the press thought performers
had the answers to all the problems of society. What can you say to
something like that? It's just absurd.' Mick Jagger took a sort of satanic
delight in the Stones' power over audiences, making the girls wet
themselves and the boys attack the police. But it was a power without
responsibility. When he and Keith Richards were busted for possession
of dope in 1965, the judge told him: 'Whether you like it or not, you're
the idol of a large number of young people, so you have grave responsibilities.' Jagger responded: 'My only responsibilities are to myself.' He
was then interviewed on TV, rather comically, by the editor of *The
Times*, the Bishop of Woolwich and the former home secretary, who

tried to gauge his creed. He told them: 'I don't want to form a code of living or a code of morals.' Rock and roll, like Romanticism, is spilled religion – the experience of surrender, with none of the ethical obligations.

Worshipping the rock idols

When rockers did try to formulate a positive 'code of living', they often expressed desire for liberation not merely from unjust social barriers, but from any barriers at all. A key influence on the philosophy of rock was Aleister Crowley, the occult practitioner, mediocre poet, bully, misogynist and paedophile. Gary Lachman has written on Crowley and his impact on rock and roll[24] – Crowley appears on the cover for *Sgt. Pepper*, and the Doors album *Doors 13*, and has been referenced by everyone from Led Zeppelin to Jay-Z. Lachman tells me Crowley embodied the rock philosophy of 'liberationism': 'It's the idea of breaking the rules, getting rid of repression, going beyond all convention. In many ways, it's an adolescent philosophy. Think of Jim Morrison's "We want the world and we want it now."' Crowley promised liberation not for everyone but for the elite, the supermen, the rock gods. 'Do what thou wilt shall be the whole of the law' for the supermen, wrote Crowley in 1905. They will delight in 'wines and strange drugs', as well as every type of sexual excess. Meanwhile the rest of humanity, 'the slaves', shall be made to bow before the supermen. This fairly accurately predicts what the cult of the pop star became – Kanye West sets himself up as a Crowleyan superman, a god, and the masses worship beneath him.

The rock star who most consciously explored the Crowleyan dark side of the rock cult was David Bowie, who created Ziggy Stardust as a pop idol to be slavishly worshipped and imitated by the masses. To some extent Bowie modelled himself on Crowley, and sang of the supermen, or *Homo superior*, who would rise up over the slaves. But he rapidly became conscious of the hollowness of the cult. He described Ziggy as 'an almighty prophet-like superstar rocker who found he didn't know what to do with it once he got it'.[25] He came to realise that dabbling with ecstatic states of consciousness solely with the intention of gaining fame and power – as Crowley would – is extremely dangerous. If you go down there with an egotistical 'set' in your mind, the subliminal mind can curse you with ego-inflation or paranoia, and tear your ego apart. Bowie nearly lost his mind – his most beautiful song, 'Word On A Wing', was recorded in the depths of cocaine-and-magic psychosis. It is the moment he gives up his will, surrenders to God, and saves himself.

Bowie realised the cult of the rock star is potentially Fascistic. Having flirted with the role of Fascist leader in the 1970s, he then satirised it in the videos for 'Fashion' and 'Blackstar', where zombie-like fans shuffle and hop in a trance to the singer's commands. That sort of idolatry makes mindless groupies of us. As John Lennon said, a few weeks before he was shot: 'Don't expect Jimmy Carter or Ronald Reagan or John Lennon or Yoko Ono or Bob Dylan or Jesus Christ to come and do it for you . . . I can't cure you. You can cure you.'

Our worship of stars is hugely unhealthy for the stars themselves. They can fall prey to god complexes, like Kanye West, becoming ever more grandiose until finally he's put into a psychiatric facility. They can destroy themselves with excess, as so many rock stars have done. They can mistake the high of crowd adulation for genuine intimacy and love, which leads to a schizoid split between your persona and inner pain. Sister Bliss says: 'If you're going on stage to fill a hole in your soul with love, the hole isn't going to go away. You can act the big star, then just be a mess the moment you walk off stage.' The cult of rock and roll is, in fact, fairly brutal for the stars – we raise them up, scream at them in adoration for a year or so, then discard them for a new idol. Then we ghoulishly visit their shrines once they've destroyed themselves.

Another risk with the cult of rock and roll is that market forces have always been eager to seize the ecstasy and squeeze from it every cent of profit they can. Behind every idol is a Simon Cowell. Governments have also tried to capture the power of rock and roll, particularly in the last few decades, when rock has gone mainstream and become respectable, used by governments for state occasions. In 2012, for example, both the Olympics' opening ceremony and the Queen's Diamond Jubilee celebration ended with Paul McCartney leading the crowd in a rendition of 'Hey Jude'. The dangerous sub-cult has become a boring national cult and heritage industry, like Christianity before it.

Today, in fact, market forces have more or less destroyed the cult of the rock star, mainly through the internet. The web first made music ubiquitous, so it became like wallpaper. And then it made music free. It's no longer special or sacred, as vinyl had once been. And we no longer revere artists or look to them to channel our dreams and re-invent our personalities – tech entrepreneurs are the new 'rock stars'. They gave us social media, where we can reinvent ourselves and connect with others directly, rather than through the medium of a band. In the age of YouTube, we're all pop stars now. Perhaps, as the cult of the rock idol disappears, we will return to the roots of music as an ecstatic participatory cult in which everyone takes part and there are no experts. We need to worship less, consume less, and play more. You may not go to church, but you can still join a choir, sing anything from Motown to Monteverdi, and get the catharsis, ego-dissolution and sheer pleasure of singing together. Or, if you're feeling really adventurous, you can go to 5Rhythms.

Strictly ecstatic dancing

It's Monday evening. I'm tired after a boozy weekend. It's dark, cold and pouring with rain. I do not feel like dancing ecstatically. And yet that is precisely where I'm headed: to a 5Rhythms session in a church hall in Tufnell Park. I'm somewhat unsure that I'll fit in. I love dancing, but can't remember the last time I danced without the aid of alcohol or drugs. I need them to get me out of my head, into 'the zone'. My usual self is a rather rational, uptight, non-intimate academic. Will I be able to get into the tribal groove, or will I stick out, a fifth wheel, a sixth rhythm? It's a big, rather empty hall, ringed by statues of goddesses holding branches. Regulars are arriving, and giving each other long hugs. They emerge from the rain wrapped up like Antarctic explorers, and strip off to yoga pants and tiny man-shorts. One bony old man is already leaping around the floor, like a geriatric jester. I stand at the side of the hall, trying to look groovy.

The master of ceremonies is Jane, an American lady who is petite and full of nimble energy. She puts on some music – a slow jazz version of 'Billie Jean' – and the 40 or so ecstatic dancers converge on the floor and start doing their thing. As you can imagine, they are all very expressive, individualistic dancers. I have no idea how to dance to a slow jazz version of 'Billie Jean'. This is the thing about post-modern spirituality: it's one long improvisation. It gets wearisome after a while, having no agreed-upon steps.

Jane gathers us into a circle. She walks around it quickly, talking in a hypnotic sort of incantation. 'We will go through five rhythms, which together form a wave. Each rhythm is associated with one part of the body. We start with "flowing", which is connected to the feet. The feet are the physical key to the conscious state. Then "staccato", connected to the hips. The hips are the physical key to the conscious state. Then "chaos", connected to the spine. Then "lyrical", connected to the hands. Then "stillness", connected to the breath. Sometimes you will dance on your own, sometimes I will invite you to connect with someone else. Go with it.' She smiles. 'There are no "right moves".'

And we're off! 'Connect to your feet, explore with your feet, stay grounded in your feet.' The music gets a bit livelier – a trance beat, building up. It's fun to dance in my bare feet, feeling the wooden floor beneath me. I feel myself getting into it, though I do wonder about the risks of athlete's foot. But it's pleasant. No one cares what I'm doing. Go with it. Let yourself go. The beat picks up – it's a good tune. I look around – everyone's into it. I remember how much I enjoyed clubbing, that moment when a good tune comes on and you look around at a dance floor filled with beaming, happy people really loving it, sharing it. You felt briefly transformed into a single organism, like coral, as the wave of the beat washed over us. How much fun was that?

'Now move your awareness into your hips. Find someone to connect with and dance together.' I am suddenly a 16-year-old at a disco, with no idea how to ask someone to dance. Plus you're not meant to use words here. It's all non-verbal. My hip-based small-talk is fairly rudimentary. Luckily a Japanese lady is in front of me and we dance for bit. She is a very good dancer and it's fun, dialoguing through dance. I explain to her that I'm a philosopher researching a book on ecstatic experiences. I say this with my hips. 'Now find a way to say goodbye and thank them.' We nod hips and spin off into the mass.

I find myself trancing. It's like my awareness moves down, spreads out, diffuses, my eyes glaze, the pupils dilate, the mind opens, the critical fire-wall comes down, the autonomic nervous system connects to the music – you can feel it on your skin, in your stomach, in your groin. You are being carried by the music. Your consciousness extends into the tribe, dancing together, seaweed bending as the wave washes over it. Then the dance carries up into the spine. The chaos stage, where we awaken 'kundalini', the spiritual energy that coils around our spine, apparently. The music becomes loud, aggressive drumming. Everyone starts to freak out, their spines gyrating and whirling. The bony geriatric is leaping around like a goat on crack. He keeps whisking past me, making me flinch. It brings me out of the trance. I start thinking again. I feel self-conscious. I notice a group of ecstatic adults who have found a children's play-house in the church hall, and now three or four of them have huddled inside it and they're shrieking with laughter. And I know it's just adults playing, but I find myself thinking, *My God, is this where the counter-culture has left us?*

After we finish, I walk home and past the news-stands announcing yet another terrorist attack. I think about Daesh, and the world of ecstatic dance seems even more infantile. But then I think, Daesh don't dance. Radical Islam is Puritan, and Puritans hate people dancing, particularly women. The only kind of ecstasy Daesh allows is the ecstasy of prayer and the ecstasy of killing. That's why Daesh attacked the Eagles of Death Metal gig at the Bataclan, 'where hundreds of pagans gathered for a concert of prostitution and vice', in the words of a Daesh press release. Their form of ecstasy is a patriarchal control-trip against any form of difference. I think of the Reverend Al Green and his homophobic church, another patriarchal control-trip. And then I think of the post-modern spiritual ecstatics who don't have any dogma at all, no maps, no intellectual or ethical systems to guide them, just the childlike experience of surrender. There *must* be a middle way, I think – a way to marry New Age play to some kind of wisdom, belief, shared ritual and authority that is not toxic or intellectually shallow.

★

It's time to dance on, deeper into the night, away from the main stage and into the DayGlo lights and fluorescent shimmering walls of the Psychedelic Wonderland.

5: Psychedelic Wonderland

It was not your usual academic conference. Greenwich University's stately campus by the Thames was flooded with dreadlocked witches, wild-haired chemists, flower-festooned Peruvian shamans, freak-out musicians, virtual-reality tech-heads, and Russell Brand, wearing a tie-dye Shiva shirt and telling anyone who would listen that he was not the Messiah. All 800 attendees had gathered for Breaking Convention 2015, the third conference on 'psychedelic consciousness, culture and clinical research'. The conference was a unique interdisciplinary marriage of the sciences, the arts and the humanities: in the morning you could see the chemist David E. Nichols presenting on the molecular structure of new LSD-type compounds (while DIY chemists scribbled his formulae in their notepads), then in the afternoon you could hear shamans talk about ayahuasca ceremonies in the Amazon, or classicists about Bacchic orgies, before dancing away at the 'Nites of Eleusis' after-party. How many academic conferences trip from the cellular to the celestial in one day?

These are exciting times for the field – some have called it a 'psyche-delic renaissance'. After a 40-year hiatus, research into psychedelics has restarted at prestigious institutions like Imperial College and Johns Hopkins University School of Medicine. And it's producing remarkable results. For example, researchers at Johns Hopkins found that, after three doses of the magic-mushroom drug psilocybin, 80 per cent of smokers in a trial gave up smoking and had still given up six months later.[1] The most successful anti-smoking therapy programmes at the moment have success rates of 30 to 35 per cent. Preliminary studies have also found psychedelics to be a very effective treatment for alcoholism and heroin addiction,[2] building on the work of 1950s psychiatrist Humphrey Osmond, who treated 2,000 alcoholics using psychedelics and found that 40 to 45 per cent went into remission. Psychedelics also show a lot of promise as part of therapeutic treatment for depression and anxiety: a small-scale study at London's Imperial College found that 43 per cent of participants with treatment-resistant depression were depression-free three months after two psilocybin trips.[3] Psychedelics seem to encourage neurogenesis[4] (the creation of new neurons), helping the brain to create new neural patterns and to unlearn habits of fear, which may be helpful in the treatment of phobias and post-traumatic stress disorder. They have also been found to have a major impact on anxiety and depression levels among those with terminal cancer − a study at UCLA noted a 30 per cent drop in depression in participants six months after one psilocybin trip and a comparable drop in anxiety. Two recent studies, by NYU and Johns Hopkins, showed that one dose of psilocybin helped 80 per cent of cancer patients recover from depression, and they were still in remission six months after treatment - that's double the recovery rate of anti-depressants.[5] How do psychedelics do this? By triggering a 'mystical experience' of ego-dissolution and sense of connection to a transcendent reality (which some call God and others don't).

One participant in the NYU study was Nick Fernandez, a 27-year-old psychology student who'd had leukaemia in his teens and still suffered with anxiety from the experience. Nick told UCLA's Linda Marsa what happened when he took psilocybin in NYU's lab:

> For the first time in my life, I felt like there was a creator of the universe, a force greater than myself, and that I should be kind and loving. I experienced a profound psychic shift that made me realise all my anxieties, defences and insecurities weren't something to worry about.[6]

Psychedelics reliably induce mystical-type experiences, comparable to some of the spontaneous epiphanies and near-death experiences we encountered in the Entrance Gate. In one psilocybin trial at Johns Hopkins University, 94 per cent of participants said their trip was one of the top five most meaningful experiences of their lives, and 39 per cent said it was *the* most meaningful experience.[7] Just one trip led to significant long-term personality changes, particularly increased openness. One participant in the UCLA terminal-cancer study told a documentary called *The Substance*: 'It fundamentally changes how you approach the world – you open up instead of negatively narrowing. The depression has lifted, I'm more trusting, intuitive, spontaneous, sociable, enthusiastic. It's almost unbelievable this happened after one day.' Beyond the undoubted medical potential of psychedelic therapy, psychedelics are an exciting tool for studying consciousness and human nature – the word 'psychedelic' literally means 'mind-revealer'. Stanislav Grof, who has researched psychedelics since the 1950s, says they can do for psychology 'what the microscope did for biology or the telescope for astronomy'.[8] So how come we had no knowledge of these mystical wonder-plants growing in our fields over the last two millennia? Should we use them for medical and spiritual purposes, or are the risks too high?

Homo sapiens' long, strange trip

Psychedelics seem to have played a central role in human culture from very early on. Paleo-anthropologists have compared the geometric patterns found on cave paintings dating back to 30,000 BC to the fractal visions people have on hallucinogenics, and inferred that early man took psychedelics – they might even have played a role in the evolution of humans' capacity for symbolic language, one of our key evolutionary advantages over Neanderthals.[9] They were certainly central to Aztec religion, in which the mushroom was worshipped as a god, and might have played a central role in the early Indian religion of the Vedas, dating back to around 2000 BC. At least a hundred Vedic hymns praise Soma, a potion described as 'the healing balm' and 'the father of poems'.

'We have drunk Soma and become immortal,' one hymn declares. 'We have attained the light the gods discovered . . . Our maladies have lost their strength and vanished: they feared, and passed away into darkness.' The mycologist Gordon Wasson has suggested the descriptions of Soma bear some resemblance to *Amanita muscaria*, a type of magic mushroom found in Asia and beyond.[10]

Psychedelics were – and in some cases still are – used in shamanic or animistic worship in South America, northern Europe, Africa and Central Asia, as a means to enter the spirit world. They might also have played a central role in classical mystery cults, particularly the Greek cult of Eleusis, in which participants drank a potion called a *kykeon*, which Wasson has suggested contained ergot, a psychoactive fungus that grows on rye.[11] Initiates at Eleusis then went on a terrifying trip to the underworld, confronting various demonic or shadow figures before experiencing a euphoric rebirth into the light as the children of Demeter. Initiation gave participants 'hope for a blessed afterlife', just as psilocybin and LSD reduce anxiety in the terminally ill today. Plutarch described the Eleusinian experience as 'wandering through the dark . . . terrors, shivering, trembling . . . after this a strange and wondrous light, voices, dances and the majesty of holy sounds and sacred visions'. And here's the account of one participant in a 2014 trial of LSD for those with terminal cancer: 'It was just really black . . . I was afraid, shaking . . . It was total exhaustion . . . like an endless marathon . . . Suddenly a phase of relaxation came . . . It became bright. Everything was light . . . It was really gorgeous . . . The key experience is when you get from dark to light.'[12]

The great forgetting

The rite of Eleusis lasted for two and a half millennia – longer than Christianity has existed – but was outlawed by the fanatical Christian emperor Theodosius in AD 391, along with every other non-Christian religious practice in the Roman Empire. And then there was a great forgetting. Psychedelics simply disappeared from Western culture for the next 1,500 years. They were not denounced or suppressed by Christian theologians – they had no knowledge at all of their existence, even though magic mushrooms were growing all that time across Europe. It's bizarre. Christianity stopped using intoxicants as a means to divine union, except incense. Psychedelics simply vanished, apart from occasional folk legends about flying witches and magic reindeer. Instead, Western culture turned to other drugs – alcohol, mainly, then stimulants, like coffee, chocolate and tobacco, and then tranquillisers, like opiates and Valium. Such substances were better suited than psychedelics to workers in the machine of industrial capitalism, energising us for repetitive work, then sedating us for mindless rest.

It was only at the end of the nineteenth century, amid the decline of Christian faith in the West, that psychedelics emerged from their long hibernation. The psychedelic revival started with the peyote cactus. Westerners had known for some time that indigenous Mexicans consumed the buttons of the cactus as part of their sacred rituals, and in 1886 the scientist Louis Lewin undertook the first scientific study of the cactus and the 'phantastical' power of the drug found in its buttons, mescaline. In 1897 the doctor and author Silas Weir Mitchell became the first-recorded white man to take mescaline, which transported him to an incredibly beautiful city of the imagination: 'Here is unlocked a storehouse of glorified memorial treasures,' he wrote. In 1953, the writer Aldous Huxley, frustrated at not having personally attained a mystical experience despite having written a whole book about them, suddenly found a short-cut to grace through mescaline. His experiences on it (and later on LSD and psilocybin) were, he decided, 'the most extraordinary and significant experience available to human beings this side of the Beatific Vision'. Psychedelics unlocked the 'doors of perception', he wrote. They released Mind-At-Large from the constriction of the ego and connected us to the Heaven and Hell within us. Psychedelics gave humans a 'gratuitous grace', Huxley suggested. They were not necessary companions on the spiritual path, but they were certainly helpful. In his last novel, *Island*, Huxley imagined an ideal society where psychedelics would once again play a central religious role. And in a final essay before his death in 1962, he suggested psychedelics could be used for mass consciousness-raising, through 'a course of chemically-triggered conversion experiences or ecstasies'.[13]

Magic mushrooms, meanwhile, came to the attention of Western society only in 1958, thanks to Gordon Wasson. In 1956, Wasson led a group of friends to Mexico to explore stories of a mushroom-worshipping cult that survived in the Mexican countryside. He persuaded a *curadera* (or healer) called Maria Sabina to include his group in her ritual. As the mushrooms began to take effect, Sabina started to sing, declaring her spiritual credentials and calling the spirits to assist them: 'The world can be cheered up, let's cheer up, let's be enlightened.'

Wasson was certainly cheered up by his trip: 'For the first time, the word "ecstasy" took on a real meaning,' he wrote. 'For the first time, it did not mean someone else's state of mind.' He felt that his soul was freed from its body and 'possessed of a divine mobility that would transport us anywhere on the wings of a thought'. It transported him to a beautiful city, much as Jewish and Christian mystics described visiting celestial cities in their ecstatic journeys. When he came down and returned to the USA, Wasson wrote an article for *Life* magazine describing his experience.[14] This drew coachloads of American spiritual seekers to Mexico, including a young UCLA anthropologist called Carlos Castaneda, who wrote a series of wildly popular books in which he described his initiation by an Indian *brujo*, or wizard, called Don Juan. Wasson 'smelled a hoax', rightly – Don Juan was a work of fiction, but that hasn't stopped his teachings being devoured by credulous Westerners to this day.

While Westerners were rediscovering psychedelic plants, scientists were beginning to synthesise entirely new chemical routes to ecstasy. In 1946, a Swiss scientist called Albert Hoffman, one of the lead researchers at the pharmaceutical company Sandoz, was researching chemical compounds of ergot. While studying one compound of lysergic acid diethylamide – LSD-25 – Hoffman felt himself becoming dizzy and was suddenly beset by 'an uninterrupted stream of fantastic pictures' lasting two hours. He wondered if the experience had been produced by the LSD, so a few days later, on 19 April 1946, he took 250 micrograms. Again he found himself becoming dizzy, so he cycled home. He later recalled:

Everything in the room spun around, and the familiar objects and pieces of furniture assumed grotesque, threatening forms. They were in continuous motion, animated, as if driven by an inner restlessness. The lady next door . . . was no longer Mrs R., but rather a malevolent, insidious witch with a coloured mask. Even worse than these demonic transformations of the outer world were the alterations that I perceived in myself, in my inner being. Every exertion of my will, every attempt to put an end to the disintegration of the outer world and the dissolution of my ego, seemed to be a wasted effort. A demon had invaded me, had taken possession of my body, mind, and soul.

His colleague called a doctor, who reassured Hoffman he was physically fine. He began to relax into the trip: 'Kaleidoscopic, fantastic images surged in on me.' He went to bed and next day arose feeling 'exhilaration, a kind of rebirth . . . When I later walked into the garden, in which the sun shone now after a spring rain, everything glistened and sparkled in fresh light. The world was as if newly created.'[15]

That was the first new psychedelic drug synthesised, but there have since been many more – Alexander Shulgin, the discoverer of MDMA, once commented that the West knew only two psychedelics in the nineteenth century: marijuana and peyote. By the end of the 1950s, it had discovered dozens. By the beginning of the twenty-first century, the number was about two hundred, and it's growing rapidly. If you look at the website Erowid, where psychonauts compare accounts of their drug experiences, there are reports about more than 800 different substances.

Psychedelics' popularisation and criminalisation

Hoffman and scientific colleagues around the world quietly studied the therapeutic potential of psychedelics throughout the 1950s. But it was inevitable, in an age of mass communication, that eventually psychedelics would go mainstream and turn the world upside down. The person many psychedelic scientists blame for what went wrong is Timothy

Leary, a Harvard psychologist who established the Harvard Psilocybin Project in 1960, with colleagues James Fadiman and Richard Alpert (or Ram Dass, as he later called himself). Their early experiments included taking psychedelics with murderers at Concord Prison – 'turning convicts into Buddhas', in Leary's words. He claimed psilocybin reduced the reoffending rate from 70 per cent to 10 per cent. But their research soon attracted the ire of the Harvard authorities, particularly when an undergraduate, Andrew Weil, wrote articles in the *Harvard Crimson* about Leary and Alpert throwing parties and giving drugs to freshmen. Leary and Alpert were fired, but this only increased their evangelical zeal to sing the gospel of psychedelics. Leary became an international guru for the LSD revolution. He told young people to 'tune in, turn on, drop out'. In his 1968 book *The Politics of Ecstasy*, Leary called for an LSD-fuelled revolution to create a 'neo-ecstatic society'. The gospel of LSD was taken up and transmitted to the masses by bands like the Beatles, the Stones and the Doors. By 1968, a great psychedelic wave seemed to sweep across Western culture, just as riots and demonstrations against the Vietnam War threatened to tear America apart. President Richard Nixon called Leary 'the most dangerous man in America', and in 1970 he announced a war on drugs and made LSD a 'schedule 1' substance, outlawing its use even for scientific research.

Almost all research into the therapeutic potential of psychedelics stopped for the next 40 years. Some psychedelic scientists today say Leary was too publicity-seeking, too incautious; he didn't give young people enough warning of the psychological risks. In at least one case, he forged results to hide the fact that some participants became psychotic. But Leary did try to create psychedelic 'guides' for people to use on trips, drawing on ancient wisdom like *The Tibetan Book of the Dead*. Indeed, it was a Leary guidebook that advised a tripping John Lennon to 'turn off your mind, relax and float downstream'.

Many other people besides Leary contributed to the mass popularisation of psychedelics in the sixties, not least Ken Kesey and the Merry Pranksters, who organised 'acid tests' in San Francisco where thousands of people drank LSD-spiked Kool-Aid from a barrel. It was also a bit rich for the US government to accuse Leary of irresponsibility when the CIA had been conducting secret LSD experiments on ordinary Americans without their consent for two decades through the infamous MKUltra project. The truth is, no one was really in control. The sixties counter-culture was an extraordinary moment of social transformation, a sudden explosion of mass ecstasy. But the supernova was not without its casualties.

How psychedelics work

Why can psychedelics be so healing and liberating, and also so traumatic and dangerous? The theory that most psychedelic researchers are converging on today is inspired by the James–Myers–Jung model of the psyche that we've explored throughout this book. James Fadiman, who worked with Leary and Ram Dass at the Harvard Psychedelic Laboratory, says psychedelics reveal that 'your ego, your personal identity, is not that big a part of you. "Jim Fadiman" is a subset of me, and the me is very, very large and a lot smarter and knows a lot more than "Jim Fadiman".'[16] Everyday ego-consciousness acts as a 'reducing valve or door on the enormous subliminal world, allowing us to focus on everyday survival and social interaction. Psychedelics open the doors to the interior mansion. They 'lower the threshold of consciousness', in Jung's words, bringing subconscious contents flooding into waking consciousness in a sort of lucid dream. Researchers are beginning to identify the neurological mechanisms by which this happens. Robin Carhart-Harris, a neuroscientist at Imperial College, has studied brain scans of people on psilocybin and noticed reduced blood flow to areas of the brain associated with the default mode network (DMN), which acts as the ego-integrator for the mind. Psychedelics reduce the activity of the DMN, dissolving the usual structures of the ego and allowing repressed subliminal mental processes to come into consciousness, including forgotten or traumatic memories.[17]

The subconscious revealed by psychedelics is very Jungian, filled with symbolic, mythopoetic and archetypal imagery.[18] Like dreams, the world of trips is somewhat lurid and cartoonish, filled with what Myers called 'strange romances'. As with dreams, the subconscious revealed by trips

Paleoanthropologists think cave paintings like these at Lascaux (from around 20,000 BC) were an early route for homo sapiens to reach altered states of consciousness.
© *Sisse Brimberg/National Geographic*

Ecstasy also had a central role in classical culture – this vase painting (**right**) shows a maenad filled with the god Dionysus.
© *The Trustees of the British Museum*

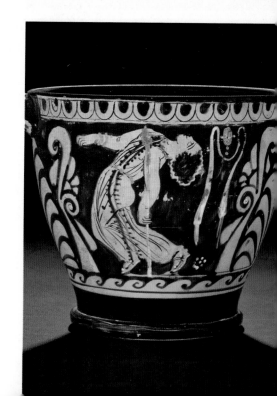

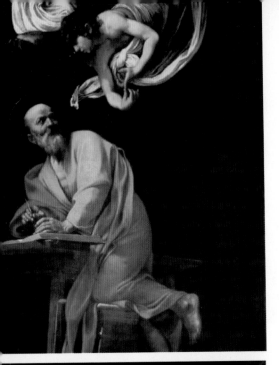

In Christian culture, ecstasy is interpreted as an invasion by God, though it could also be demonic possession or human imagination.

Two examples from Caravaggio – **above**, Saint Matthew and the ecstasy of creative inspiration. **Below**, Saint Paul and the ecstasy of sudden conversion.

Ecstasy – or 'enthusiasm' as it became known – has been ridiculed and pathologized over the last five centuries of western intellectual culture.

On the left, Hogarth's 'Enthusiasm Delineated' (c.1760) mocked the unbridled emotionalism of Methodist services.

On the right, a late-19th-century photo from the Salpêtrière clinic in Paris showing a hysteric patient in ecstatic attitude. Western psychiatrists often interpreted spiritual experiences as symptoms of mental pathology.

Planche XXIII.

ATTITUDES PASSIONNELLES

EXTASE (1878).

Despite the marginalisation of ecstasy in Western culture over the last five centuries, it has kept taking new forms.

Above, a 19th-century Methodist camp meeting in the US.
© *Courtesy of the New Bedford Whaling Museum*

Below, rock and roll secularized the ecstasy of charismatic Christianity and brought it to the masses. This is the audience at a Beatles concert in Plymouth in 1963. © *Mirrorpix*

Since the Reformation, westerners have sought new forms of enchantment and transcendence outside the church, through the arts.

Above, virtual reality offers a new technology for ecstasy, blurring the boundary between the real and imagined. © *Emilio Morenatti/AP Photo/Shutterstock*

On the right, Shakespeare's theatre offered a playful, sceptical space for ecstasy (this is Vivien Leigh as Titania in a 1937 production of *A Midsummer Night's Dream*). © *Photograph by JW Debenham. Courtesy of the Mander and Mitchenson Collection at the University of Bristol*

The Sublime – awesome encounters with nature – became a replacement for Christian ecstasy in western culture from the 18th century onwards.

On the left is Caspar David Friedrich's 'Wanderer Above the Sea of Fog' (c.1818). © *bpk | Hamburger Kunsthalle | Elke Walford*

Extreme sports have also been embraced as a means to ecstatic experiences in nature – the image **below** is from Werner Herzog's 1974 documentary about a ski-jumper, *The Great Ecstasy of Woodcarver Steiner*. © *Deutsche Kinemathek – Werner Herzog Film*

The Romantic counter-culture explored ecstatic experiences through poetry, free love and intoxicants. **Above** is a frontispiece by William Blake, a keen practitioner of sexual spirituality.

Below is a photo from the 1969 Woodstock festival. Such experiments in ecstasy became a mass phenomenon during the 1960s.

The dark side of ecstasy: one of the oldest human means to heightened consciousness is violence and blood sacrifice, either against oneself or others.

Above, ecstatic nationalist movements like Nazism offer ecstasy through the worship of the state and its Leader, and through a narrative of sacred war against demonised outsiders. © *Corbis Historical/Getty Images*

Below, an image of the myth of King Pentheus, torn apart by the demented followers of Dionysus. © *2017. Kimbell Art Museum, Fort Worth, Texas/Art Resource, NY/Scala, Florence*

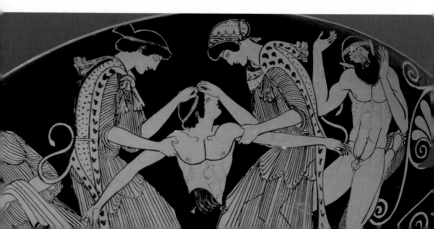

is soaked in movies, books and other culture. There is often a rather bombastic sense of a mythical landscape through which the tripper must journey, like the hero of a medieval romance, encountering gods and monsters in their quest. These encounters might veer in an instant from being insanely funny to utterly terrifying. Everything becomes meaningful and significant; everything reveals hidden patterns and connections. People often encounter what Jung called the 'shadow' side of the personality – the wounded or repressed aspects of the psyche. Psychedelic therapists draw on the Jungian idea of confronting and integrating the shadow, assuring them there is no such thing as a bad trip – in fact, difficult trips may be the most therapeutic. Dr Bill Richards, a psychologist at Johns Hopkins Medical College's psychedelics lab, told the BBC: 'We often say that if, during a psychedelic session, some monster appears, you should say, "Hello, monster, why are you here? What can I learn from you?"[19] If you go towards it, there is integration and healing. If you run away from it, it's like running away from your own shadow. You can develop panic and paranoia, and you could well end up in a psychiatric emergency room.' Ego-dissolution can be a terrifying experience. You are plunged into the ocean of the subconscious, and if the ego resists, it can feel like drowning. Alexander Shulgin warned that the 'unexpected eruption of unconscious energies' can be very harmful to those 'whose inner core or sense of self is not sufficiently developed . . . [Such people] spend much of their lives, after such an eruption, in places of confinement.'[20]

Ego-death and soul-loss

I've had first-hand experience of the dangers of psychedelics. I was a teenager in the early 1990s, when MDMA became widely available, when magic mushrooms and LSD were being taken in large quantities, and 'psychedelic trance' was all the rage. My friends and I fell in love with the music and stories of the 1960s counter-culture – Tom Wolfe's *The Electric Kool-Aid Acid Test* was the closest thing to our Bible. We started experimenting with LSD much too young, at 15. And we had some incredible experiences. I remember picking and eating magic mushrooms in a field in Gloucestershire: the more I ate, the more mushrooms appeared around me. I felt a great wave of electric energy sweep through my body and I collapsed in laughter. There, beneath me, was a mini-Constantinople of mushrooms. For the next six hours, it was like my friends and I were transformed into shaggy-legged satyrs, running and laughing through the woods in Bacchic abandon. We ended up lying on our backs in a field looking at a sky of astonishing beauty in which I saw an infinity of couples making love. It felt like a vision of Heaven. We felt connected to an animate nature teeming with sexual energy and intelligence, and this goddess was communicating with us, revealing her secrets.

A year after that mushroom trip, my best friend had a psychotic breakdown on LSD. He was diagnosed with paranoid schizophrenia and locked up. Since then, he's been stuck in a 30-year bad trip battling demons and psychiatrists, a nightmare he has endured with remarkable courage. Another friend was found naked in the streets of Goa, insisting he was the god Shiva. A third joined a Gnostic cult. A fourth jumped off a cliff while tripping, and died. At least ten of us suffered medium-to-long-term psychological damage, including me. I had a bad trip when I was 18. I started to get scared at an acid techno party and later went into full-blown paranoid psychosis at a friend's after-party. I was convinced everyone at the party was dissecting my personality (this was a delusion) but was too paranoid to move. I finally plucked up the courage to leave and limped back to my parents' flat in the blank grey morning. Home had become strange, unfamiliar, uncanny. Nowhere felt safe. I was too frightened and ashamed to tell my parents or friends what had happened, which was a big mistake. My mental health got worse over the subsequent weeks, though it subsequently cleared up. Then, in my first year at university, the buried trauma from this experience came out in nightmares, panic attacks, mood swings and moments of dissociation. I was later diagnosed as suffering from post-traumatic stress disorder, but shamans would call it 'soul-loss'. It took me several years to get better – in fact, I didn't start to recover until after the skiing accident I described in the Entrance Gate.

My friend's schizophrenia and my own psychological problems may have happened anyway, but I don't think psychedelics made them any easier. We were far too young to be messing around with the numinous, and we paid far too little attention to the 'set and setting' in which we took psychedelics. Data suggest we were unlucky to have experienced long-term mental health problems,[21] but if psychedelics are ever accepted as a medical treatment, we need to recognise how to manage bad trips and who should steer clear of psychedelics altogether.

The treasures behind the dragon

Clearly there are monsters down there in the underworld. But there are also treasures. By lowering the threshold of consciousness, psychedelics allow people to intervene in habits and patterns that are usually subconscious, automatic and chronically resistant to conscious efforts to change. They bring insight, help people to confront and accept repressed experiences or emotions, and allow them to choose to think, feel and live differently. This can free them from chronic negative ego-patterns, like alcoholism or depression. Psychedelics may also help to heal psycho-immune disorders, perhaps because psychedelics take us into a highly suggestible trance state in which we may be able to affect our autonomic nervous and auto-immune systems.[22] We can also enter this psychedelic-induced state of trance for creative inspiration – the ancient Indian verses of the *Rigveda* call Soma (which historians of religion think refers to a magic mushroom) 'the father of poets'. Psychedelics sharpen what Aldous Huxley called 'aesthetic consciousness', enhancing our powers of deep noticing and giving us an exquisite sense of the beauty of the arts and the natural world. On Huxley's first trip, he lost himself in wondrous contemplation of a print of a Vermeer painting, while pioneering psychologist Havelock Ellis said he never fully appreciated the poetry of Wordsworth until he took mescaline.

Psychedelics unfetter our imagination, allowing us to be the artistic creators of our own reality. The psychiatrist Oliver Sacks wanted to experience the colour indigo and so, after taking LSD, amphetamine and cannabis, he turned to the white wall in his living room and exclaimed: 'I want to see indigo – now!' He writes: 'As if thrown by a giant paintbrush, there appeared a huge, trembling, pear-shaped blob of the purest indigo. Luminous, numinous, it filled me with rapture: it was the colour of heaven.'[23] Most importantly, psychedelics reveal the power of our attitude to our conscious experience – what psychedelic scientists refer to as 'set'. A narrow attitude of egotistic fear, grasping or aversion can rapidly take us into a Hell of panic and paranoia. But we can just as rapidly be released from Hell if we let go and accept the journey. Then we're transported to a blissful sense of connection with other beings, both human and non-human. The musician Sting says of an ayahuasca trip: 'The normal barriers that separate "me" from everything else have been removed, as if every leaf, every blade of grass, every nodding flower is reaching out, every insect calling to me . . . This sensation of connectedness is overwhelming.'[24] And we may get a sense of connection to some bigger Self – which people may call the Atman, Buddha-nature, Logos or God – some cosmic energy or sparkling luminous awareness to which everything is connected. Like people after near-death experiences, trippers often return from the underworld insistent that, in the words of Aldous Huxley, 'Love is the primary and fundamental cosmic fact.'

Return to an animist cosmos?

Psychedelics reveal fascinating things about the psyche and the subliminal mind. But do they reveal anything reliable about the external world?

After psychedelic trips people are more likely to agree with statements like; 'there is a living presence in all things', 'everything is connected' or 'I was in touch with an ultimate reality beyond time and space'. People often come back from trips with a sense of connection between their personal consciousness and a transcendent reality (or God) which is filled with love. That may be the reason why psychedelics dramatically reduce depression and anxiety in the terminally ill. Roland Griffiths, head of Johns Hopkins Medical School's psychedelics lab, told me at Breaking Convention: 'Not everyone necessarily becomes convinced there's an afterlife, but quite often they become open to that possibility for the first time. That's a big change from the total certainty that they are facing annihilation.' This poses a conundrum for modern science – on the one hand, psychedelics heal depression and anxiety in the terminally ill, far better than any other treatment. On the other hand, they appear to do this by inducing beliefs that are contrary to mainstream science, such as belief in an animate cosmos or transcendent reality filled with love. Is this a dangerous delusion, a useful placebo, or perhaps a genuine insight? Does it matter, if it reduces people's suffering?

In fact, psychedelics point beyond traditional materialism in a more radical sense in that they take people into a cosmos that is teeming with 'spirits', or discarnate intelligences. A survey of 800 trippers by Elena Fountoglou and Tamara Freimoser found that 46 per cent of ayahuasca-takers reported 'encounters with suprahuman or spiritual entities', as well as 36 per cent of consumers of dimethyltryptamine (DMT), 17 per cent of LSD-takers, and 12 per cent of psilocybin-takers. Similar percentages reported 'experiences of other universes and encounters with their inhabitants'.[25] How should scientists make sense of these spirit-encounters? One could take them simply as hallucinations – the word that French psychiatrist Jean-Étienne Dominique Esquirol introduced in 1817 to refer to delusory visions. This was how the psychiatrist Oliver Sacks understood his own drug-induced visions – on one belladonna trip, he discussed the philosophy of Bertrand Russell with a spider before seeing his parents land in his garden in a helicopter. Both his parents and the philosophical spider turned out to be hallucinations. One could interpret psychedelic encounters with spirits as projections of one's own mythopoetic subconscious. Psychedelic therapist Bill Richards suggests we view any monsters we meet on trips as aspects of our own psyche to be welcomed and integrated, and this seems a much healthier attitude than seeing them as demons who might actually destroy us. And yet there is still the issue of why people who take DMT often report meeting the same sort of creature: mechanical elves. As Terence McKenna put it, 'You get elves – everyone does.' There was even a panel at Breaking Convention devoted to the topic 'Are DMT elves real?' – one of the more unusual academic panels I've been to. The majority of the audience thought the elves were real.

The ontological status of the spirits encountered on trips is a thorny question for the young field of psychedelics studies, which is trying to establish itself as a respectable, publicly funded scientific field after its 40-year hiatus. As anthropologist Jack Hunter told Breaking Convention: 'Belief in spirits is the cut-off point between the primitive and the modern.' Since the seventeenth century, science has defined itself by its ability to replace animist with mechanical explanations for natural phenomena, thereby liberating us from what astronomer Carl Sagan called 'the demon-haunted world'. If psychedelics are taking us back into such a world, it will face an uphill battle to gain scientific acceptance and public funding – although there's no reason to interpret these beings as 'spirits': they may be alien intelligences, something Sagan was far more willing to believe in. Personally, I think the entities one occasionally meets on psychedelics are usually projections of one's own subconscious. But who knows?

The discernment of spirits

Perhaps a more practical question for the field would be: are encounters with these beings harmful or healing? Psychiatrist Rick Strassman conducted the first major trial of DMT at the University of New Mexico Hospital in the 1990s.[26] More than 50 per cent of participants reported encounters with beings – elves, dwarfs, insects, clowns, crocodiles and snakes – in an environment usually described as a hyper-advanced technological world. It was not like a dream, participants insisted. It was as real, vivid and detailed as waking reality. And, on the whole, these were not encounters of love. The beings' attitude was one of detached scientific curiosity. They examined the humans as we might examine a frog. Some participants reported being dismembered and anatomised. 'I clung to the idea that all was God and that God is Love,' said one participant. 'Even here?' replied the beings, as they feasted on his emotions. Mostly, the beings simply wanted to communicate with humans, and seemed frustrated at our lack of comprehension.

Strassman was 'baffled and nonplussed' by these accounts. As a Buddhist, he'd been expecting encounters with pure consciousness, not machine elves. He gently suggested to his participants that the beings were aspects of their subconscious, but the participants were stubbornly insistent and eventually he came round to their view that the beings were real. 'How can we tell if these beings are for us or against us?' he asked Breaking Convention, as he reflected on his findings. 'Will we try to weaponise them? Will they try to weaponise us?' Strassman has ended up going back to his native Judaism, because the Bible describes how to discriminate between the various discarnate beings one encounters and how to defend oneself from malevolent beings. 'When opening yourself to spiritual worlds, it's not all love and light,' he says. 'It's important to know how to protect yourself, how to pray.' Also at Breaking Convention I heard psychedelics author Daniel Pinchbeck describe how he felt possessed after one trip on dipropyltryptamine (DPT) and needed an exorcism to be cleansed. Several audience members said they'd had similar possession experiences.

This raises the question: when we take psychedelics, are we messing with forces or powers that we don't understand, that we are not necessarily qualified to face? Albert Hoffman, the discoverer of LSD, wrote: 'The fundamental question very much occupies me, whether the use of these types of drugs . . . could not indeed represent a forbidden transgression of limits.' Are psychedelics a divine sacrament, or the forbidden apple? Should we keep clear of psychedelics and stick to lager and Chardonnay? Well, alcohol kills over three million people a year, according to the World Health Organisation. In terms of the risks and the benefits of alcohol and psychedelics, there is no comparison: psychedelics are far safer and better for us. It is always somewhat dangerous to go beyond the ego and explore the world beneath. But remaining in the confines of the ego is even more dangerous – we get bored, depressed, suicidal and destroy the planet in our fantasies of ego-domination. Considering the benefits from psychedelics, I think it's likely they will return to the mainstream of our culture over the coming decades. The challenge is to create what Imperial College's Robin Carhart-Harris calls 'controlled spaces to lose control', where we can help people get the benefits of psychedelics, while mitigating the risks.

Set and setting

Timothy Leary left two rules for guiding trips to successful outcomes. First, know what you're taking, and know your dosage. The effects of LSD can range from a microdose of 10 micrograms, where the effect is mental clarity and mild euphoria, to a large dose of 200 to 600 micrograms, where the effect is vivid hallucinations, profound ego-dissolution and mystical experiences. Second, as previously mentioned, we should pay attention to the mindset we bring to a trip and the setting in which it takes place.

Paying attention to mindset means we shouldn't treat psychedelics as a party-drug, a high, a gas. It's a therapeutic experience, a cathartic experience which may involve difficult encounters with repressed or shadow aspects of the psyche. Rather than simplistically dividing trips into 'good' or 'bad', and getting freaked out if a trip starts to feel scary, we should remember the words of Rick Doblin, head of the Multidisciplinary Association for Psychedelic Studies (MAPS): 'A difficult trip is not the same as a bad trip.' He suggested we should think of it like a therapy session: a really difficult session might be powerful and therapeutic, while if you spend the entire trip giggling it might mean you didn't go very deep. We can try to prepare our set, clarifying our intention before we begin with prayers or invocations, or purifying our intentions with fasting, as the initiates of Eleusis did. The key intentions to strengthen are surrender, equanimity and love. Love is the ladder that seems reliably to take trippers from the darkness to the light.

Next, the setting. Leary suggested people find a quiet, protected place, with people they love and trust, or with a trusted guide. My big mistake was doing LSD when I was too young, at a techno warehouse party where I didn't really know anyone, then going to an after-party where, again, there was no one I really trusted who could guide me out of my bad trip. Tripping unlocks the subliminal mind, which is highly suggestible — that's why cult-leaders like Charles Manson used it to brainwash his followers. So it's important you trust the guides before putting your mind in their hands.

Priests or psychiatrists?

Who are the guides we would trust with such a powerful experience? Laura Huxley, wife of Aldous, asked, 'Who should be entrusted with the tool box – priests or psychiatrists?' One possible 'controlled space' for psychedelics is a medical clinic. The therapeutic potential of psychedelics appears to be huge, and the decriminalisation of medical marijuana in several US states shows that the legalisation of psychedelic treatments is possible, or even likely. But there's some way to go. Existing trials have been small, with fewer than a hundred participants. It would take a large-scale trial, lasting several years and involving at least a thousand participants, to get government approval for psychedelic treatments. That would cost around £1 billion and funding would need to come from a major pharmaceutical company. The other likely breakthrough is in palliative care for the dying: if you have terminal cancer, why shouldn't you have access to a treatment that dramatically reduces depression and anxiety? Rick Doblin of MAPS looks forward to a day when there are psychedelic therapy centres on the high street. At the least, there are now 'psychedelic harm reduction tents' at many festivals, so that people on bad trips can be guided through the experience by sympathetic and experienced helpers, rather than carted off to psychiatric wards and pumped full of anti-psychotics. There is also a website, Tripsit, where people can log on and talk to volunteers if they're really high and feel scared. Most of the time, people freaking out on psychedelics just need some reassurance and empathy, and they'll be okay.

What one notices about the existing medical centres for psychedelics is how spiritual or religious they are. The medical becomes spiritualised. This is because the outcome of psychedelic experiences is so connected to setting – to the ritual, performance, music and symbolism in which a tripper is immersed. NYU's lab, for example, conducts a ritual in which ropes are tied together 'to symbolise the interdependence of all beings', before the patient is handed the psilocybin in a silver chalice. Other labs use Buddha statues and stone carvings of mushrooms to set the mood. All pay a lot of attention to music too – Imperial College employs a PhD student just to study the effects of different types of music on psychedelic consciousness. It's all a long way from the rather sterile atmosphere of the modern hospital – closer to a religious ritual, in fact.

Could one develop a psychedelic 'controlled space for losing control' that is explicitly religious? Could one trust one's consciousness not to a neuroscientist or psychiatrist but to a priest or shaman? In 1966 Timothy Leary abandoned the Harvard lab, created the League for Spiritual Discovery, and wrote a book called *Start Your Own Religion*. In subsequent years, other psychedelic cults mushroomed, including the Psychedelic Venus Church, the Church of the Toad of Light, and the Family of Charles Manson. They were not unmitigated successes. The problem, perhaps, was that psychedelic culture was too subversive and transgressive to create a stable central cult. Doblin said: 'Psychedelics need to move beyond the counter-culture and think how to integrate into society. One possible precedent is the ancient Greek cult of Eleusis.' He's not the first psychonaut to suggest a revival of Eleusis. Albert Hoffman also wrote: 'Only a new Eleusis can help mankind survive the threatening catastrophe in nature.' The classicist Carl Ruck, who coined the term 'psychedelics', is hoping to restart the Eleusinian Mysteries in the original location and wants to launch a 'Gaia Project' there to create 'a new covenant with Earth'. Well, stranger things have happened.

But starting a new religion is a tricky business. Rather than relaunching the worship of Demeter/Gaia, how about integrating psychedelics into the existing Christian cult? There was one famous study in 1962 called the Good Friday Experiment, when Harvard theology student Walter Pahnke gave psilocybin to several trainee priests. Twenty-five years later, many of the priests still said it was one of the most spiritual experiences of their life.[27] However, on the whole Christian theologians have dismissed the idea that you can get to God through a chemical compound. The scholar R. C. Zaehner dismissed Aldous Huxley's trips as 'profane mysticism', although the theologian Walter Stace was more sympathetic, arguing: 'It's not like a mystical experience, it *is* a mystical experience.'[28]

The Purging Plant

I can't see Catholic or Anglican churches integrating psychedelics into their rituals anytime soon. But local churches in South America have been more willing to syncretise the Christian with the psychedelic. In the 1930s, an illiterate Brazilian peasant called Irineu Serra had an eight-day vision on ayahuasca, a psychedelic potion made from a vine, which inspired him to create rituals where people drank ayahuasca, sang hymns and performed communal dances. Santo Daime churches have spread all over the world, and are legal in Holland and some parts of the US. Men and women all wear white, take the potion, then lie down on mattresses in separate parts of the church or tent. Each participant is given a bucket to vomit into – the 'purgation' is quite literal and physical. In between the tripping and the puking, participants are expected to take part in the ritual singing of hymns written by Irineu and his followers, which praise God, the Virgin Mary, Jesus and Santo Daime (which means 'Saint Give Me'). There is a moral foundation for the trips – an emphasis on the virtues of 'firmness', on 'concentration', on doing the rituals in the right way. One psychologist friend of mine has taken part in a Santo Daime ritual and said the trips were both terrifying and wonderful – a journey from demonic darkness into heavenly light, climaxing in a realisation of 'Love as the central cosmic fact', in Huxley's words.

Another friend, a successful author I'll call Clara, journeyed deep into the Peruvian jungle to take part in a twelve-day ayahuasca retreat at the Temple of the Way of Light, one of the leading centres for ayahuasca medicine. She had just had her fifth miscarriage, was also struggling with obsessive compulsive disorder, and was looking for a way to heal and become a mother. She says: 'There were 20 of us in the group, including a UN translator, a Canadian engineer and an ex-nun. I was the only one who'd tried psychedelics before. We all had stuff to deal with, and we were all very nervous.' They were met by the *maestras*, Shipibo-Indian healers, most of them women. That first evening, they gathered in the *maloka*, or ceremonial space, for the first of seven night-long doses of *la purga* – the purging plant. 'You purge by puking, shitting and crying. And you also purge whatever emotional baggage you've been carrying around.'

The first night, Clara lay on her mattress, next to her puke-bucket, in a state of grief and terror. 'I'd written a novel about a war, and spent years researching about grief. I realised my subconscious drew me to this topic as a way of exploring my own grief for the babies I'd lost in miscarriages. The plant showed me that the way to move on was to have a ceremony, like the ceremony of the Unknown Soldier.' She was also taken to a knot of fear in her solar plexus. 'I'd been afraid my whole life, going back to when I was eight and had been abused by a music teacher. I was taken back to that situation. I could see him leering over me, the spittle on the side of his mouth. But this time, I stood up and said no. As I did, the man shrank and went into my stomach. I felt this toxic presence in my colon. I went to the toilet and I shat him out. I could see him in the toilet, and I covered him in compost.' Sometimes, during the trips, the *maestras* would sit beside Clara and sing *icaros,* songs of the spirits. They said that ayahuasca enabled them to see a person's energetic body, to see where there was physical or psychic illness. Their songs could guide the spirits to heal Clara's womb, cleansing the darkness with light. 'I saw all these extraordinary things come out of my womb – one boss who'd been very bullying to me, whose negative energy I'd apparently internalised. I even coughed up Virginia Woolf, who represented to me the idea that female writers must be childless.'

Clara had been held back by subconscious emotional patterns – some from her past, and some she felt were from her ancestral past – which were deeply embedded in her body. The plant helped her enter this subliminal world and unblock ego-patterns in a way that was profoundly healing. Her obsessive compulsive disorder has never been as bad again, and she says all the other participants felt liberated too. She says: 'Ayahuasca is a laser-guided missile going straight to the source of pernicious anxieties. It's simple, natural, but also the most advanced technology you could ingest.' Did it change her religious beliefs? 'We were told that any entities we met were manifestations of our own minds, but that's a moot point. What is the nature of mind? Where is it located? I'm an animist – I think we're in a conversation with the natural world, with plants, trees, rocks, water, that they possess a subjectivity as valuable as my own.'

As for me, I'm wary of going back to the Psychedelic Wonderland after my bad trips. I was sorely tempted to try ayahuasca as part of my research for this book but felt I'd been given a lucky break by my near-death experience and didn't want to blow it again. Besides, doing an ayahuasca trip just to get material for a book didn't seem the purest intention. I particularly advise you to steer clear of psychedelics if you have a history of psychosis in your family. Please don't even think of doing psychedelics before you're 25 – your identity hasn't properly formed yet so it's too soon to dissolve it. Psychedelics may be useful to Western culture at this particular historical stage because we're stuck in ego-consciousness and have lost a way beyond that. Trips may have an important role in moving us towards more of an interconnected consciousness where we feel re-connected to nature. And psychedelic treatment for the terminally ill may radically alter our attitude to death. But we shouldn't see psychedelics as the *only* way to divine reality. They're a short-cut, little more than a temporary holiday from the ego unless we work to integrate our insights. The spiritual practice most religious traditions say we need to learn, if we want to go beyond the ego in a more permanent sense, is contemplation. Take a deep breath, and follow me to the Contemplation Zone.

6: The Contemplation Zone

I arrived in Ödeshög just as the snow was beginning to melt. A minibus picked me up from a bus station, in the middle of rural Sweden, and drove me to the meditation centre. It was a small walled enclosure containing four buildings, a pebble courtyard, and a little muddy forest at the back. The other participants on the course were already there, 30 women and 29 men, milling around, talking excitedly. It was the last time they'd be allowed to talk for the duration of the course. For the next 10 days, pretty much the only voice we'd hear would be that of a dead Burmese businessman called S. N. Goenka, who helped to popularise the South East Asian Buddhist meditation technique known as Vipassana.

We signed in, handed in our wallets and phones. We'd taken a vow to follow the centre's rules for the duration of the course: no fags, no booze, no drugs, no meat, no talking, no reading or writing, no interaction with the opposite sex. We also agreed to follow the meditation schedule every day. When I saw the schedule, my heart sank.

4 a.m.	–	Morning wake-up gong
4.30 – 6.30 a.m.	–	Meditate in the hall or in your room
6.30 – 8 a.m.	–	Breakfast break
8 – 9 a.m.	–	Group meditation in hall
9 – 11 a.m.	–	Meditate in the hall or in your room, according to the teacher's instructions

11	– 12	–	Lunch
12	– 1 p.m.	–	Rest and interviews with teacher
1	– 2.30 p.m.	–	Meditate in the hall or in your room
2.30	– 3.30 p.m.	–	Group meditation in hall
3.30	– 5 p.m.	–	Meditate in the hall or in your room, according to the teacher's instructions
5	– 6 p.m.	–	Tea break
6	– 7 p.m.	–	Group meditation in hall
7	– 8.15 p.m.	–	Dharma talk in hall
8.15	– 9 p.m	–	Group meditation in hall
9	– 9.30 p.m.	–	Question time in hall
9.30 p.m.		–	Lights out

I had some meditation experience, but was I really capable of medi-tating for ten hours a day for ten days? I must, I told myself. Do it for the book. After all, I was in the middle of the Swedish countryside, where was I going to run to? I sat next to an old man at dinner on the first evening. It was his fifth Vipassana retreat. I asked him how his first had gone. 'I . . . I'm not sure I should tell you,' he replied. I insisted. 'Well . . . I kept on having these very disturbing visions of Hell. But it passed. Everything passes.' I sighed and stirred my lentil stew, wondering what Balrog would emerge from my own subconscious. The psychedelic author Terence McKenna once remarked: 'Nobody ever went into an ashram with their knees knocking in fear of the tremendous dimension they were about to enter through meditation.' But we should.

The decline of Christian contemplation

It's hard to pinpoint a precise moment when Christian contemplation began to decline, but I'd suggest it was roughly when Henry VIII first laid his eyes on Anne Boleyn. If Anne had been slightly less hot, we might still have a functioning Christian contemplative infrastructure in the UK. Before the Reformation, there were more than 800 monasteries and nunneries around England and Wales, some a millennium old, where at least 10,000 people devoted themselves to *la vita contemplativa*. They developed a rich literature of contemplative practices for ecstatic journeys into the 'abyss' of consciousness. They sought to open the doors to the mansions of their soul: 'Narrow is the mansion of my soul,' wrote St Augustine. 'Enlarge Thou it, that Thou may enter in.' They created metaphor-maps to describe the soul and guide people through it – the soul as garden, or castle, or ark, or festival. Medieval contemplatives were the depth-psychologists of their day, exploring the further reaches of the soul in order to connect to God in ecstasy. Contemplation was for everyone, not just monks and nuns. According to St Bonaventura, it was what God made us for. Monastic houses turned out beautifully illustrated 'books of hours' for the aristocracy to use in contemplation, and best-selling mystical self-help books like *The Little Book of Eternal Wisdom* for the urban laity. Peasants would also learn the basics of contemplation from mystery-plays (one of which features Contemplatio as a character) and through pilgrimages to monasteries.

England's monastic culture stretched back all the way to AD 527, but it took Henry's enforcer, Thomas Cromwell, just five years to asset-strip the monasteries and nunneries, gutting some of their priceless libraries. The dream-culture of contemplation evaporated like mist in the morning sun. Previously, the 10,000 monks and nuns praying round the clock were thought to be the central spiritual pillar upholding the nation. Yet what did God do when Henry removed and sold off this pillar? Nothing. England carried on, prospered even.

It wasn't all Anne Boleyn's fault, of course. Reformation thinkers, like Martin Luther and Erasmus, had long criticised monasteries for their idleness, their hypocrisy, their elaborate contemplative exercises, their corrupt trade in relics and intercessionary prayer. Where did Jesus say that his followers should sit on their bums in luxurious buildings and spend all day contemplating? Historian Diarmaid MacCulloch suggests the Reformation left Protestant Europe without 'any structured form for either meditation or contemplation'.[1] The Catholic Church also became suspicious of contemplation, which began in the sixteenth century to be labelled 'mysticism'. It was seen as something illicit, over-emotional, possibly heretical. The Church had always suspected those contemplatives like Meister Eckhart – a fourteenth-century

Dominican – who seemed to advocate a direct relationship with the divine, unmediated by the Church. In the fevered atmosphere of the Counter-Reformation, this led to a campaign against 'mystical theology'. The Bishop of London, Richard Chartres, tells me: 'One of the most feared things as far as the reformed Roman Church was concerned was the whole realm of mystical experience – why else did the Church put St John of the Cross in jail? The great spiritual mind of sixteenth-century Spain was persecuted because his kind of mystical exploration is a threat to rigid control, bureaucratic church authority, and the over-definition of mystery in the interest of polemics.'

The Protestant and Catholic churches became more rationalised in the seventeenth century, and the old idea of following a contemplative path to ecstasy was seen as unhealthy and dangerous – hence the Catholic Church's condemnation of Quietism, a popular movement of intense prayer.[2] In the eighteenth century, anti-religious writers such as Diderot and Matthew Lewis mocked monks and nuns as repressed or lascivious perverts. Ecstatic visionaries such as St Bridget had been the great heroes of medieval culture, but now they were seen as deluded and mentally ill. Nineteenth-century psychiatrists, such as Joseph Breuer, insisted that St Teresa of Ávila was 'the patron saint of hysteria'.[3] Once, medieval culture had followed Aristotle's idea that there are two great paths: the contemplative life and the active life. But the legacy of the Reformation and the Enlightenment was a decisive turn away from *la vita contemplativa*, a turn outwards to *la vita activa*. Meditating for the entire day seemed at best navel-gazing and at worst a recipe for insanity. The Western model of the psyche also changed decisively: Christian contemplatives had tried to map a vast interior space, the 'abyss' of interior consciousness, partly by exploring altered states of consciousness, like dreams, visions, voices and imaginative journeys. But such ecstatic voyages came to be seen as dangerous and pathological. In a materialist universe, there is no Holy Spirit out there, no 'buried treasure' in our souls. We should rely on our instrumental rationality to control the material world and not pay too much attention to our imagination, dreams or inner life. The Western psyche shrank to the rickety shed of the ordinary ego.

The Eastern invasion

That situation was never sustainable – the urge to transcend the ego seems to be deep in human nature. Very gradually, Eastern contemplative practices began trickling into Western culture to fill the vacuum left by the decline of Christian contemplation. It began in the eighteenth and nineteenth centuries, as Western powers occupied Asian countries and Orientalists began to translate sacred Asian texts such as the *Bhagavad Gita,* the *Dhammapada* and the *Upanishads*. These texts appealed to Western free-thinking intellectuals, like Blake, Thoreau, Schopenhauer and T. S. Eliot. In the 1950s, the American Beats got into Buddhism, and Jack Kerouac had a vision of 'a great rucksack revolution, thousands or even millions of young Americans wandering around . . . all of 'em Zen Lunatics'.[4] And then, in the 1960s, Eastern contemplative practices swept through Western culture with all the ferocity of the grey squirrel. Eastern gurus travelled to the West in the late 1950s and 1960s and taught their respective practices: B. K. S. Iyengar brought modern yoga, Bhaktivedanta Swami Prabhupada brought Hari Krishna, Maharishi Mahesh Yogi brought Transcendental Meditation, D. T. Suzuki brought Zen, Osho brought his neo-tantra, and Chogram Rinpoche brought Tibetan Buddhism. At the same time, many Western backpackers followed the Beatles' example and journeyed to India to search for enlightenment in various ashrams.

Back in the 1950s, Goenka was a Burmese millionaire businessman. He turned to Vipassana when he was suffering from terrible migraines that left him addicted to morphine. He was an excellent student, and his master eventually gave him a mission to teach Vipassana to other lay-people around the world. Goenka moved to India in the 1970s, where his Vipassana centre attracted several Westerners who would go on to be leading figures in Western Buddhism, such as Jack Kornfield, Joseph Goldstein and Ram Dass. Kornfield and Goldstein set up the Insight Meditation Centre in Massachusetts in the late 1970s, offering similar ten-day and two-week retreats inspired by Goenka's course. In the spring of 1979, a researcher at the University of Massachusetts medical school called Jon Kabat-Zinn attended a two-week retreat at the Insight

Meditation Centre. On day ten, he had a 'vision' for the development of a secular medical meditation technique he would call 'mindfulness':

> I saw in a flash not only a model that could be put in place, but also the long-term implications . . . namely that it would spark new fields of scientific and clinical investigation, and would spread to hospitals and medical centres and clinics across the country and around the world, and provide right livelihood for thousands of practitioners.[5]

That year, Kabat-Zinn created his eight-week Mindfulness-Based Stress Reduction (MBSR) course, which incorporates aspects of Vipassana and yoga, designed not to reach Nirvana but to improve our health.

The science of mindfulness

Kabat-Zinn later became part of a small group of 'contemplative scientists', who met with the Dalai Lama for biannual dialogues organised by the Mind and Life Institute. The Institute was the brain-child of Francisco Varela, a Chilean biologist who learned Tibetan meditation in the 1970s and thought it could play a central role in the scientific exploration of consciousness. Varela outlined a new approach to consciousness-research, which he called 'neuro-phenomenology'. It would study consciousness from the third-person perspective of science (particularly neuroscience) and from the first-person perspective of experience (particularly the deep experience of trained contemplatives). Varela's approach, which owes something to William James and to Aldous Huxley's vision for 'neuro-theology', is now the dominant methodology for studying consciousness, according to philosopher Owen Flanagan.[6]

In 1987, Varela organised the first Mind and Life Institute dialogue with the Dalai Lama. Over the next 15 years, the Institute brought together the Dalai Lama and some of the West's leading psychologists: Aaron Beck (founder of CBT), Paul Ekman, Allan Wallace, the neuroscientist Richard Davidson and others. Eventually, the Dalai Lama remarked: 'All these discussions are highly interesting, but what can we contribute to society?' His Holiness believed that contemplative science could play a crucial role in forging a new spirituality for the faithless. He encouraged Davidson to use neuroscience to study the positive effects of meditation. Davidson took on the mission, and a 2002 study of French monk Matthieu Ricard found high activity in his left pre-frontal lobe, an area of the brain that may be associated with positive emotion, and unusually high amounts of synchronised gamma waves, which may have a connection to positive emotion and compassion.[7] These results were seized on excitedly by the Western press – finally, hard, empirical, material evidence of the health benefits of spiritual wisdom! 'Buddhists lead scientists to the seat of happiness,' read one headline about the Ricard study. 'Is this the happiest man alive?' read another. During the noughties, contemplative science went from a fringe scientific endeavour to a major academic research field, attracting vast amounts of funding. In large part, this was thanks to Kabat-Zinn's MBSR course. It created a standard template for an eight-week secular intervention, which scientists could test to see how it affected a range of emotional or behavioural problems. In 1991 only one scientific paper was published on mindfulness. In 2013 there were 549, many of them funded by the Mind and Life Institute.[8]

'His Holiness has instructed us'

In 2012, the Institute held its first public conference, the International Symposium on Contemplative Studies (ISCS), which 700 academics attended. In 2014, it held the second ISCS in Boston, which I attended. It was a huge conference, with more than 1,600 attendees, mainly academics working in contemplative science. 'When we started in the 1970s, there were fewer than ten people working on contemplative science on the planet,' remarked neuroscientist Richard Davidson in amazement, as he gazed out over the packed conference hall. The ISCS had at least 300 presentations on how mindfulness apparently helps people cope with depression, negative thinking, anxiety, insomnia, chronic pain, addiction, binge eating, PTSD, ADHD and suicidal ideation, while also enhancing people's resilience, happiness, productivity, compassion, care for the environment and capacity for self-transcendence. The science of mindfulness has now inspired 41 mindfulness centres at American medical colleges, where doctors and patients learn how to meditate.[9] This is revolutionising American medicine, by showing the deep connections between mental and physical health. At ISCS, there were also representatives from the UK's booming mindfulness movement, which is based on a therapy called mindfulness–CBT, developed by Professor Mark Williams of Oxford's Mindfulness Centre and now available free on the NHS.

No wonder the delegates at ISCS seemed a little giddy. This wasn't just academic research, this was what *Time* magazine called 'the mindfulness revolution', and it was going to save the world from misery and planetary destruction. The conference was a strange mixture of the academic and the spiritual: one hall was used for poster sessions in the morning, and yoga sessions in the afternoon.

'What journey brought you here?' one delegate asked me, staring deeply into my eyes.

'I . . . flew with Virgin Atlantic,' I replied.

'No, what *spiritual* journey?'

All sixteen hundred delegates rose in reverent silence as the Dalai Lama took the stage. 'This is the most exciting moment of my life,' a psychologist next to me said. Several scientists began their talks with phrases like 'His Holiness has instructed us'. The Dalai Lama told the hall: 'There are one billion non-believers in the world. The only way to educate them about inner values is through scientific research. They don't care what a monk says.'

The contemplative scientists burned with a sense of spiritual mission. 'We are living at a time of environmental crisis,' Kabat-Zinn told the hall, before leading us in a guided meditation. 'The only change that will make a difference is a transformation of the human heart.'

Beyond academia, mindfulness is mushrooming throughout popular culture, in apps like Headspace, in courses for employees at companies like Google and Goldman Sachs, in the US Army, in schools and prisons, and in high-street gyms and spas. You can find books and courses on mindful parenting, mindful eating, mindful sex, mindful knitting, mindful colouring, mindfulness for pets. You name it. Thanks to mindfulness, yoga, Transcendental Meditation and other Eastern practices, contemplation has made a stunning return to Western society. Eastern contemplative practices have flourished by presenting themselves as secular evidence-based techniques to improve health, happiness and productivity. Tibetan Buddhist teachers like the Dalai Lama may believe in spooky things like the non-material nature of consciousness, reincarnation and karma, and even fruitier things like astrology, magic and ecstatic prophecy, but His Holiness is prepared to bracket off those beliefs as 'Buddhist business'. 'In 20 years,' he told the Mind and Life Institute, 'we never discussed reincarnation.' Indeed, Dr Williams's best-selling book on mindfulness-CBT doesn't mention the Buddha once.

This resolutely secular approach means mindfulness can be championed by Western politicians and technocrats who think Western culture desperately needs a post-Christian set of values and practices for the good life but who know secular liberal governments can't promote a religion. In 2014, an All-Party Parliamentary Group on Mindfulness in the UK launched a report called *Mindful Nation* – the same year, as it happens, that Christians became a minority in the UK. The report argued for the expansion of mindfulness in the NHS, schools, companies and prisons. Three ministers spoke at the launch of the report and at least 80 MPs and members of the House of Lords now practise mindfulness. Secular mindfulness seems to be becoming the new established religion for post-Christian Britain. 'In the long-term, Christianity will be gone,' says Lord Layard, the government adviser who helped get mindfulness-CBT into the NHS. 'Meditation is the nearest thing we have to fill the void. Apparently something like 10 per cent of the population now meditates. I don't know if we'll all become Buddhist, but Buddhism has good practices, and it doesn't assume the existence of miracles.'

How does mindfulness work?

There are many different forms of meditation, which affect the mind and body in different ways. Just slowing and deepening your breathing has a relaxing effect on your autonomic nervous system, switching it from the sympathetic nervous system (used for fight-or-flight) to the parasympathetic nervous system (used for rest and healing).[10] Repeating a mantra in your mind is a form of self-hypnosis, which helps the mind and body to relax.[11] You can also foster feelings of love and gratitude through various forms of affective meditation.[12]

Mindfulness and Vipassana, by contrast, try to sharpen people's self-awareness. First, you train your attention to be settled and collected. Initially, one's ego-consciousness is incredibly scattered – problem-solving, ruminating on things in the past, fantasising about things in the future. You bring the mind back repeatedly to the breath, as if you were training a puppy. You then use your collected attention to scan the body, up and down, investigating any sensations you feel. You bring an attitude of curiosity and equanimity to whatever arises, whether it's a pleasant sensation or a painful one. As you observe the sensations, you realise they never stay quite the same: they're always changing. This realisation of impermanence may help overcome ego-attachment and ego-aversion – if a depressed feeling comes, don't panic, it won't last for ever. You may also notice a connection between your attitude of equanimity and the sensation itself; when you accept a sensation with equanimity, it transforms. You can practise a similar technique with your thoughts and feelings: when a negative thought or feeling arises you can welcome it, observe it, and see how it changes. Dr Mark Collins, in his book on mindfulness-CBT,[13] compares the approach to Rumi's poem, 'The Guest House' (translated by Coleman Barks):

> This being human is a guest house.
> Every morning a new arrival.
>
> A joy, a depression, a meanness,
> some momentary awareness comes
> as an unexpected visitor.
>
> Welcome and entertain them all!
> Even if they're a crowd of sorrows,

who violently sweep your house
empty of its furniture,
still, treat each guest honourably.
He may be clearing you out
for some new delight.

If our ego is like a rickety old shed, then the planks of the shed are our habits of attachment and aversion. We believe things like 'I *must* be happy, popular and successful, and I *mustn't* be unhappy, unpopular and a failure.' We imprison ourselves in our rigid beliefs of how we must be, how we must feel, how the world must treat us. And when reality turns out different, we become panicked, ashamed, angry and depressed. This strong aversion to reality only increases our suffering – we end up 'an outcast from the unity of nature', in the words of Stoic philosopher Marcus Aurelius.

In some ways, mindfulness is similar to CBT, which is unsurprising, considering the similarities between Buddhism and Stoicism. CBT teaches people to use their rationality to examine their rigid beliefs, and ask themselves Socratic questions, like 'Why must I always be liked by everyone?' Mindfulness teaches a similar equanimity and cognitive distancing from our rigid ego-beliefs. But instead of disputing negative beliefs, as Stoics do, Buddhists simply *observe* thoughts and sensations as they come and go. And mindfulness, like Vipassana, has a much stronger emphasis on the body than Greek philosophy. It teaches people to be aware of what S. N. Goenka calls 'the physical unconscious'. Our attachments and aversions are often strongest at a physical level. We get attached to the pleasant physical sensation that comes from smoking, or drinking, or binge-eating, or drugs, for example. We might also carry around a lot of subconscious physical stress and unhappiness in our body, without entirely being aware of it. Through focused attention on the body, we can bring this 'physical unconsciousness' into consciousness, and transform our physical sensations through focused insight and equanimity. This focus on the 'physical unconscious' is arguably much more transformative than CBT's narrow focus on our thoughts.

Raptures and hell-visions

There are proven benefits to practising this sort of meditation every day – it has been shown to be particularly beneficial in preventing relapse after recovery from long-term depression. There's also some evidence that it improves mood and attention, reduces stress and boosts our immune system. However, there is a risk of thinking of mindfulness as some sort of miracle cure that we can use to reduce stress and boost productivity instantly. That much was pointed out by S. N. Goenka, who first got interested in Vipassana as a cure for his migraine. His teacher told him that Vipassana wasn't a health cure, it was a way to purify the self in order to go beyond the ego and attain Nirvana. This was what Buddhist meditation was designed to do. And, as we saw in the Psychedelic Wonderland, the journey beyond the ego can be pretty wild. One may experience full-bodied raptures or hellish visions, and if you're attached to your ego-shed and just wanted a bit of a spring-clean, you could be in for a shock.

We're particularly likely to encounter these wilder fringes of human consciousness if we go on a meditation retreat. A 1979 study by the Buddhist teacher Jack Kornfield found that 95 per cent of students on a three-month retreat and 40 per cent of students on a two-week retreat reported experiences of rapture or bliss (described as *piti* in the Pali texts). These apparently arise as the mind settles and deepens beyond ego-consciousness. But students also reported painful experiences: the return of difficult emotions and traumatic memories, autonomic dysfunction in breathing, shaking, insomnia, nightmarish visions of violence or orgies. Kornfield writes:

> Unusual experiences . . . are the norm among practiced meditation students. Over 80 per cent of our three-month students reported such experiences as part of their normal meditation process. From our data it seems clear that the modern psychiatric dismissal of these so-called 'mystical' and altered states as psychopathology – referred to as ego-regression to an infantile state or labeled as psychic disorder – is simply due to the limitations of the traditional Western psychiatric mental-illnesses oriented model of the mind.[14]

Buddhism, like Christian mysticism, offers itineraries telling meditators what to expect along the road. One of the most useful is the *Visuddhimagga*, written in Sri Lanka in around 350 AD. It describes various stages on the path: once the mind is sufficiently trained and collected, it reaches the 'access level', which brings 'strong feelings of zest or happiness' (I'm quoting Daniel Goleman's excellent book *The Meditative Mind*)[15] and may also bring visions of deities, demons, corpses and so on, which can be 'as realistic as talking to a guest who comes on a visit'. Keep going, the book tells us, and don't be distracted by the visions. Then the meditator reaches the 'first *jhana*'. *Jhana* is difficult to translate but means, roughly, a state of deep absorption or concentration. This brings a prolonged feeling of physical rapture – electric thrills, waves of joy, the hair standing up on your skin, combined with a calmer bliss. Eventually one reaches the second *jhana* – more rapture and bliss, though without any verbal thoughts. Then comes the third *jhana*, where the meditator goes beyond the coarser physical manifestations of rapture and feels a higher state of bliss and equanimity. At any of these stages, the meditator may think they have reached Nirvana, because they feel so good. However, these states are just 'pseudo-Nirvana', and there's a risk of becoming attached to them or proud of them, and losing one's progress. The advanced meditator eventually reaches a stage where she or he realises everything arises and passes, even ecstasy, and goes into a state of disenchantment and despondency, in which 'the meditator's world of reality is in a constant state of dissolution'. Her or his mind is filled with terror, disgust, fear, despondency, emptiness. In one text, this is called the 'roll–up–the–mat' stage, because the meditator just wants to go home and curl up in a ball. But this 'Dark Night of the Soul' is just a stage before a higher state of unity and integration. You just need to keep going. Still, imagine how scary it would be to find oneself in that stage of dissolution without being warned about it and without knowing if it would ever end.

At Brown University's contemplative studies department, Dr Willoughby Britton has spent the last decade studying the difficult or negative experiences people can have through meditation. At ISCS, Dr

Britton told us: 'Westerners are mainly using contemplative practices for health and well-being. But that's only a tiny slice of the possible effects of meditation – we should be aware of the full range of experiences that can result.' She said the commonest negative experience – as with psychedelics – is the return of repressed traumatic memories, or Jung's 'shadow'.

Other difficult experiences include cognitive confusion and problems with planning, hallucinations, loss of narrative identity, loss of sense of agency, de-realisation, de-familiarisation, extreme anxiety, panic, rage, mania. Meditators can also experience physical issues – insomnia, breathing irregularities, involuntary movements, sudden rushes of energy that shake the body. They can come back from retreats and find it difficult to relate to other people, or to return to their job. They can feel that they have lost their sense of self.

Britton's project focuses on the most extreme cases, in which problems lasted for an average of at least three years – in one case, the problems continued for more than 20 years; 68 per cent of these problems arose during or after a retreat, but in 30 per cent of cases the people were only practising for an hour a day. Even in standard eight-week mindfulness programmes for depression and anxiety, such as the NHS now runs, 40 per cent of people say they had some difficult experiences, particularly the return of repressed memories. The most difficult experience, of course, is to lose your ego when you weren't expecting to. Britton interviewed a schoolteacher who lost her sense of self for nine years. She said: 'I had no centre. I was gone, I was lost, there was nothing there. In the house I had to hold on to furniture. In retrospect it was really living in Hell.' There's often little support for people who go through these dark stages on the path – even in Buddhist communities. However, the grass-roots community of meditators on the internet is increasingly open about what it's like to go through the 'Dark Night', as hundreds, maybe thousands, of long-term meditators have now experienced it. It appears that treating meditative practice as a tranquilliser is like treating LSD as an aspirin. It *may* cure your headache, but it will probably take you on a much deeper trip than that.

The Burmese torture–camp

Each morning at Ödeshög, we woke to the sound of the gong at 4 a.m., walked through the darkness to the dharma-hall, and arranged ourselves on our cushions, like roosting chickens, pulling blankets round our shoulders, getting comfy and focusing our minds. For the entirety of day one, we practised *samadhi*, or concentration, focusing our attention on the nostrils and breath. On day two, we focused our attention on our nose. On day three, we just focused on our upper lip. Ten hours of meditation on our upper lip. It was initially very difficult to focus. Ego-consciousness kept racing off to the past or the imagined future, returning like a puppy bringing sticks. But, gradually, the mind calmed down and agreed to focus on the task at hand (there was nothing else to do). The quality of consciousness became clearer, 'more subtle', as Goenka put it in his evening video-talks. By day three, I was able to focus my attention more or less continuously for an hour on the upper lip, noticing the subtle sensations playing around there.

Every evening, Goenka spoke to us from beyond the grave. He died in 2013, but the courses at his 170 centres use videos of him teaching. Every meditation session is also guided by a recording of him, and begins and ends with his resonant baritone chanting in Pali. During his evening video-talk on day three, the ghost of Goenka told us to prepare ourselves for day four, when we would finally learn the Vipassana technique, and make a 'deep surgical incision' into the unconscious. It would be dark, difficult, scary, but it would also be profoundly healing.

The next morning we gathered nervously in the dharma-hall. Goenka led us through the 90-minute meditation: we should concentrate on our head, then our face, then our shoulders and arms, then our throat, then our stomach, and so on . . . It was a big let-down. His instructions moved too fast for me to really concentrate on each body part, and wasn't this just a 'body-scan'? Where was the deep dive into the unconscious we'd been promised? I was annoyed after that session, annoyed with that overweight burping Burmese businessman, and all the Western sheep who chanted '*Sadhu* [agreed]' after his Pali chanting, even though they'd no idea what they were agreeing to. It was so boring, having nothing to focus on except your own mind. The other men wandered around the courtyard in the breaks, staring blankly at a tree or the sky, like post-lobotomy patients. I couldn't remember what day it was. Were there five or six days left? I found myself getting irritated with my fellow meditators, even though we never spoke. The guy with lank hair in my room banged around like a maniac when I was trying to sleep. How I hated him. The guy who meditated behind me, with the dry mouth. It was like I could hear every movement of his dry tongue on loudspeaker.

Things got harder in the next session. We were told there was a 'new rule' – three times a day we would do 'sittings of great determination', in which we should try not to move for the whole hour. For some masochistic reason, I decided to do these sittings cross-legged, even though I could barely sit cross-legged for ten minutes because of a metal pole put into my leg after my skiing accident. For all of us, these sessions were intensely uncomfortable and painful. 'I thought meditation was meant to be . . . relaxing!' one lady complained to the assistant teacher in a quavering voice. We were told to be aware of whatever sensations arose – whether gross (painful) or subtle (pleasurable) – and observe them with 'a calm and equanimous mind'. This would overcome our deep-seated ego-habit to react to physical sensations with craving or aversion, which was at the root of all our suffering. 'Always remind yourself that every sensation is impermanent,' Goenka told us. 'It is *anicca*, the law of impermanence. All is *anicca, anicca, anicca*.'

So there I sat, hour after hour, doing these circuits round the body, from head to toe and toe to head. I'd do roughly four circuits in an hour. The pain in my thighs and buttocks would start midway through circuit two, at the 20-minute mark. By 30 minutes it was quite painful. By 45 minutes it was agony. During the last five minutes, my body would be shaking from the pain, there'd be tears in my eyes, a feeling of nausea. I'd be conscious only of the pain, stabbing, awful, unbearable pain, in my knee or feet or buttock or thigh. Surely it must be an hour by now! Why didn't the chanting begin? I'd open my eyes and glare at the assistant teacher. Play the goddamn chanting! Finally I'd give up, unlock my legs, and the pain would vanish. And then the chanting would begin. We went through three of these 'sittings of great determination' a day. Why put myself through this torture? Surely there was nothing ennobling about the pain: it was just my body warning me I'd injure myself. We were told that observing gross sensations without aversion 'purified' the accumulated *sankharas* (habits of craving and aversion) of the past. Pain is the purifying fire – instead of whipping ourselves, like medieval monks, we would observe our physical and emotional pain 'with a calm and equanimous mind'. We would learn that both gross, solidified sensations and subtle sensations were *anicca*, or impermanent – they arose and passed away. The sensations might be fast, pleasant treble vibrations, or slow, painful bass vibrations, but they were all part of the same cosmic song of *anicca*. This realisation would liberate us from our attachment and aversion. We would eventually achieve a blissful state called *bhanga*, in which our whole body would dissolve into pleasurable subtle vibrations and waves of joy – the sort of limb-melting ecstasy that the Christian mystics had spoken of. It sounded marvellous. Meanwhile I was in agony.

Don't get attached to the rapture

On day six, I managed to get to the hour-mark without moving my legs. I dragged my attention grimly around four body-circuits, my limbs quivering with the effort, until Goenka's chanting came in at the end of the hour as a blessed relief. And then, on day seven, something strange happened. It was another hour-long meditation, the pain was building, I was observing it and reminding myself it was impermanent. And then something shifted. It was like a light dawned within me, literally, and a cool breeze spread over the top half of my body – it was sufficiently pleasant that I no longer felt bothered by the pain in my legs. And then, when I observed the 'gross sensations' of pain in my legs, which seemed so solid and permanent, they dissolved too, into subtler sensations. Even my feet woke up from their deep-frozen sleep. Everything in my body dissolved – everything except my left buttock, which remained stubbornly clenched. I observed it, willing its dissolution, but it held out. After that, the sessions became easier, though it was not a linear progress – sometimes I'd have a great session, and decide I'd become a very wise and advanced being, and in the next I'd wipe out after 30 minutes. It was constantly humbling and humiliating.

On day ten, we got to speak to each other. The noise was deafening after nine days of silence. We were told to dedicate our practice to loving-kindness and the liberation of all beings. I felt ashamed of losing my rag with my roommate – I'd actually called him a dick at one point when he'd woken me up. He turned out to be very nice, not the demonic egotist I'd imagined. He told me he'd found the retreat extremely difficult because of returning traumatic memories, but he'd got through it. It had been very physically and emotionally painful for most of us. For two people, it was too much – they checked out early. One seemed to have had some kind of psychotic episode, wandering in the woods all night. But others had more 'ecstatic' experiences – a girl told me she'd felt as if she was coming up on MDMA by day nine. Another guy, who had never meditated before, said that at one point his attention had shifted and he'd found himself in sort of a giant space filled with light. Goenka, in his videos, had repeatedly warned us to avoid attachment and aversion to any sensations that arose. He said it was particularly dangerous to get attached to any ecstatic experiences – subtle vibrations, electric thrills, waves of pleasure and joy. If we got attached, we'd become 'sensation-addicts', chasing the thrills, and just create more ego-attachment for ourselves, more suffering when the thrill was gone.

I got a lift back to Gothenburg with a girl called Laura, who told me this was her second retreat. On her first, six months ago, she'd experienced a ten-day ecstatic high, her whole body vibrating with ecstatic waves of pleasure. She'd bounced into this retreat expecting another high, and instead it had been hard and painful. But she'd realised this was all part of the work.

I realised that I, too, had become hung up on ecstasy in the course of writing this book. There are two risks in our culture. The first – perhaps the main risk – is that we pathologise ecstatic experiences and push them away in aversion, ending up shut off in our narrow ego-prisons. But the second risk is we become too *attached* to ecstatic experiences. We end up thrill-seekers, 'sensation-addicts'. This seems to be a particular risk in the Western subcultures that have preserved a more positive attitude to ecstatic experiences, particularly charismatic Christianity and the New Age movement. How could one not get attached to ecstasy, when each moment of rapture is interpreted as a visit from Jesus, proof you're saved, a sign that 'God is on the move'? How could you not end up chasing such moments and feeling desolate in their absence? A few Christian mystics warn us not to be seduced by 'spiritual delights'. Marguerite Porete, the thirteenth-century French mystic, warned that the stage of 'inebriation' – 'so dangerous, noble and delicious' – is just an intermediary stage on the soul's journey, which it must go beyond, relinquishing its pleasure and falling 'from Love into nothingness', until finally it attains a higher unity beyond duality.[16] But Porete and similar ecstasy-sceptics are, I'd suggest, a minority voice in Christian culture – she was burned at the stake, after all.

Christian mindfulness?

So what can we take from the Contemplation Zone? Once again, I'm reminded of the importance of 'set and setting'. First, meditation shows us the power of 'set' – the power of attitude and intention to modulate consciousness. I saw that so clearly in my experience of physical pain, which would either spike into unbearable agony, or transform into bearable calmness, depending on my attitude from moment to moment. We need to strengthen our determination for the long journey, and we need to practise equanimity, not get despondent when we encounter difficulties, or too jubilant when we experience rapture. And we need to purify our intention with moral precepts – too often, mindfulness is stripped of any ethics. We need to turn outwards, to dedicate our practice to the welfare of others.

I'm also reminded of the importance of 'setting' – the context in which we practise. All of our practice was hugely supported by the context of the Ödeshög centre, the military strictness, the kindness of the volunteers – all of whom worked for free – and the daily teaching and chanting of Goenka. But I found it far harder to practise Vipassana outside that context, back in London. We were told all we needed to keep up the practice was to meditate for two hours every day, while also giving up booze, meat and sexual impropriety. How hard could that be? It proved quite hard. My practice has dwindled to 40 minutes a day of very patchy concentration. What's strange is that, after the intense military supervision of the retreat, we were left to our own devices outside the meditation centre. There is not much of a Vipassana community at all, in stark contrast to Christian life. The one Vipassana sitting group I attended in London, people gathered in a hall in silence, meditated for an hour, then left in silence. If this is the West's new religion, it seems highly puritan, individualist, ascetic, stripped of any ritual or community. Where are the carol services and jumble sales? Where is the pastoral care, for those who might have psychological difficulties after a retreat?

I wondered if it was possible to integrate a mindfulness practice into a Christian theistic context. Clearly, many people do. Professor Mark Williams, the co-creator of mindfulness-CBT, is also an honorary canon at a church in Oxford. He says he thinks mindfulness could actually be a blessing to the Church, helping to deepen people's practice and their connection to God.[17] The Church desperately needs a return to its contemplative roots – perhaps mindfulness is a way back. However, contemplative scientists have tended to be derogatory towards Christian contemplation. In one of the first articles of contemplative science, in 1982, researcher Edward Maupin set the tone when he wrote: 'In general, many of the traditions of prayer and meditation within Christianity have consisted in a kind of blabbing at God.'[18] At the ISCS in Boston, I was struck by the near-total absence of any presentations on Christian or classical Greek contemplative practices – 95 per cent of the presentations explored Buddhist meditation. I asked Thomas Coburn, emeritus president of Naropa University and a veteran of contemplative studies, about the weird absence of Western contemplation from the conference. He replied: 'Sooner or later, contemplative studies needs to deal with the fact that most contemplatives are theists. Most academics have grown up in a Judeo-Christian background and have rejected it. They're either not interested in Judeo-Christianity or outright hostile towards it.'

The lack of interest in Christian contemplation may also be because there is not much of a living tradition in the West. We see the ruins of once great monasteries lying around the English countryside, 'like the peaks of a vanished Atlantis drowned four centuries deep', as Patrick Leigh Fermor put it.[19] I asked the Bishop of London where I could learn to practise Christian contemplation today and was told: 'Alas, we do not have many places where one can go today – we are very needy.' However, there are still some people who try to practise 'mystical theology': there are groups dedicated to following Julian of Norwich's teachings, or those of Meister Eckhart, or St Ignatius's spiritual exercises, or the Orthodox hesychast tradition, or the Centering Prayer of Father Thomas Keating. And there are still many monasteries and nunneries, some of them centuries old, where people can go to stay for free. Of course, most Christian contemplative techniques are very much focused on the person of Jesus Christ – you meditate on His wounds, or visualise scenes from the gospels, or imagine yourself in a rapturous and erotic marriage to Him (more on this in the Tantric Love Temple). It's hard to see how such methods could ever be turned into a secular therapy, as Stoicism has been turned into CBT and Buddhism into mindfulness. Perhaps the closest thing is the surrender to a Higher Power in 12-step recovery programmes.

The contemplative university

Aldous Huxley wrote that 'A society is good to the extent that it renders contemplation possible for its members.'[20] Perhaps we need new centres for contemplative research and practice – new monasteries for a multi-cultural society. Like the Mind and Life Institute, these centres could research and practise wisdom techniques from both a scientific and a humanities-based perspective, then disseminate those practices to the wider community, as monasteries used to do. Such centres could research not just secular Buddhism, but practices from Christianity, Greek philosophy, Islam, Judaism, Taoism and so on.

This new sort of wisdom centre is beginning to appear in academia, at contemplative studies departments in American universities, like

Brown and Virginia, at UK mindfulness centres in Exeter and Oxford, and in organisations like Mind and Life. These centres are a return to the original model of academia, as found in Plato's Academy or medieval schools, like the Abbey of St Victor, where academics didn't just rationally analyse the outer world, but also tried to transform their own consciousness to find wisdom and ecstasy. But then Henry VIII seized the assets of monasteries and handed them over to universities, those factories of knowledge and emotional dysfunction. We need to return to the old model of the university as a hive of contemplative wisdom.

This would be a shift beyond Max Weber's model of the disenchanted academic toiling away at the objective classification of the external world. Instead, academics would work to transform their own and other people's consciousness, and become the prophets of a new evidence-based spirituality. Weber himself warned against this trend, and his warning is worth heeding. In his lecture 'Science as a Vocation', he warned that science 'is not the gift of grace of seers and prophets dispensing sacred values and revelations, nor does it partake of the contemplation of sages and philosophers about the meaning of the universe'. Who, he asked, believes that science leads to happiness, 'aside from a few big children in university chairs or editorial offices'? He insisted that 'only a prophet or a saviour can give the answer [to the meaning of life]. If there is no such man, or if his message is no longer believed in, then you will certainly not compel him to appear on this earth by having thousands of professors, as privileged hirelings of the state, attempt as petty prophets in their lecture-rooms to take over his role.'[21]

Today, there is a lot more optimism that academic scientists, like Jon Kabat-Zinn, Mark Williams or Richard Davidson, could create an evidence-based spirituality that might somehow replace religion. This was the hope of William James, Frederic Myers, Aldous Huxley, Alister Hardy, Timothy Leary and others mentioned in this book. But the risk of this project is that it turns academia into a religious cult, which overhypes its findings, and hides negative results – there is already evidence that some mindfulness researchers and journals have done this, as have some psychedelic scientists. We need to make sure that the field of contemplative studies is open to what Weber called 'inconvenient facts', including the fact that the journey beyond the ego is not easy or safe, that there may be casualties. We need to be humble about what contemplative science can objectively prove – brain scans may show that experienced meditators have higher levels of gamma in the left pre-frontal cortex, but does that mean they're happier or more virtuous? 'How do you know if someone is really enlightened?' the Dalai Lama asked the ISCS. 'It's not a status conferred by an institution, like a degree. You need sustained observation of a person for over a year. It's like spying.' Round-the-year spying may be doable in a monastery but is unlikely to get past a university ethics committee. These are questions to be grappled with along the way - I still think the way to transcend the four-century war between Western science and religion is through academic research into the ecstatic.

Now let's turn to the most controversial aspect of ecstatic experience: its connection to sexuality. Both Goenka and Nicky Gumbel tell us to overcome our sexual desires in order to advance spiritually. Sexual desire is apparently the great enemy on the path to ecstasy. But could there be an alternative path, which embraces sexuality as the ultimate route to ecstatic consciousness? Let's find out as we swing into the Tantric Love Temple.

7: The Tantric Love Temple

'So, a few practicalities before we get under way. First, no nudity in the front office between nine and six, when the postman and deliveries come. We don't want to shock the local village.'

I'm in Dorset at a 'conscious sexuality' festival. Two hundred people have gathered for five days of dancing, hugging, emoting and shagging, with workshops on everything from eight-hand massage to mindful self-pleasuring. A lot of the talk at the festival revolves around the Love Lounge, a polyamorous playground for nighttime frolics.

'Have you been to the Love Lounge yet?'

'We had an amazing time in the Love Lounge.'

'Would you . . . like to come to the Love Lounge?'

The festival is at a place called the Osho Leela house in Dorset. Leela, from the Hindu *lila*, meaning play. Osho was a famous Indian guru, also known as Bhagwan Shree Rajneesh, who helped to introduce 'neo-tantra' to the West in the 1970s. He grew up in a strict Jain family in post-independence India, but rejected his austere upbringing to become one of the most controversial gurus of the 1970s. He set up an ashram at Pune, near Mumbai, and taught a life-philosophy that was perfectly pitched for hippie refugees looking for something to commit to. Osho was charismatic, rebellious, humorous and radical. He claimed to have become personally connected to the divine, and to be able to bring his followers to a realisation of their own divinity. Many spoke of their first encounter with Osho (or Bhagwan) as a spiritual shock – they gazed into his luminous eyes and felt their ego dissolve in love. Here is his first disciple, Ma Anand Sheela:

> That moment all disappeared. All that existed was me and Bhagwan. Everything in me melted. I had never experienced such feelings in my life . . . I felt elated . . . After this meeting all I could do was breathe for Bhagwan, eat for Bhagwan, sleep for Bhagwan, be for Bhagwan . . . I was possessed by the passion for Bhagwan.[1]

Osho initially rejected religions as old-fashioned and dogmatic – 'My whole effort is to create a religionless religion.' Instead, he wanted to wake up his followers to their own divinity, using 'crazy wisdom' – jokes, paradoxes, shock. 'Leave your shoes and mind at the door,' read a sign at the entrance to the meditation hall. He embraced experimentation, developing his own 'dynamic meditation', which involved five stages of intense shouting, shaking and dancing. He would also transmit his spiritual energy in rituals, placing his hands on the heads of his followers to send them into spasms of bliss. He taught them that all previous religions had got stuck in a sado-masochistic repression of the body, sexuality, materialism and pleasure. But he taught a new philosophy, which combined spiritual transcendence with sensual pleasure. He declared:

> My concept of the new man is that he will be Zorba the Greek and he will also be Gautam the Buddha: the new man will be Zorba the Buddha. He will be sensuous and physical, in the body, in the senses, enjoying the body and all that the body makes possible, and still a great consciousness . . . he will be Christ and Epicurus together.[2]

Part of this marriage of transcendence and sensuality was tantra, originally an esoteric branch of Buddhism and Hinduism in which elite adepts could reach enlightenment through transgressions, like eating meat, drinking wine or consuming semen and menstrual fluid. In traditional tantra, sex took place in arcane rituals in which the male attempted to reverse the flow of semen while visualising deities, thereby reversing the flow of energy from their genitals to their 'crown chakra'. But Osho developed what he called 'neo-tantra', a tantra for the masses, focused on achieving a 'cosmic orgasm' in which one's ego dissolves and the divine arises:

> All the religions are against sex, afraid of it, because it is such a great energy. Once you are in it you are no more, and the current will take you anywhere . . . In deep love people are afraid of becoming mad, or of dying . . . The abyss opens its mouth, the whole of existence yawns, and you are suddenly there and you can fall into it . . . In love you are not, the other is also not: then only, suddenly, the two disappear.

This sounds a lot more fun than drinking menstrual fluid. Westerners flocked to the Pune ashram to become sannyasin, donning orange robes and acquiring exotic new names. One American sannyasin recalls: 'We had a feast of fucking, the likes of which had probably not been seen since the days of the Roman Bacchanalia.' In some ways, the ashram was the Indian twin of Esalen, the Californian commune that pioneered a body-focused spirituality of massage, dancing, meditation and group sex. Like Esalen, the ashram ran expensive workshops on everything from Reiki to primal-scream therapy. Like Esalen, it ran 'encounter sessions' in which people stripped naked and confronted each other to try to release their hang-ups. But at Osho's ashram, these sessions were even more experimental than at Esalen. People screamed, fucked, beat each other up, and emerged with bruises and broken bones.

From wonderland to Fascist state

In 1981 Osho and his followers moved to the desert outside Antelope, Oregon, to build a new utopia, Rajneeshpuram. More than 3,000 sannyasin moved there, and started building a city in the desert. Within two years, they had constructed a dam, planted saplings, cultivated organic farming plots, built houses, restaurants, a hotel, a barber's shop and a crematorium. It was funded by a network of Osho-owned meditation centres and discotheques around the world, and by more illicit activities: Osho followers were the first to introduce MDMA into Europe in the 1980s, and rich potential funders were sometimes spiked with a pill before being taken to meet the guru. At its height, at least 15,000 people came to the Rajneeshpuram annual festival, and the ashram made hundreds of millions in revenue. But things started to go wrong.

The local residents in Antelope were frightened by the thousands of orange-clad hippies who descended on their quiet rural neighbourhood. Osho suffered from ill health and became addicted to Valium and nitrous oxide. While he retreated into a stoned silence, the ashram was run by his leading disciple, Ma Anand Sheela, and a coterie of other women, who proved inept at public relations and local politics. They tried to take over the political system in Antelope to make sure they got planning permission for their projects. They moved sannyasin into the local town to get them on the voting register, took over the council, and renamed the town Rajneesh. They shipped homeless people into the ashram by the hundreds, dosed them with tranquillisers, and bussed them into town to vote. They trained a gun-toting 'peace force' to protect the ashram. Perhaps in response to threats of violence from locals, they resorted to violence themselves, poisoning local officials and local restaurants with salmonella, in the largest incident of bioterrorism on American soil. Ma Anand was equally paranoid about her fellow sannyasin, tapping their phones and even attempting to kill Osho's personal doctor when he threatened her authority. The utopia transformed into what Osho himself called 'a small Fascist state'.

In 1985, Ma Anand was arrested in Germany for attempted murder, and Osho was deported to India for tax evasion. The city of Rajneeshpuram eventually became a Christian summer camp. But Osho carried on attracting followers in India, insisting he had no knowledge of Ma Anand's nefarious activities. He died in 1990, but the Pune ashram has flourished into the 'Osho multiversity', a sort of spiritual Disneyland where visitors pay 20 pounds for a day ticket, take an AIDS test, and then are free to dip into whatever spiritual practice or encounter session they fancy, before recuperating in their five-star Osho guesthouse with a massage. He preached a new spiritual capitalism and, sure enough, an empire of Osho products has arisen – Osho books, Osho DVDs, Osho radio, Osho TV, Osho apps, Osho Zen Tarot cards.

Semi-conscious sexuality

Today, in Dorset, the Osho Leela centre is a far cry from the Fascist state of Rajneeshpuram. The managers seem to have much more tact in their dealings with the locals. There is a lot more emphasis on creating 'safe spaces' and 'held spaces'. Some of the old radicalism remains – I tried the 'Aum meditation', a two-and-a-half-hour journey through 14 stages. First we screamed at each other, with an Iggy Pop lookalike screaming, 'I'm better than you, you ginger-bearded fuck!' at me for two minutes. Then we hugged and asked for forgiveness. Then we looked deep into each other's eyes and said we loved one another. Then we freaked out. Then we cried. Then we laughed. We were guided through intense emotions, like buttons on a TV remote. And the strange thing is, I felt each emotion. Are we so easily manipulated?

Later, I went to a cacao ceremony, where we sat in a circle and solemnly invoked the goddess Mama Cacao and asked her to bring us healing. We were then each given a glass of gloopy cold cacao, and told to lie back and surrender. Gradually, people started to moan, writhe and sob, until the whole room seemed to be screaming, laughing and crying. I sat up and looked around. One of the guides asked if I was okay. Of course I was. I'd just had a cup of cacao, which is barely psychoactive at all, yet people were rolling around as if they were on ayahuasca. I guess they just wanted permission to let go – it could equally have been a ritual involving a packet of crisps.

The festival was intense. There was a lot of staring into each other's eyes, a lot of long hugs, a lot of sharing and crying. Which is fine, and potentially healing for a recovering Stoic like me. But, I wondered, does the process of 'clearing blockages' ever actually end? Or is it an endless exorcism, like peeling an onion? The other issue was that most of the attendees were in their 50s and 60s. Osho Leela is next to an old people's home, and it felt like the tantric care-home of the future, where pensioners could gather for nude saunas and leather play. The advanced years of the devotees led to a certain amount of angst. 'My libido is declining,' one ageing sannyasin wailed. 'And who am I then, besides a quite amusing guy? I'm nowhere near tantric bliss . . . I'm not even at moderate joy.' The problem was that many of the older attendees wanted a younger partner, so it felt like a cougar version of musical chairs. I noticed one attractive woman of my own age in the first workshop, who looked familiar. I approached her and asked: 'Do we . . . er . . . know each other?'

'Hi, Jules,' she replied. 'Yes, we went on two dates. You don't remember?'

I was mortified. It seemed the epitome of 'unconscious sexuality'. Was I sleep-walking through my love-life? We decided not to pair up for the next intimacy exercise. Instead, I wandered into a 'cuddle party' – a roomful of baby-boomers writhing on a floor, like a bingo hall on Quaaludes. I was wedged between a middle-aged lady and a man in his 70s. I couldn't bring myself to cuddle him and made my excuses. Eventually I found myself cavorting on a mattress with a therapist from Guildford. I discovered it's surprisingly easy to generate instant intimacy with a complete stranger. But how real is it? Beneath all the polyamorous play, a lot of people seemed to be looking for more-or-less-traditional monogamous love. It was confusing to know what all these intense emotional encounters meant. Was it meaningful and long-lasting? Or was it just play?

A brief history of sex and ecstasy

The philosopher Roger Scruton has observed: 'The sexual revolution of modern times has disenchanted the sexual act. Sex has been finally removed from the sacred realm: it has become "my" affair, in which "we" no longer show an interest. This de-consecration of the repro-ductive process is the leading fact of modern culture.'[3] On the other hand, the philosopher Simon May argues we have made a religion out of sexual love, to fill the vacuum left by God.[4] We can't decide if sex is the main obstacle on our spiritual journey or, in Susan Sontag's words, 'the oldest resource available to human beings for blowing their minds'.[5]

In the pagan world, sex was one of the main ways that the spirit-world intersected with human affairs. The gods sexually desired humans, and descended from Olympus to seduce or rape us, as Zeus raped Ganymede, Europa, Leda and others. This divine intercourse blurred the boundaries between gods and humans, and created semi-divine heroes, like Heracles and Theseus, who helped to advance human evolution. Sex also blurred the boundary between humans and animals – humans in classical mythology have sex with goats, bulls, eagles, swans, even clouds. In fertility cults, sexual energy was venerated as part of the life-giving power of the Earth. In the cult of Eleusis, celebrants bore models of giant phalluses to symbolise the sexual energy of nature; in the cult of Astarte, they worshipped a curvaceous goddess who resembled an extra from a Russ Meyer movie. The ancient Greeks, like other Mediterranean cultures, recognised there was something transgressive and gender-bending about religious ecstasy. Dionysus was portrayed as a cross-dresser, the male followers of Cybele also wore dresses, the prophet Tiresias became a hermaphrodite. To allow a god within you is to be penetrated, unmanned, to become a bisexual or hermaphrodite. In the classical world, then, sexual love is a powerful, playful, disruptive demonic force, associated with the goddess of love Aphrodite and her son Eros, who robs us of our reason. Civilised society must try to placate this disruptive force and guide it into stable channels.[6]

This acceptance and worship of sexuality began to be questioned in the fifth century BC, in the ascetic rationalist philosophy of Pythagoras, Plato and, later, the Stoics.[7] These philosophers tried to liberate the soul from the body through ascetic practices, to bring it into union with divine reason. Plato suggested that we should control Eros – desire – and guide it up from erotic love for a beautiful human to intellectual love of beauty, truth, goodness and other rational concepts. The Platonic and neo-Platonic philosopher surrendered to the ecstasy of love, but it was an intellectual, non-physical union with the Impersonal Divine. The Stoic, meanwhile, denigrated sex as 'the expulsion of some mucus' (in the words of Marcus Aurelius). Sex for the Stoics was an embarrassing and disgusting reminder of our animality, to be controlled and transcended so that we remain self-possessed and rational.

This first sexual revolution was initially confined to the philosophical elite. But when Christianity became the official religion of the Roman Empire, it preached an asceticism for the masses. Jesus was in some ways a transgressive figure, challenging the death sentence for adultery, hanging out with a former prostitute. But He was no sexual libertarian: if anyone has lustful thoughts about someone else's spouse, He warns, they've already committed adultery. It's better to 'lose one part of your body' (like your eyes, or your penis) than for your whole body to be damned through lust. St Paul was even more of a puritan. The body rebels against the soul, dragging it down to earth with its bestial desires. We must practise continence, preferably celibacy, as we wait for the End Times. If you can't wait, get married and have sex, but only to produce children. Homosexuality and lesbianism are abhorrent sins. The early fathers continue this puritanism: St Augustine's whole struggle to come to God is a struggle to overcome his sexual desires. Gregory the Great decreed that married sex is only sinless when there is no pleasure involved. The early Christian theologian Origen went so far as to castrate himself, a practice common enough among early Christians that it had to be outlawed in the fourth century. The flesh must be mortified with ascetic practices – fasting, flogging, hair-shirts, beds of nails. The Devil sends lustful images to tempt the holy, and they must repel them, as the Irish St Kevin repelled the peasant girl who amorously approached him by pushing her off a cliff. The attainment of spiritual ecstasy requires the rigorous control of sexual desire.

The Christian vice-police

Christian mystics, influenced by Plato and Plotinus, try to guide their desire up from created things to ecstatic and erotic union with the Lord. In Platonic mysticism, this union is intellectual and impersonal, but in Christian mysticism, it's often intensely personal, visual and sensual. 'There is no point at all,' wrote mysticism scholar R. C. Zaehner, 'in blinking the fact that the raptures of theistic mystics are closely akin to the transports of sexual union.'[8] The erotic mysticism of the Middle Ages reminds me of erotic fan-fiction like *Fifty Shades of Grey*: the contemplative imagines themselves into the world of the Bible, then visualises Christ as a handsome lover, coming into the bridal bedroom to sweep them up in His arms and kiss them. Here is Hadewijch, a thirteenth-century mystic, meeting Jesus in prayer: 'Then he came to me himself and took me completely in his arms and pressed me to him. And all my limbs felt his limbs in the full satisfaction that my heart and my humanity desired.' Here's Richard Rolle, a cross-dressing four-teenth-century Yorkshire mystic, imagining becoming the bride of Christ: 'Come down, Lord. Come, Beloved, and ease my longing. See how I love, I sing, I glow, I burn.' The moment of religious ecstasy, for erotic mystics, is a moment of erotic penetration by the Lord. As religious scholar Jeffrey Kripal remarks, 'the history of erotic mysticism privileges a homoerotic structure and "exiles" heterosexuality'.[9] However, heterosexual male contemplatives might visualise an erotic union with female figures, like 'Lady Wisdom' or 'Lady Poverty'.

But while a handful of mystics were lost in erotic reverie, the rest of the population had to control their desires – or else. As legal historian Eric Berkowitz writes: 'From the reign of Emperor Constantine to the present, the Christian notion that sexual love brings spiritual death has been the cornerstone of Western sex law.'[10] Any sex outside marriage was a sin against God, and threatened the entire community with the sort of divine punishment that flattened Sodom and Gomorrah. Because of the threat of divine punishment, what you did in the bedroom was everyone's business, and misbehaviour must be brutally suppressed. Berkowitz writes: 'All sex outside marriage was illegal, and the Church, state and ordinary people devoted huge energies to suppressing and policing it.' Cases against adultery, fornication or prostitution accounted for 60 to 90 per cent of all litigation in the later thirteenth century. Adultery was punished by public flogging or capital punishment – the last person to be executed for adultery in England was hanged in 1654, while homosexual sex remained a crime until the 1960s.

Courtly love and Enlightenment fucking

One sees the beginnings of a shift from Christianity's negative attitude to sex in the eleventh century with the development of courtly love in southern French courts. Troubadour poets developed the idea – in part derived from Ovid's *Ars Amatoria* – that romantic love could be an ennobling, stylish and spiritual game, with its own rules and rituals. The Damsel becomes a secular replacement for God – distant, perhaps cruel, but omnipotent and perfect. One glance or smile can send her lover into raptures. By the Renaissance, poets like Shakespeare and John Donne celebrated the ecstasy of romantic love. The lovers, when they're in bed together, create their own world in which they immerse and dissolve themselves – this is the idea behind the beautiful bedroom scenes in *Romeo and Juliet* or Donne's 'The Sun Rising', both gorgeous celebrations of pre-marital sex. However, the lover's journey beyond the ego can be humiliating and dangerous – to be 'blasted by ecstasy' in Shakespeare means to be driven mad by love-sickness.

These literary conventions were acceptable in the theatre or court, but people's actual sexual behaviour was still ruthlessly policed by church courts. That changed, finally, in the seventeenth and eighteenth centuries. During the Enlightenment, religious belief became less a matter of state control, and more a matter of private conscience – 'the care of each man's salvation belongs only to himself', in the words of John Locke. Church courts became less powerful, and urban populations expanded, allowing people to move from gossiping villages to the relative anonymity and liberalism of cities. Enlightenment culture shifted from a terror of divine punishment to an interest in natural morality and earthly pleasure. Nature was seen as a wise teacher, and what could be more natural than heterosexual sex (homosexuality became even more repressed during the Enlightenment because it was deemed to be unnatural)? As John Wilkes wrote in 1754: 'Life can little more supply, than just a few good fucks and then we die.' The Enlightenment embraced what historian Roy Porter called 'the rational quest for sexual joy'.[11] Pornography became more widely accepted and available – books about celebrity courtesans became bestsellers, while Londoner John

Shebbeare noted 'every print-shop has its windows stuck full with indecent prints to inflame desire through the eye'. Prostitution became decriminalised, in part because of the rise of standing armies – when evangelical campaigners tried to shut down brothels, soldiers beat them up. As historian Faramerz Dabhoiwala has argued, it was during the Enlightenment that sex became privatised and de-sacralised.[12] Sex was liberated, but also became a matter of less sacred significance. It was just fucking.

The Romantic counter-enlightenment and mystical sex

However, sex was not totally de-sacralised. In the second half of the eighteenth century, radical Christian groups embraced sex as a means to divine union. This celebration of mystical sex goes back to the thirteenth-century Brethren of the Free Spirit, who insisted that, since Christ has freed us from sin, we can embrace 'perfect liberty' through nudity and polyamory. In the mid-eighteenth century, a German aristocrat called Count Zinzendorf formed a religious group called the Moravians, who were a key influence on John Wesley and on contemporary charismatic Christians, like Holy Trinity Brompton. The Moravians were influenced by Kabbalist mystical practices in which one visualised the divine body while making love, as a means of drawing down God's energy and releasing it on Earth. The Moravians would visualise the body of Christ as an androgyne, with a phallus and a vagina-like 'side-wound', and then imagine themselves erotically uniting with Jesus, either entering his side-wound or being entered by him. Like Jewish Kabbalists, Moravians saw marital sex as the best path to divine union. Moravian couples would frankly discuss their sex lives in small groups, a practice that 'anticipated to some degree modern "group therapy"', in the words of theologian Colin Podmore.[13] The intense group ecstasy of Moravian 'love feasts' occasionally spilled over into orgies. The son of Count Zinzendorf, Christel, created a radical group of young Moravians who cross-dressed, strummed guitars and indulged in ritualised bisexual play in the 'blue chamber' of Zinzendorf's castle. When Count Zinzendorf found out what was happening, he closed the group down.[14]

Sacred sex remained part of radical spirituality in the late eighteenth and early nineteenth centuries. Swedish mystic Emmanuel Swedenborg experimented with Kabbalah and tantra, which he came across through reports from European travellers in India. He taught himself to restrain semen ejaculation by tensing the cremaster muscle, which he believed could redirect sexual energy to his mind, sending himself into a trance in which he could connect to angels. William Blake, who was influenced by both the Moravians and Swedenborg, preached a philosophy of free love in which sexual repression was a hateful part of political, economic and spiritual enslavement. Repression makes us ill: 'He who desires but acts not, breeds pestilence.' God wants us to be virile, liberated, sexually playful beings: 'The head Sublime, the heart Pathos, the genitals Beauty, the hands & feet Proportion.' Mystical sex – using the methods of Kabbalah and tantra – is the best way to heal our psychic wounds and return to Paradise. We should learn to frolic naked in the Garden of Love, as Blake and his wife Catherine did in their garden in Surrey. Unfortunately, Puritan priests have spread a spirit-killing religion of sexual repression:

> And priests in black gowns were walking their rounds
> And binding with briars my joys and desires.

Other Romantics raised romantic love to the status of a secular religion, comparable to medieval courtly love. Rousseau's Romantic novel, *La Nouvelle Héloïse*, was a European bestseller and helped to create a new cult of sentimentality, in which the aim was not so much the attainment of the beloved as the enjoyment of one's own exquisite feelings. Its success helped foster a steady flow of romantic novels, films and pop songs that continues to this day, in which heroes and heroines search for The One – Mr Darcy, Heathcliff, Stella – who will lift us from the tedium of our lives, redeem us and complete us. As philosopher Simon May notes, in Romanticism the idea that God is love is replaced by the idea that love is God. For high Romantics, like Wagner or the poet Novalis, ecstatic union with The One can only really take place in death, when our souls are liberated from our bodies and we can truly unite. 'In death is love most sweet,' writes Novalis in *Hymns to the Night*. 'What bliss, what sensual delight does thy life provide which would outweigh death's ecstasies?'

The modernist sexual revolution

The pendulum of sexual liberty swings back in the nineteenth century. Victorians were not quite as prudish as the twentieth-century stereotype suggests, but the Victorian middle class prided itself on its respectability, and developed a cult of the domestic family. The Victorian housewife was expected to be an 'angel in the house', an embodiment of the virtues of piety, purity, domesticity and submission. Sex should be enjoyed, but within the confines of marriage. The Victorian male, however, might secretly be allowed more sexual liberty beyond the bounds of his class and family, with working-class prostitutes (male or female), with maids or with exotic women at the periphery of empire – but there was always the anxiety that one's misdemeanours would intrude into the sanctity of family life, as they do in *Jane Eyre* or Ibsen's *Ghosts*. Sex was less an object of religious superstition, and more a public health concern – masturbation and sexually transmitted diseases were objects of particular medical anxiety. Victorian culture seemed schizophrenic: there was a sentimental worship of marital love, while Victorian novels and poetry tend to mention sex only through coy allusions or euphemisms.

This coyness radically changes in the modernist sexual revolution from 1890 to 1930. A new openness towards sex emerges among modernist bohemians. The Bloomsbury set typified this frank experimentalism, as recalled by Virginia Woolf:

> It was a spring evening. Vanessa and I were sitting in the drawing room . . .
>
> Suddenly the door opened and the long and sinister figure of Mr Lytton Strachey stood on the threshold. He pointed his finger at a stain on Vanessa's white dress.
>
> 'Semen?' he said . . . With that one word all barriers of reticence

and reserve went down. A flood of the sacred fluid seemed to over-whelm us. Sex permeated our conversation . . . the old sentimental views of marriage in which we were brought up were revolutionised.[15]

The idea that sex could be an ecstatic voyage beyond the ego and into the spirit-world occurs again and again in modernism.[16] The American poet Laura Riding searched for an orgasm so powerful she could stop time. Surrealists like Max Ernst, André Breton and Salvador Dalí used sex and sexual imagery as a way to throw off the shackles of the civilised ego and magically connect to the creative subconscious. Occult practitioners, like W. B. Yeats and Aleister Crowley, used sex magic as a way to channel spirits and demons. And Edwardian researchers of spiritualism, like Frederic Myers, noted the arousal of female mediums when they were in trance states. At seances, spirit-possessed mediums flirted, cuddled and even shagged male attendees, as if ecstasy had given them permission to sidestep their society's conventions.[17]

In the 1930s, the psychologist Wilhelm Reich, a wayward disciple of Sigmund Freud, developed the idea that all of society's social and emotional problems could be solved if we just shook loose our sexual repressions and achieved 'cosmic orgasm'. Sexual repression made us ill – Reich said he felt unwell if he didn't orgasm at least once a day. We needed a 'sexual revolution' to complement the social revolution of Marxism-Leninism. Reich became more and more mystical, believing he could see the sexual energy of the universe, and channel it into people through a specially designed 'orgone box'. Although he was quasi-psychotic, Reich realised what Freud didn't: that we can find catharsis through the body and, in particular, through orgasm.[18]

D. H. Lawrence and the religion of sex

The greatest prophet of mystical sex in the modernist revolution was D. H. Lawrence. His psychology is close to that of Myers, James and Jung in that he believed there is a greater subliminal Self beyond the conscious ego, to which we could connect for healing and fulfilment. He writes:

> This is what I believe . . . That my soul is a dark forest. That my
> known self will never be more than a little clearing in the forest.
> That gods, strange gods, come forth from the forest into the clearing
> of my known self, and then go back. That I must have the courage
> to let them come and go.[19]

Like Reich and S. N. Goenka, Lawrence believed this subliminal self
is deeply embodied, and we can access it through physical exercise,
particularly sex. Sexual love enables us to go beyond the conscious ego
and be born again through the darkness of the other, as he describes
in *The Rainbow*:

> His blood beat up in waves of desire . . . The reality of her who
> was just beyond him absorbed him. Blind and destroyed, he pressed
> forward, nearer, nearer, to receive the consummation of himself, he
> received within the darkness which should swallow him and yield
> him up to himself . . . It was the entry into another circle of
> existence, it was the baptism to another life . . . At last they had
> thrown open the doors, each to the other, and had stood in the
> doorways facing each other . . . it was the transfiguration, the
> glorification, the admission.

There's a lot that's annoying about Lawrence, but *The Rainbow* is an
extraordinary book – a Bible told through the sex lives of three gener-
ations of a rural Midlands family. Lawrence describes sex in a sacramental
language that could easily be ridiculous but which he manages, on the
whole, to make hypnotic and enchanting. Here, from *The Rainbow*, is
a post-coitus bedroom scene between Will and Anna, lying in bed after
their marriage. As in Shakespeare and Donne, the lovers turn their
bedroom into a blissful Otherworld:

> As they lay close together, complete and beyond the touch of time
> or change, it was as if they were at the very centre of all the slow
> wheeling of space and the rapid agitation of life, deep, deep inside

them all, at the centre where there is utter radiance . . . And now, lo, the whole world could be divested of its garment, the garment could lie there shed away intact, and one could stand in a new world, a new earth, naked in a new, naked universe. It was too astounding and miraculous.

The problem, in Lawrence's view, is that Western civilisation has become too rational, too obsessed with instrumental control and social prestige. We have lost the capacity to get out of our heads. As a result, we are going mad, taking out our restlessness on each other and on the planet. We need to open to the wisdom of the body: 'Real knowledge comes out of the whole corpus of the consciousness; out of your belly and your penis as much as out of your brain and mind.' In *Lady Chatterley's Lover*, the gamekeeper Mellors declares: 'I believe if men could fuck with warm hearts, and the women take it warm-heartedly, everything would come all right.' But Lawrence became more and more pessimistic and apocalyptic about Western civilisation, seeming to think he and his wife Frieda were the last warm fuckers on Earth, and the rest of the human race were better off wiped out.

The sixties search for the perfect orgasm

During the sexual revolution of the 1960s, the sexual experimentalism of modernist bohemians became a mass phenomenon, in large part thanks to the development of the contraceptive pill and abortion clinics, but also to the loosening of religious and social taboos over individual behaviour. Roger Scruton claims that the sixties was when sexual reproduction became privatised and de-sacralised. This is not quite true. First, as we've seen, sex was de-sacralised earlier, during the Enlightenment. And second, the sixties' sexual revolution was not one revolution but several, often moving in clashing directions.

Certainly there was a move to disenchant and rationalise sex. Sexologists such as Alfred Kinsey, the research team Masters and Johnson, and the psychologist Albert Ellis tried to bring the light of reason to sexual behaviour, to remove obfuscations and religious taboos and enhance human control over desire. This move towards 'sexual rationalism' was not really interested in sex as a means to ego-obliterating ecstasy: sex should be a means to rational pleasure, and sex education would help challenge superstition, increase knowledge, and make us all masters and mistresses of our own pleasure. Sex entrepreneurs like Hugh Hefner also tried to rationalise and commodify sex. Censorship laws were loosened through campaigns to get books such as *Lady Chatterley's Lover* published. The liberalisation of censorship enabled the rise of adult magazines like *Playboy* and adult films like *Deep Throat*. Sex became much more visible through the use of erotic imagery in advertising and pop culture. If sex is privatised and freed from religious control, then why shouldn't the free market move in to cater to our desires? Again, this trajectory is less about ecstatic surrender and more about control – in this case, the control of the free market.

However, another movement within the sixties sexual revolution viewed sex as an ecstatic liberation from the ego and a vehicle for the utopian transformation of society. This trajectory embraced the idea – found in Wilhelm Reich and D. H. Lawrence – that bad sex was responsible for all the neuroses and evils of civilisation. If we could just shake off our inhibitions and have a really good orgasm, everything would be groovy – this was one of the central ideas behind the San Francisco 'Summer of Love'.

Part of the mystical sex revolution was the Reichian idea that adults need to overcome their sexual hang-ups on their journey to spiritual fulfilment. Sexual exploration could take place at locations like Esalen, the Big Sur commune where seekers congregated in hot tubs to explore their boundaries; or in sex cults like Osho's ashram or the Children of God, a radical Californian sect in which group sex was seen as central to spiritual worship. If you didn't want to join a cult, you could still go to a swinger club or commune to get a taste of polyamorous paradise. Here is journalist Herbert Gold describing a famous Californian sex commune called Sandstone in 1975: 'The large water-bed domain has a cathedral ceiling . . . A sign says: PLEASE, BEYOND THIS POINT, SPEAK ONLY SOFT WORDS OF LOVE. It seems to be an injunction that is observed by the faithful . . . the couples couple on the water-bed chapel, heated to 80 degrees . . . the water-bed peace that passeth understanding and maketh inner space.'[20] And here is Steve Ostrow describing his Continental Baths in New York, a swinging club that was eventually renamed Plato's Retreat: 'The world comes here now to feel the release of decades of pent-up sexuality, all those years of inhibition are splattered, if you will, against my walls! . . . We're close now to total sexual liberation.'[21]

The dark side of the Swinging Sixties

Yet 'total sexual liberation' proved difficult to attain. Feminists pointed out that, in many instances, the sexual revolution left women just as objectified and oppressed by men as ever – they had been liberated, but only to dress up as bunnies and serve drinks at Hugh Hefner's Playboy mansion. Feminist critics of the porn industry seized on the testimony of Linda Lovelace, who said she'd been forced into performing in *Deep Throat*. Rock and roll culture often degenerated into teenage girls worshipping and being abused by male rock stars and DJs. Quaaludes – the love-drug of the sexual revolution – were used by sexual predators to loosen girls' inhibitions, not always with their knowledge or consent. The San Francisco Summer of Love was a field-day for rapists – 'Rape is as common as bullshit on Haight Street,' one observer commented. At the extreme, sex gurus like Charles Manson or Osho forced female followers to sleep with whomever they chose for them. Inside the Children of God (since renamed the Family), female devotees were forced to have sex with men in order to convert them and raise money for the Church, in a practice known as 'flirty fishing'.

Sexual liberation revealed some nasty corners of human sexuality. In 1971, Germaine Greer organised a Wet Dream Festival as a sort of pagan ritual of polyamory, but was 'sickened' when some of the films shown depicted bestiality, coprophilia and sadism. Champions of total sexual liberation argued that children should be introduced to sex at an early age, encouraged to explore their own sexuality, and even incorporated into sex play with adults. Philosopher Michel Foucault argued against any regulation of sex, including paedophilia, insisting that 'it's quite difficult to lay down barriers' as 'it could be that the child, with his own sexuality, may have desired the adult'.[22] The leader of the Children of God preached that sex with children was healthy and natural, and many children were serially abused in the cult during the 1970s. This kind of child abuse was the most disturbing consequence of the sexual revolution. But a more widespread social change was the steep rise in divorce and single-parent families, and a new belief that pursuing one's own spiritual and sexual fulfilment was more important than maintaining family stability. The sexual revolution was not always great for children.

And then there was the peculiar rise of BDSM (bondage and discipline/domination and submission/sado-masochism) in San Francisco leather bars in the 1970s, in which men (and, later, women) searched for what Foucault called 'limit experiences' in which the ego is obliterated. Why, in an era of sexual liberation, were people so keen to be bound and gagged?

The agony and ecstasy

The strange thing one notices about the Enlightenment sexual revolution is the sudden fad for flogging and spanking. It crops up in novels like *Moll Flanders*, in pornographic prints, and in brothels – one madam even owned a flogging-machine. It's as if, after 15 centuries of Christian sexual repression, the old infrastructure of discipline and punishment returns as erotic play. The Marquis de Sade predicted this – amid the Enlightenment's attempt to rationalise sex, he saw that the death of God doesn't necessarily lead to a utopia of rational, egalitarian pleasure-seeking. If we embrace the law of nature, nothing is forbidden. If you get off on the suffering of another, how is that forbidden by nature? Cruelty, 'very far from being a vice, is the first sentiment Nature injects in us all'.[23] His heroes get acute pleasure from transgression – anal sex, incest, torture and blasphemy. Although they're atheists, they preserve the idea of God for the thrill of disobeying Him. They create a religion in reverse – all that was forbidden by Christianity is now sacred: 'heavenly ass'; 'heavenly fuck', 'heavenly incest'; 'Holy frigging God, what ecstasy!' De Sade ends up embracing the philosophy of Fred West and

Ted Bundy: the ultimate high is the taboo of sexual torture and murder.

In the twentieth century, French writer Georges Bataille likewise explored a dark sexual ecstasy born of transgression. He insisted the 'whole business of eroticism is to destroy the self-contained character of the participators as they are in their normal lives', to rupture the ego through transgressive sex and violence, thereby attaining 'divine ecstasy and extreme horror'.[24] Bataille called for 'organisations that have ecstasy and frenzy as their goal (the spectacular death of animals, partial tortures, orgiastic dances etc)'. Like De Sade, Bataille didn't believe in God but still got a thrill from transgressing His rules and rituals. Around the same time, Aleister Crowley suggested that the best way to ecstatic states of consciousness was through transgressive sexual violence – humiliation, flogging, rough sex, black magic rituals. You see BDSM feature in many New Age rituals, from Wicca to chaos magic.[25] For Pauline Réage, author of the masochist classic *Story of O*, BDSM became a sort of private religion: the heroine, O, deifies her lover, makes a god of him, and then experiences the joy of total surrender. The world is narrowed to the blissful simplicity of serving the Master or Mistress. The more O's god demands of her, the more she can surrender her ego and abase herself before him. The old monotheism has been rejected, but returns as erotic play.

The way of pain

Practitioners of BDSM discovered a technology of ecstasy previously found only in religious cults: the way of pain. The artist Grayson Perry declared: 'I see a lot of religious practices as offshoots of kinky sex.'[26] How often in religious cults around the world does ecstatic union with the divine involve self-mortification, self-flagellation, cutting oneself, stabbing oneself, threading needles through one's face, body or genitalia, starving oneself, tying oneself up, lying on nails, wearing hair-shirts, embracing lepers, and generally mortifying the flesh? The Lord 'favours those who do violence to themselves,' wrote St Teresa of Ávila.[27] Kinksters take this ancient technology and secularise it, creating their own private cult. They discover, as I discovered at Ödeshög, that pain is never just pain: it can be transformed according to the attitude or 'set' one brings to it. Christian mystics turned it into 'sacred pain', a purifying fire that brought them closer to God. BDSM practitioners use pain as a means to ecstatic pleasure and ego-dissolution. Kink author Geoff Mains writes: 'Pain of any form becomes sheer ecstasy. Needles through the flesh. Hot candle wax dribbled over alligator clips . . . The frontier between pain and pleasure has been crossed.'[28]

There are physiological mechanisms underlying the ecstasy of submission known as 'subspace' in BDSM. Extreme pain overwhelms the sympathetic nervous system, while the relief of pain activates the para-sympathetic nervous system, leading to a flood of endorphins and opiates in the body, similar to the high athletes feel after intense work-outs.[29] On a phenomenological level, pain absorbs the attention and annihilates the self: the essayist Elaine Scarry notes how, in extreme pain, 'the created world of thought and feeling, all the psychological and mental content that constitutes both one's self and one's world . . . ceases to exist'.[30] There's also a ritualistic dynamic to BDSM. As with religion, BDSM practitioners have discovered that the 'setting' of ritual and role-play is incredibly mind-absorbing and trance-inducing: they develop their own mask-and-costume ceremonies, their own elaborately choreo-graphed scripts. They make the dungeon an Otherworld in which they are totally absorbed. Anthropologists of religion have found that the more painful sacrifices a religion demands of us, the more strongly we emotionally bond to it.[31] Something similar appears to be true in sexual relationships.

Many humans want something or someone to surrender to; they want to bow, worship and give up their freedom and their bodies to a strong god or goddess figure. And others are more than happy to play the god-role – not like gurus, who play the god-role all the time for real, but as a Master or Mistress, who plays the god-role temporarily, for fun. As one BDSM teacher suggested to me, all sex has a shadow side. If one denies that shadow, then the desire for power or submission can emerge unconsciously, in unacknowledged power games or, at the extreme, in the dangerous worship of gurus. Sexual abuse by spiritual teachers is unfortunately widespread – a 1985 survey by Jack Kornfield of 54 spiritual teachers (mainly Buddhist) found 63 per cent admitted to having sex with students.[32] In BDSM, this shadow side of religion – the desire for sexual power and submission – is consciously acknowledged and explored through play.

Perhaps kinksters have discovered a healthy, safe way to achieve surrender. While early psychologists of BDSM insisted such behaviour was the pathological product of self-hating neurotics, recent surveys have suggested BDSM practitioners are just as well adjusted and happy, if not more so, than the general population.[33] BDSM post-*Fifty Shades* is rather mainstream and plain vanilla, sold in high-street stores, taught at endless workshops and video-tutorials. There's a mature emphasis on learning the etiquette, learning how to play well, learning to create 'safe spaces'. De Sade would be appalled.

Yet, naturally, the world of shadow play has its own shadow side. Any path that involves playing with ego-destruction is going to attract the hardcore who get bored with plain vanilla and want to try rocky road. Foucault himself was fascinated by the emergence of chemsex in San Francisco. 'I met an attractive young man who told me that he and many others go to the baths a few times a week, frequently under the influence of uppers and amyl . . . These men live for casual sex and drugs, incredible!'[34] Foucault got into the chemsex leather scene when he knew he was likely HIV positive. The threat of death only made the sex more exciting. A recent *Vice* documentary, *ChemSex*, shows that, alas, Foucault was a prophet for a dangerously destructive trend in the gay community, where people get addicted to the toxic transcendence of drug-fuelled BDSM orgies, often with the knowledge they might get 'pozzed up', i.e. infected with HIV. One participant says: 'Everyone leaps on each other and you dissolve in this sweaty mass of sex and lust, and you'll lose yourself . . . and that's when it feels like bliss. You do another shot of GHB, and everyone is back there, it's fantastic.' Drug-fuelled orgies are okay if they're done safely and . . . er . . . in moderation, but the problem, to which many in the documentary testified, is that there are people in the scene who don't respect the consent, safety or feelings of others. And the high is so high it becomes addictive. One recovering addict declares: 'When you've had that and you go back to sex when you're not on drugs, you think . . . Is that it?'

The troubled legacy of the sexual revolution

Today, most of us still find occasional moments of spiritual ecstasy through sex. In an online survey I did in 2016, with 323 respondents, 77 per cent said they thought sex is or can be a spiritual experience; 60 per cent reported experiencing ego-dissolution or merging with their partner during sex; 59 per cent said they sometimes got the shakes or shivers during sex; 17 per cent said they sometimes hallucinated during sex; and 10 per cent said they felt an erotic connection to a spirit or god during sex. Experiences of sexual ecstasy have barely been studied by academics, except by a psychologist called Jenny Wade. Her book *Transcendent Sex* explores moments where people found themselves in utterly altered states, connecting to divinities, or being transported to hallucinatory realms.[35] Wade suggests such experiences happen to about one in eight people, although my survey suggests ego-dissolution through sex may be more common than that.

The legacy of the sexual revolution is not so much the de-sacralisation of sex as the rejection of priestly control over it. Sex has been privatised, like spirituality. Many Western churches tried to fight a rearguard action against the sexual revolution, leading to the culture wars of the 1980s and 1990s. But they lost. That's one of the main reasons for the decline of church congregations in just about every Western country since the 1960s. The sexual revolution fundamentally changed our attitudes to sex: we're relaxed about birth control, fine with masturbation, and generally accepting of homosexuality – indeed, a 2015 YouGov poll of British 18 to 24 year olds found that 50 per cent did not identify as 'exclusively heterosexual'. We're also comfortable with kinky sex. While Alfred Kinsey was so shocked by BDSM he didn't even ask people about it, 75 per cent of respondents in my survey said they had either tried BDSM-lite play in the bedroom (spanking, being tied up, etc.) or fantasised about it.

However, while we've liberated our pleasure from the control of priests, we still worry about the power of the free market over our desires. In my survey, 74 per cent of respondents thought Western society had become over-sexualised. Respondents worried about the effect of a hyper-sexualised pop culture on young girls. They worried about the availability and effect of hardcore porn on teenage boys. Feminists worried that porn encouraged violence against women, but in fact the most popular porn sites feature sexualised mother-figures (Freud was right, after all!). The new technology of smartphones and apps like Tinder have made casual sex so easy that we suffer from the paradox of choice. And yet, in the supermarket of desire, we also cling to a Romantic belief in The One (the most popular dating site in the UK is called 'Soulmates'). I wonder if a legacy of Romanticism and the sexual revolution is an expectation that romantic love should always be ecstatic – there may be rare moments of ecstasy in marriage, but there is an awful lot of laundry too.

But the more positive legacy of the sixties sexual revolution, hopefully, is that we have become less ashamed of sex, more accepting of consenting adults' differing sexual choices, and more intelligent about how to give ourselves and each other pleasure. And that ultimately strengthens married life. One friend tells me: 'You reach this point after a few years of marriage where the raw animal desire has died down, and that's when a lot of marriages get in trouble. Tantra taught my wife and I how to improve intimacy by doing basic things like breathing in and out at the same time while looking into each other's eyes. It's made our love-making far more intimate and powerful. If more people learned basic tantra, it would save marriages.'

The occasional ecstasy of parenting

There's a final type of ecstasy I want to consider in this chapter, which is the ecstasy of love between parent and child. One of my tutors at university was Lesel Dawson: she gave me my deep love of Shakespeare. While she was finishing her book on Elizabethan love-sickness, she gave birth to her first child, Jamie. He was born two months prematurely, and was immediately taken from Lesel after birth and put into an incubator. She says: 'I didn't know how I would respond when I was taken to see him. But the minute I saw him, I felt someone had punched me in the stomach. I felt sick with love. Finally I got to hold him. That was the only thing that made me feel okay.' She'd spent the previous few years examining the 'radical decentring of self' that the Elizabethans described in love-sickness,[36] and here she was, experiencing something similar through motherhood: 'There's a very intense period at the beginning, where you really feel a blending of your self with theirs, you feel blissed out, totally absorbed in the "baby-bubble". It could become addictive. It's intensely physical and sensuous – your body responds to their call by lactating. For a long time after I stopped breast-feeding, emotional events would trigger lactation in my breasts.' Lesel says the experience of ego-merging fades as the children grow up and separate, but she remains permanently changed by motherhood. She says: 'Parenthood is hard, it's a grind, you often feel miserable and exhausted. But it comes with these pearls of physical and emotional experiences that are fantastic. They're moments of bliss in a landscape of drudgery.'

★

It's time to head on. Having touched on the relationship between pain, violence, sacrifice and ecstasy, let's go deeper, and darker, as we head to the Mosh-Pit to explore the ecstasy of war.

8: The Mosh-Pit

Omar Hussein grew up in Wycombe, an unexceptional schoolboy who later worked as a security guard in Morrison's hardware store. He felt, he told the BBC, 'like a lost sheep, not knowing where I was going, waking up every day doing the same old things'.[1] He became more serious about his Islamic faith; initially, his friends said, it steadied him and made him more mature. But he rapidly became drawn to the more radical fringe of Islam and voiced his support for Daesh on social media. His outspokenness landed him on a police watch list, but he was still able to travel to Turkey in 2014, despite Special Branch confronting him at Heathrow airport. Suddenly his mundane life felt like a secret-agent movie. He was thrilled to be arriving in the utopia of Daesh. He told the BBC: 'Going to the airport, you're happy cos you're leaving the land of disbelief and immorality, and you're going to the land of jihad. That's like Paradise, man.'

When he arrived, was the 27-year-old put off by the bloody reality of life under Daesh – the fighting, the repression, the gruesome public executions? On the contrary, it was a high. 'I've witnessed a few beheadings and that,' he said. 'I've seen hands being cut off. The best feeling ever is to kill a disbeliever. If he disbelieves in Islam, then one of the most beautiful feelings is to go into battle and point the barrel of your gun at him. I'm doing a deed which I love and which God loves.' He added: 'Going into battle, running headlong, killing the enemy, you actually get a buzz from it. It's a beautiful feeling, man . . .'

It's the midnight hour at the Festival of Ecstasy, and we come to the darkest aspect of ecstatic experience: the ecstasy of violence and war. 'War,' wrote the French knight Jean de Bueil in 1465, 'is a joyous thing.' It is 'one of humankind's great natural highs', notes sociologist Barbara Ehrenreich.[2] The German military author Ernst Junger wrote: 'Once again: the ecstasy . . . The enthusiasm of manliness bursts beyond itself to such an extent that the blood boils as it surges through the veins and glows as it foams through the heart . . . it is an intoxication beyond all intoxication, an unleashing that breaks all bonds. [In combat] the individual is like a raging storm, the tossing sea and the roaring thunder. He has melted into everything.'[3] One of the best accounts of the ecstasy of war is an article by Vietnam veteran William Broyles Junior, called 'Why Men Love War'. He writes:

> A lieutenant colonel I knew, a true intellectual, was put in charge of civil affairs, the work we did helping the Vietnamese grow rice and otherwise improve their lives. He was a sensitive man who kept a journal and seemed far better equipped for winning hearts and minds than for combat command. But he got one, and I remember flying out to visit his base the night after it had been attacked by an NVA sapper unit. Most of the combat troops had been out on an operation, so this colonel mustered a motley crew of clerks and cooks and drove the sappers off, chasing them across the rice paddies and killing dozens of these elite enemy troops by the light of flares. That morning, as they were surveying what they had done and loading the dead NVA . . . on mechanical mules like so much garbage, there was a look of beatific contentment on the colonel's face that I had not seen except in charismatic churches. It was the look of a person transported into ecstasy. And I – what did I do, confronted with this beastly scene? I smiled back, as filled with bliss as he was.[4]

War, as the philosopher John Gray has noted, is a form of play, in which one can put off one's usual identity and the normal constraints of morality, and be transported into an altered state, aided by costume, face paint, music, drugs and the intense sensory overload of battle.[5] War, says the journalist Chris Hedges, has 'a *Midsummer Night's Dream* quality to it'.[6] We speak of the 'theatre of war' and, like theatre, it lets people dress up and lose themselves. War is 'often embraced as a release', Gray writes. It offers people several forms of ecstatic experience, but I'm going to highlight four: combat flow, ecstatic togetherness, participation in sacred myth, and what I call 'blood-catharsis'.

Combat flow

In the late 1980s, the American literary journalist Bill Buford became fascinated by English football hooligans, and joined a firm of Manchester United-supporting hooligans, hanging out with them on and off for eight years, and observing various punch-ups and riots. Violence, he realised to his horror, gave him a 'peak experience': 'I had not expected the violence to be so pleasurable . . . the pure elemental pleasure was of an intensity that was unlike anything else I had experienced before.' Violence absorbs the mind and annihilates the ordinary self: 'The human mind is never at rest in the present; it is always roving, recalling, remembering, selecting, adding, forgetting . . . I am attracted to the moment when consciousness ceases: the moments of survival, of animal intensity, of violence . . . the present in its absoluteness.' He added: 'This is, if you like, the answer to the hundred-dollar question: why do young males riot every Saturday? They do it for the same reason that another generation drank too much, or smoked dope, or took hallucinogenic drugs, or behaved badly or rebelliously. Violence is . . . their mind-altering experience.'[7]

We're already familiar with Mihály Csíkszentmihályi's concept of 'flow': when a person is focused on a challenging yet enjoyable task, they can attain a state of trance-like absorption. Their consciousness – usually scattered, diffuse and anxiously self-monitoring – becomes utterly and blissfully fixated on the task at hand. In the last few years 'flow' has become something of a secular religion among Positive Psychologists, sportspeople and entrepreneurs, but what's less often discussed is that one of the surest avenues to flow is war. The threat of death triggers a heightening of consciousness that often feels euphoric.

Winston Churchill wrote: 'Nothing in life is so exhilarating as to be shot at without result.'[8] Yuval Noah Harari, historian at the Hebrew University of Jerusalem and author of *Sapiens*, has collected various accounts of 'combat flow', like the following from Shawn Nelson, an American soldier fighting in Mogadishu in 1993:

> It was like an epiphany. Close to death, he had never felt so completely alive . . . The only thing he could compare it to was the feeling he found sometimes when he surfed, when he was inside the tube of a big wave and everything around him was energy and motion and he was being carried along by some terrific force and all he could do was focus intently on holding his balance, riding it out. Surfers called it The Green Room. Combat was another door to that room . . . In those hours on the street he had not been Shawn Nelson, he had no connection to the larger world, no bills to pay, no emotional ties, nothing. He had just been a human being staying alive from one nano-second to the next.[9]

One of the things that draws young Muslims to Syria, perhaps, is the search for more flow through risking their lives on an adventure. Csíkszentmihályi tells me: 'At the moment, all the focus is on academic performance in high school, and if you're not successful in that one domain of cognitive skill, there's so little to do. That's why young people become easily seduced into drugs and violence.' It is a thrill to travel to Syria and feel you're at risk. Umm Umar, a 16-year-old British Muslim grooming others to join her in Daesh, wrote on Twitter: 'Your Iman [faith] will get sooo high during the border crossing. Big adrenaline rush . . . The sickest thing I've ever done in my life is cross that Turkish border . . . I'll never forget that night.' Battle brings a blissful release from the iron cage of rational bureaucracy. Abu Sumayyah Al-Britani, a young British jihadi who joined Daesh, complained that back in the UK 'you need road tax, you need this, you need that and blah, blah, blah . . . For me to be here it's freedom. It's really, really fun. It's better than that game Call of Duty.'[10]

Ecstatic togetherness in war

Violence and war give us a strong sense of connection to our fellow combatants. We feel intense love for our 'band of brothers'. Jean de Bueil wrote in 1465:

> We love each other so much in war . . . A sweet joy rises in our hearts, in the feeling of our honest loyalty to each other, and seeing our friend so bravely exposing his body to danger in order to keep and fulfil the commandment of our Creator, we resolve to go forward and die or live with him.[11]

James Jeffrey, a British lieutenant who served in the Iraq War, wrote:

> It all made for an intoxicating experience and was possibly, sad to say, the best thing I, and I imagine others, had ever done. Ever since it has been like something has gone out of my life for ever. For it wasn't just the unparalleled sensory spectrum, there was a communal satisfaction, tapping into a primordial core, which came from taking part. That blissful sense of community started with the soldiers, wonderfully skilled and maddeningly headstrong, insubordinate at times but ultimately doggedly looking out for each other.[12]

There is a sense of the transcendence of one's little ego in the big family of the army or the state, a 'casting aside of our little selves to live under the august grace and the enhancing of the genuine life of the people of a State', as the Japanese Ministry of Education put it in 1937. The German nationalist Heinrich von Treitschke wrote: 'The grandeur of war lies in the utter annihilation of puny man in the great conception of the State, and it brings out the full magnificence of the sacrifice of fellow country-men for one another.'[13] In war, we feel less lonely. Chris Hedges wrote: 'The communal march against an enemy creates a warm, unfamiliar bond with our neighbours . . . wiping out unsettling undercurrents of alienation and dislocation.' Indeed, as war correspondent Sebastian Junger pointed out in his book *Tribe*, the suicide rate and violent crime rate in New York went down after the 11 September attack: people felt less alone and hostile to one another when they had a common mission and a common enemy.[14]

This is another of the pull-factors that attracts young Western Muslims to join Daesh: the search for social connection and the yearning to belong. To be a Muslim in the West is, according to the Daesh propaganda magazine, a state of 'strangeness': the Muslim 'is a stranger amongst Christians and liberals, a stranger amongst fornicators and sodomites, a stranger amongst drunkards and druggies'.[15] Western Muslims may feel feared and hated by the rest of Western society, while their fellow Muslims are oppressed abroad. Online groomers for Daesh use the techniques of cult indoctrination to love-bomb potential recruits and make them feel special and chosen. Their true family is waiting for them in Syria, they are told. Daesh videos show new arrivals ripping up their passports, symbols of their old compromised identities. Daesh's in-house magazine, *Dabiq*, is full of photos of young mujahideen arm in arm – jihad is one long bromance. New arrivals feel themselves born again as brothers and sisters of the Ummah, the mystic tribe of Islam. It's a rejection of the atomisation and loneliness of modern society and a return to what Karl Popper called the 'magic tribe',[16] where we're all one big, happy family united in God. A poem by Ahlam al-Nasr, a young Syrian woman who has become the official poet of Daesh, celebrates this sense of supranational ecstasy:

> My brother in India, you are my brother,
> as are you, my brothers in the Balkans,
> In Ahwaz and Aqsa,
> in Arabia and Chechnya . . .
> My heart stretches out to them . . .
> We are all one body,
> this is our happy creed . . .[17]

War as a sacred myth

War, as the journalist Chris Hedges put it, 'is a force that gives us meaning'. Scott Atran, an anthropologist who has studied the lure of radical Islam, wrote: 'ISIS's caliphate project . . . speaks directly to those who feel their lives are worthless, spiritually corrupted, empty, boring, or devoid of purpose and significance, and who see no value in their own societies. It promises, in short, salvation and ultimate meaning through total commitment to a sacred cause.'[18] When a group or nation goes to war, we can find that normal critical thinking is suspended and individuals and whole societies move into what the war-psychologist Lawrence LeShan calls 'mythic reality'.[19] Frederic Myers describes the subliminal mind as 'mythopoetic' – it is fond of bombastic narratives of quests, adventures and ultimate battles. War takes us into this mytho-poetic trance. We move into black-and-white thinking, in which the world is neatly divided into Us and Them. We are the embodiment of absolute goodness; They are the embodiment of evil. This rejection of ambiguity and simplistic division of the world into heroes and villains – what Daesh calls 'the elimination of the Grey Zone' – is deeply satisfying to our story-loving subconscious.

Daesh becomes a dream-world in radicalised Muslims' minds – a utopia, Heaven on earth. Dr Katherine Brown, an expert in Islamic radicalism at King's College London, compares the allure of Daesh to the attraction of the Soviet Union for young Westerners in the 1930s: it promises a 'perfect world' where they can be 'perfect people'.[20] This dream of perfection becomes a sort of trance-like obsession in would-be jihadis' minds, much as Jerusalem appeared as a city in the sky to the first Crusaders. One ex-jihadi told Atran that when he thought of Daesh 'immediately, my mind would conjure images of two armies fighting each other on an open plane. Warriors wielding their swords and riding along on beautiful horses.' Online groomers promise more material temptations too – for the girls, the chance to marry a dashing warrior, for the boys, the chance to have multiple wives and sex slaves. Everyone will get their own mansion. Everyone will get their own jeep. It's portrayed as an 'Islamic Disneyland', as one ex-jihadi puts it contemptuously. 'Don't let yourself get hypnotised by their sweet talk,' she warned.[21]

The flipside of this ecstatic utopia is a demonisation of the Other. The West, Israel, the Kurds, the Yazidis, gays and any opposing Islamist groups become demonic deviants. Mythical thinking readily turns into apocalyptic thinking: this is a final showdown between Good and Evil. Daesh followers believe they are in the End Times, as predicted in Muslim texts written centuries ago. According to prophecy, the Mahdi (a sort of Muslim Messiah) will appear, the one-eyed redhead Antichrist will rise up, there will be a terrible battle with the forces of Rome, Jesus will descend on a white horse, Constantinople will fall, and finally 'the shade of this blessed flag will expand until it covers all eastern and western extents of the Earth'. It's bonkers, of course, but similar apocalyptic predictions inspired countless bloody millenarian uprisings during the Middle Ages and the Reformation.[22] Apocalyptic thinking is still quite entrenched in the modern psyche – according to the Pew Research Centre, half of all Muslims outside the West believe in the imminent coming of the Mahdi,[23] and 41 per cent of American Christians also believe in the imminent Rapture.[24] The sense that everything is happening according to prophecy gives people a terrible ecstatic certainty in a world of risk and complexity. There is a divine plan! It is written! Even if we don't literally believe in such stories, our mythopoetic subconscious loves them – that's why apocalyptic myths like *The Lord of the Rings* or *The Matrix* are still so popular today. The idea we can play a leading role in a cosmic struggle is much more exciting than the modern materialist idea that there is no divine plan and nothing you do makes any cosmic difference (so go back to stacking shelves).

Blood-catharsis

Finally, and most darkly, humans seek catharsis through blood-sacrifice. We've looked at many forms of catharsis in this book. As I've discussed, humans living in complex societies carry a shadow, made up of feelings of shame, anxiety, resentment, aggression and guilt, which their society forces them to repress. One of the oldest methods humans have used to purge these negative pent-up feelings is to project them onto an animal or human, make them a scapegoat, then kill them. This blood-sacrifice supposedly purges and cleanses the community of its moral pollution and pleases the gods, who are hungry for blood. Sacrificial killing, according to the classicist Walter Burkert, 'is the basic experience of the sacred'. Sacrifice literally means 'to make sacred'.[25]

Pleasing the gods and purging your sins through blood-sacrifice is an ancient and widespread practice. It was only transcended relatively recently in Christianity – where Jesus becomes the *über*-scapegoat, whose blood-sacrifice renders any further blood-sacrifices unnecessary.[26] 'It is finished,' in the words of the Gospel of John. Instead of pulling out a victim's still-beating heart and eating it each Sunday, Anglicans can partake of the Body of Christ by sipping some wine and nibbling some bread – a substitute of a substitute. Buddhism and Greek philosophy take the transcendence a step further: instead of blood-sacrifice, we can transcend suffering and find bliss through self-sacrifice and inner struggle.

However, this transcendence of blood-sacrifice is a mere 2,500 years old. Humans have been carrying out blood-sacrifices a lot longer than that. And, in many ways, we prefer the old method of blood-catharsis to the new-fangled innovations introduced by Plato, the Buddha and Jesus. So, in times of crisis we go back to the tried and tested. Christians have repeatedly reverted to mass blood-sacrifice, as in the witch trials or the Crusades. The knights and peasants of the Crusades were assured that the more they 'killed for Christ', the more sins would be expiated. When they finally arrived in Jerusalem, they killed every Muslim man, woman and child in the city. 'In and around the Temple of Solomon, the horses waded in blood up to their knees, nay up to the bridle. It was a just and wonderful judgement of God.'[27] Later Crusaders, even if they didn't reach Constantinople, contented themselves with murdering as many Jews as they could find on the way.

Islam has not traditionally had the same emphasis as Christianity on atoning for sins through shedding blood (your own or someone else's). Muhammad did apparently suggest that those who give their lives fighting for Islam go straight to Paradise, but there is not the suggestion that the more blood you spill, the greater your reward, and killing non-combatants was forbidden. But Islamic culture has become much bloodier in the last three decades. The cult of the suicide-bomber was launched by the Ayatollah Khomeini in the Iran-Iraq War as a tactic to resist Iraq's superior firepower. He promised suicide-warriors 72 virgins in Paradise and connected their sacrifice to the Shiite cult of martyrs. Suicide-bombing was adopted as a religious practice and resistance strategy by Hezbollah and by Sunni groups like Hamas and Al-Qaeda, then went viral in Iraq, with two suicide-bomb attacks every three days in 2008. In the last few years, Daesh has taken the glorification of blood-letting a stage further, with its gruesome YouTube videos of executions, tapping into a deep human desire to see one's enemies humiliated and mutilated.

Today, Islamism seems obsessed with blood-catharsis. 'There is no liquid loved by Allah more than the liquid of blood,' declared the radical preacher Abu Hamza.[28] A Palestinian jihadi, Rabie Shehada, said in a YouTube video: 'I swear we are a people who love drinking blood.' Daesh has repeatedly insisted that killing non-Muslims, including non-combatants, is 'a form of worship to Allah'. Graham Wood noted in *The Atlantic*: 'The Islamic State is committed to purifying the world by killing vast numbers of people.'[29] It delights in rituals of mass execution – prisoners' throats are slit like those of sacrificial animals. Blood-sacrifice purges the body of Islam of deviants, and brings the Ummah together in awe and euphoria, what Scott Atran calls 'the Terrorist Sublime'. It also guarantees those who commit the murders a place in the highest realm of Paradise. Islamist mass murder arises from toxic religious dogma, certainly, but it can also arise from a tragically twisted psychology – American Muslim Omar Mateen apparently struggled with the shadow of homosexual desires,[30] so he tried to purge himself of guilt by killing 49 people in the Orlando gay club he frequented. This is what Jung called projection – we can't confront our shadow, so we project it onto others and attack them.[31]

The secular state as an antidote to ecstasy

So what should we do about ecstatic violence? You could try to banish collective ecstasy altogether. That's what many Enlightenment thinkers tried to do: all collective ecstasy is 'enthusiasm' and religious enthusiasm rapidly leads to violence, as the seventeenth-century Wars of Religion supposedly showed. The modern secular state was put forward by Enlightenment thinkers, like Thomas Hobbes, as the antidote to the violence of the Wars of Religion.[32] How does the antidote work? First, the state establishes a monopoly on violence, so we can't go around killing each other for faith, revenge or honour. Only the state can do that. Second, the secular state privatises religion, pushing it out of the public sphere. Prior to the Enlightenment, power was shared between the Church and the Crown. But this, argued Hobbes, creates a fatal ambiguity – do people owe their allegiance to God or Caesar? The solution was to get rid of God or, at least, to reduce religion to a handful of simple ethical propositions on which everyone could agree. All claims to personal revelation were 'idols of the brain', Hobbes insisted. Humans don't have one foot in this world and another in the spirit-world. *This* is the only world there is, and in this world, the state is an all-powerful Leviathan.

Enlightenment thinkers also tried to make politics more rational and humane, phasing out witch-trials, attacking cruel practices, like slavery or public executions, and developing the idea of human rights. They encouraged public education because science 'is the great antidote to the poison of enthusiasm and superstition', in Adam Smith's words. And, particularly in the Scottish Enlightenment, they attacked the utopian idea of the perfect state. Instead of trying to make a New Jerusalem on Earth, thinkers like Smith and David Hume settled for creating a functioning state of material well-being where humans can try to find a bit of happiness. Private vices, like casual sex, luxury spending, alcohol, prostitution and popular entertainment, should be tolerated, because they are good for economic growth, and economic growth means more jobs, which means the masses are less likely to fling themselves into ecstatic death-cults. The End Times are not coming, so instead of waiting for the Rapture, we should try to improve our lives here on Earth. This was a new and radical idea at the time.

Hand in hand with the evolution of the secular state went a psychological change, which the sociologist Norbert Elias called 'the civilising process'.[33] Civilised states required their citizens to become better at self-control and emotional repression. We must become polite, self-conscious and even-tempered to flourish in stable, commercial, civilised societies. God is replaced by Public Opinion – we behave ourselves not out of fear of divine punishment but because we desire the approval of others and fear their rejection. To seek others' approval, we must control our temper and not attack any of the millions of strangers we find ourselves living among. If you lose your temper and punch someone in a medieval society, it's not that big a deal. If you attack someone in the modern civilised state, people will think you're weird, you might lose your job, you might get sent to prison or the psychiatrist's clinic. A video of you losing it might even appear on YouTube. So we don't lose it, however much we want to. The desire to kill is still quite wide-spread: a survey in 2000 found that 60 per cent of male undergraduates admitted to recent fantasies of killing someone, and 32 per cent of female undergraduates.[34] But most of us don't act on those impulses.

Nationalist ecstasy

The modern state is an incredibly successful invention. As Steven Pinker chronicled in his recent book, *The Better Angels of our Nature*, there has been an astonishing decline in violence throughout human history.[35] The first leap forward was the shift from hunter-gatherer societies to agriculture-based city-states in the Bronze Age, which led to a five-fold decrease in the rate of violent deaths. Then the emergence of the modern disciplinarian state led to a ten- to 50-fold decrease in the rate of violent homicides between 1500 and the present day. However, it's something of a self-serving Enlightenment myth that the Wars of Religion were caused by faith. Many historians argue they were more driven by the emergence of competing nation-states than religions.[36] Neither did the secular nation-state banish ecstatic violence. It's more accurate to say that the state asserted a monopoly on violent ecstasy, which it channelled into a new civil religion – the ecstatic worship of the nation-state and its leader. And these new gods were just as blood-thirsty and apocalyptic as the old.

Take the French Revolution, a key moment in the emergence of the secular state. This was not the creation of some calm, rational *philosophes*. It was the creation of mass ecstasy and mass terror.

The historian Alexis de Tocqueville noted:

> No previous political upheaval, however violent, had aroused such passionate enthusiasm, for the ideal the French Revolution set before it was not merely a change in the French social system but nothing short of a regeneration of the whole human race. It created an atmosphere of missionary fervour, and indeed, assumed all the aspects of a religious revival . . . it developed into a species of religion, albeit a singularly imperfect one, since it was without a God, without a ritual or promise of a future life. Nevertheless, this strange religion has, like Islam, overrun the whole world with its apostles, militants and martyrs.[37]

In an attempt to sustain the popular mood of ecstatic unity and national rebirth, the Jacobins tried to forge a new 'civil religion'. It appointed the painter David to organise endless festivals – the Festival of Federation, the Festival of Unity, the Festival of Reason, festivals for martyrs and heroes. Like the Catholic Church, the state used all the artistic effects at its disposal to create an 'empire of images': it commissioned paintings, sculptures, operas, national monuments. The festivals promised citizens that they could achieve immortality through their membership of the nation. David wrote about his painting of the martyr Le Peletier: 'Just look at the crown; it's the crown of immortality. The nation can confer it on any of its children.'[38] It also popularised the military parade: thousands of soldiers paraded in drilled unison on Bastille Day, giving the soldiers an intoxicating sense of ego-loss as they marched in time, and the spectators a dizzying sense of national power.[39]

But the best way the Jacobins discovered to make the state sacred and awesome in the eyes of the population was through human sacrifice. The sacrifice of martyrs was celebrated, but even more exciting was the bloody and public sacrifice of enemies of the state. The emphasis on human sacrifice was right at the heart of the new 'rational revolution'.

Robespierre suggested that violence would 'purify the earth that has been soiled and recall to the earth Justice'. Another leading Jacobin, Fabre d'Églantine, cried: 'In the towns let the blood of traitors be the first holocaust to liberty.'[40] Public executions were necessary, according to the Jacobin Georges Danton, 'to appease the people of Paris'. They were 'an indispensable sacrifice'. The emphasis on human sacrifice as catharsis and purgation is there in 'La Marseillaise', the French national anthem, which declares: 'Let impure blood water our furrows'.

Worship of the Glorious Leader

The idol that some modern states have raised up in place of God is the divine leader, monarch, emperor or Führer. Napoleon was inspired by the classical cult of divine dictators, like Alexander and Caesar, and consciously developed a cult of himself as national genius, which continues to this day. Other national leaders inspired just as much ecstatic devotion. This is the moment that Count Rostov catches sight of the Russian emperor in a military parade in Tolstoy's *War and Peace*: 'he experienced a feeling of tenderness and ecstasy such as he had never known before . . . "Oh to die, to die for him," thought Rostov.'[41] This cultic worship of 'great men' (or women) becomes, in the nineteenth century, a substitute for Christianity,[42] and flowers in the twentieth century with the totalitarian personality cults of Hitler, Mussolini, Stalin, Mao and Hirohito.

The Nazi Party was particularly adept at creating a cult around the Führer. Hitler was a gifted demagogue but, as Ian Kershaw has explored, the 'Hitler myth' was more the creation of astute propaganda than the product of some magical charisma on Hitler's part. In 1927, before Hitler had become the Führer, Rudolf Hess was musing that the party needed 'a great popular leader . . . similar to the great founder of a religion'.[43] Joseph Goebbels agreed that the Führer would be the 'fulfilment of a mysterious longing'. By the early 1930s, the socialist journal *Das Freie Wort* noted the appearance of domestic shrines to Hitler. By the mid-1930s, Führer-worship had spread across Germany. 'The whole of Munich was on its feet,' noted the left-wing Sopade group after one

Führer-rally. 'People can be forced to sing, but they can't be forced to sing with such enthusiasm.' Following another mass rally in Cologne in 1936, Goebbels noted with satisfaction: 'One had the feeling that Germany had been transformed into a single great church.' The Führer had become, in the popular imagination, a messenger from God, a 'Führer without sin'. Hitler knew how to stimulate popular ecstasy through appeals to national greatness and a beery *Volkisch* mysticism: 'I feel you and you feel me!' He understood the desire to feel our small selves dissolved within an enormous crowd. And he also understood the power of demonisation and the dark catharsis of violence. The Reich would be made sacred and eternal through the purgation and extermination of millions of internal and external enemies.

One sees a similar ecstatic devotion to the emperor Hirohito in Japan. Many Japanese in the 1930s also thought of war as a 'purifying exorcism, a cleansing ablution', in the words of one wartime Japanese writer. One encounters the same yearning to sacrifice oneself and one's enemies in Britain upon the outbreak of the First World War: 'kill Germans – kill . . . the good as well as the bad, the young men as well as the old . . . I look upon [the war] as a war for purity, I look upon everyone who dies in it as a martyr.' So preached the Bishop of London in 1914.[44] The cult of the strong-man seems to be making a resurgence today, with the online adulation of 'god-emperor' Donald Trump. Much of the worship seems designed to shock liberals, but it's worrying to see videos of American neo-Nazis saluting to cries of 'Hail Trump!'[45]

Alternative channels for ecstatic nationalism

Ecstatic violence, then, is still with us in the modern, secular, rational state. It's just taken new forms, created new gods. However, a secular democratic state is still the best defence we have against ecstatic nationalist violence, particularly through the existence of a free press, a free parliament and an independent judiciary. There will always be psychopaths, like Hitler, but they are able to do less damage if a free press can report on their crimes, failures and the ugly reality of war. War psychosis

– the descent into simplistic myths and the yearning for redemptive blood-sacrifice – easily spreads through a population, but it tends not to last long once you start losing. The Führer myth didn't last beyond Stalingrad, and the mystique of Daesh is rapidly fading as it loses territory. The myth of Putin, by contrast, has endured for almost two decades, thanks to a state-controlled media.

But it's not enough to condemn the ecstasy of extremism. We need alternative outlets for ecstatic experience, including nationalist enthusiasm. Otherwise life feels boring, depressing, atomised and meaningless. As Norbert Elias noted, the 'civilising process' has psychological side-effects. 'Life,' he wrote, 'becomes less dangerous, but also less emotional or pleasurable . . . the battlefield is, in a sense, moved within.'[46] This 'war within' can lead to a permanent 'inner unrest', compulsions, addictions, depressions, anxieties and a constant sense of the artificiality and immorality of the civilisation in which we live. We long for excitement, connection, meaning, ecstasy. 'The fulfilment of a human need . . . for enjoyable excitement . . . is one of the basic functions which human societies have to satisfy,' Elias wrote, near the end of his life. The 'neglect of paying attention to this need is one of the main gaps in present approaches to mental health'.[47] Education in science and critical thinking is important. But what young people really crave is adventure, excitement, flow. 'The main goal of a truly civilised education,' writes the psychologist Mihály Csíkszentmihályi, 'is to teach children to experience flow in settings that are not harmful to self and others.'[48]

Elias suggested we need 'mimetic substitutes' for war, which give us a similar excitement without the fatalities. Religion is one substitute we've looked at – Jesus as substitute-scapegoat. However, as we've also seen, religion often reverts back into its old tendency to blood-sacrifice. The arts are another mimetic substitute: Elias thought that, as civilised societies exerted more control over people's violent tendencies, people learned to play out their repressed desires in the dream-world of books, theatre, film, computer games and virtual reality. Again, however, the arts are not a fail-safe antidote to the violence in human nature. There's been a long and unresolved debate over the last 50 years about whether violent movies make viewers more or less aggressive, whether they're a cathartic release or an instigator of more violence. Rock and roll has also been an important alternative arena for collective ecstasy over the last 60 years: better to worship Queen or Prince than the Führer. The ecstatic community of rock and roll is international, inclusive and, on the whole, non-aggressive, in stark contrast to Fascism or jihadism. There is a theory (unproven) that one of the reasons English football hooliganism declined in the late 1980s was that many 'casuals' ended up taking E and dancing to acid house.

Sport as an outlet for ecstasy

The mimetic substitute that Elias thought most important to modern societies was sport. It's become an important arena for ecstatic experience in the last 50 years, including nationalist ecstasy. Indeed, if you search for 'ecstatic' in Google News, the main place you find it is in the sports pages. Like war, sport ticks various ecstatic boxes – the need for catharsis, flow, togetherness and sacred myths. But it meets these needs with far fewer fatalities. It is one of our best 'controlled spaces to lose control'.

Of course, if we look back to the history of sport in the medieval period, it wasn't exactly a *substitute* for bloody violence and war. Rather it was a *supplement*. Until very recently, sports like football were little more than 'beastly furie and extreme violence', as one observer of a football riot put it in 1531.[49] The state tried repeatedly to ban the 'bloody and murderous practise' of football between the fourteenth and the nineteenth centuries. It was only in the mid-nineteenth century that English public schools evolved rules for boxing, football and rugby. At that point, such sports became more than simply excuses for a riot. They demanded a balance between the urge to release one's emotions and destroy the opposition, and the need to exert self-control, skill, discipline and virtue in pursuit of victory. Again, however, public-school sports weren't a substitute for war, they were a supplement. They trained young men to serve the empire. In fact, the playing fields at Eton are even named after parts of the Middle East – one field is called

Mesopotamia, while a small muddy stream is grandiloquently named the Jordan.

Sweat-catharsis

Modern sport generally doesn't offer the catharsis of blood-sacrifice, which war does, with the exception of hunting, shooting and bull-fighting. What it offers instead is 'sweat-catharsis'. It offers humans a place for intense physical exertion in which we can 'work out' the stress, tension and discontent of civilisation, in a manner similar to the catharsis of dance. We exorcise through exercise; it's become our preferred means of altering our emotions, transforming our consciousness and purging ourselves of nervousness, angst and self-loathing. We gain spiritual merit along with a hot body (these two become merged in the modern mind). People go to the gym for their daily or weekly spiritual practice; they've turned in their millions to yoga, of course, but also to jogging, cycling, weight-lifting, and to new sweaty blends of sport and spirituality, like Zumba, Tough Mudder and SoulCycle. The personal trainer has become the new priest. 'I want the next breath to be an exorcism,' urges the Master Trainer to the whooping congregation at SoulCycle. 'I want you to go into a trance! Disappear!'

Some new forms of spirituality have grown up around sport, like the Sri Chimnoy movement, in which runners seek self-transcendence by running 3,100 miles round a block in New York over 52 days.

How does this sweat-catharsis work? Probably through multiple mechanisms. First, strenuous exercise overwhelms the sympathetic nervous system and activates the parasympathetic nervous system, releasing endorphins and endocannabinoids, and giving us a sense of calm and mastery over the flesh. When we exercise intensely with others, we share this endorphin rush and feel bonded to our fellow athletes.[50] As in dancing, our breath and heartbeat may also become synchronised with those of other participants (particularly in rowing). The more exhausted we are, the less mental energy we have for neurotic worrying. We may achieve what neuroscientists call 'transient hypo-frontality', in which less blood goes to the pre-frontal cortex of our brain and we shift into a blessed quiet.[51]

Achieving flow in sports

Sport, like war, can give us access to flow states. The tennis coach Timothy Gallwey was one of the first psychologists to recognise that. His 1974 classic *The Inner Game of Tennis* applied Zen and Daoist wisdom to sport. Gallwey writes: 'the greatest efforts in sport . . . come when the mind is as still as a glass lake'. The author Geoff Dyer, who has spent a lifetime chasing 'peak experiences', tells me: 'If you asked me where I'm most in the zone, obviously it would be playing tennis. That absorption in the moment, I just love it.' For me, too, tennis is more than just a game: it's a form of contemplation or therapy, a way to turn off the analytical mind and become reconnected to body-consciousness. I love how my body can choose exactly the right shot, then execute it in an instant, in a way that my rational-analytical mind could never do.

Some intrepid humans have discovered that, if you're really chasing flow states, the best way is through situations where your life is in jeopardy. Extreme sports like surfing, snowboarding and bungee-jumping have become hugely popular since the 1960s, offering people the chance to induce a near-death experience amid the sublime and terrifying grandeur of nature. The mountaineer and BASE-jumper Dean Potter, who died in an accident in 2014, reported: 'When I'm really in tune with it, deep in the zone, I get to a place where I disappear completely, where I merge with the rock, when time slows down, my senses are unbelievably heightened, and I feel that oneness, that full-body psychic connection to the universe'.[52]

Getting into the zone gives athletes a sense of catharsis. Big-wave surfer Jeff Kalama says (in the documentary film *Riding Giants*): 'There's something about riding a 60-to-80-foot wave that commands so much focus and attention that it's the only thing that matters for a few seconds. It's very purifying because as far as you're concerned nothing else exists.'[53] Extreme sports are also a search for rites of initiation and male bonding in a time of peace. An example of this is the Dangerous Sports Club, created by some ex-public-school boys at Oxford in the 1970s. The club invented bungee-jumping, and also pioneered BASE jumping, riding down ski-slopes in home-made vehicles, and being thrown out of medieval catapults, all the while wearing top hats and tails and quaffing champagne. It was as if, in the absence of empires to defend in war, these young men had to resort to hurling themselves off bridges. The less intrepid of us, meanwhile, can reach vicarious experiences of flow by marvelling at elite athletes' superhuman abilities. David Foster Wallace suggested watching Roger Federer at play was a spiritual experience, because his gifts – the ability to slow down time, to choose exactly the right shot, to exhibit so much grace under pressure – seem beyond-human.[54] We worship the elite athlete as an epic hero in the classical sense – a supremely gifted person in which the human mingles with the divine. We say Lionel Messi is 'from another planet'.

Ecstatic togetherness and sacred myth

Sport, like war, also offers people an ecstatic sense of unity and love with others. Like war, it's a socially sanctioned way for men to express their love for each other. For the last three years, I've been running philosophy workshops at Saracens Rugby Club – the team are the English and European champions. I've been struck by the bond between the players. As coach Joe Shaw puts it, 'The extra 5 per cent is that we love each other.' That love, it seems to me, comes partly from the fact that rugby is one of the very few places – outside war – where men can recreate the primitive experience of hunting in a pack, putting their body on the line for each other in pursuit of a shared goal. Occasionally, as in a hunting pack, teams can move into a sort of tele-pathic 'super-consciousness'. My favourite example of this is the Barbarians' famous try against New Zealand in 1973, when seven players linked up to run a try from their own 22. Carwyn Jones, the Lions coach, subsequently said: 'The try was a demonstration of a game at that almost super-conscious level.'[55]

Even if we don't play sport, we can experience a vicarious sense of togetherness through spectating. We may feel small, insignificant and mortal, but on Saturdays, at the stadium, we feel a blissful sense of dissolving into the tribe of the club or the national team, united in love of our club and hatred of the opposition. We can chant together, sing together, feel that we will 'never walk alone'. We can assert our tribal identity with face-paint, colours, flags, tattoos. Our lives may be brief, but we are part of a club with a long and glorious history – pundits in this sense are like the bards of oral tradition, reminding us of epic battles of old. And when we die, something of us will live on in the club, which must be why so many fans want their ashes scattered on the hallowed turf of their club pitch.

Personally, I don't buy into the cult of the sporting fan. Worshipping the nation-state is bad enough; worshipping Watford FC seems ridiculous. But sports certainly are incredibly absorbing. They're machines for generating stories – stories of redemption, the triumph of the underdog, the incredible comeback, the search for perfection. Geoff Dyer wrote that, if an alien anthropologist saw the remains of human civilisation, they would assume a football pitch marked some sort of sacred place – the lines, the markings, the posts at either end. And they do.[56] Like the games of war, religion and theatre, sport offers a set-apart space for dream-play. The lines we draw and the rules and rituals we create are somewhat arbitrary; it's the absorption and improvisation that we bring to the play.

When sporting ecstasy becomes toxic

However, as with every other variety of ecstasy, there are risks to the ecstasies to be found in sports. They can easily become co-opted by the free market. Corporate interests are eager to make sports as lurid and commercial a spectacle as possible, and to encourage the worship of elite athletes as gods. That can be unhealthy for both the players and the fans. Sport can be a means of escape into a mythical fantasy of heroic, invincible athletes, the 'rise of the superman', as one recent book on flow in sports puts it. This idolatry leads to completely overblown rhetoric among commentators – Simon Barnes, writing in *The Times* about Andy Murray's Wimbledon victory in 2013, enthused that it was as if 'some mythical, mystical quest had been achieved . . . it really seemed as if this really was the Holy Grail'.[57] We live out our schoolboy fantasies through elite athletes, and when they win we ask them eagerly, 'How does it feel?' to enjoy a vicarious ecstasy. We are sure they must be feeling 'a bliss beyond all earthly concepts of joy', in Simon Barnes' words. But the truth is more complicated. In fact, athletes often report feeling depressed or dissociated once they've achieved their career goals. They are greyhounds who've caught the mechanical rabbit. What will they chase next?

Laird Hamilton, the big wave surfer, has said: 'I question [who I am] all year long, except when it's 30 feet and I'm out surfing.' When he's not surfing, his wife says, he is depressed, 'like a dragon-slayer when there are no dragons to slay'.[58] This is the risk of a culture obsessed with winning, with highs, with 'pushing the envelope' and finding the 'ultimate experience'. It becomes a bipolar culture, chasing the ecstatic highs but then plunging into deep depression for long periods in between. The emotional cost of the cult of sports is that players become burned out. Three-fifths of Premiership football players go bankrupt after retiring, according to a charity for ex-players.[59] Many slump into depression or addiction. Old age is not kind to sporting heroes – like rock stars, they are disposable idols for our dream-projections.

A more ecstatic liberalism

2016 was not a good year for sports. The Euro2016 football champion-ship was marred by fighting between Russian and English fans – the Russian hooligans were apparently trained in military-style camps. And the Olympics were rocked by revelations of widespread doping, both by the Russian state and (according to details hacked by Russian intel-ligence) many other nations as well. It's a reminder that sometimes the mimetic violence of sport spills over into actual violence, and that sport can be co-opted by nationalist regimes looking to enhance their own prestige.[60]

And yet sporting festivals play an important role in maintaining social cohesion: they are one of the few places where a multicultural nation can experience collective ecstasy. Modern Britain is sometimes confused about its national identity and what exactly its citizens have in common.

But, in 2012, there was a genuine sense of national togetherness at the Olympics, in the opening ceremony's celebration of our rock and roll heritage, in the stadium triumphs of Jessica Ennis, who is of mixed race, and Mo Farah, who was born in Somalia. Indeed, the Olympics and the World Cup are unique opportunities for the whole world to join together in collective excitement.

Sports are an outlet for things people used to get from war: catharsis, flow, tribal belonging, sacred myth. However, on its own sport is not a sufficient outlet for collective ecstasy and transcendence. We also need more of a sense of transcendence in our politics. At the moment, political elites seem to have no long-term vision for the future, other than more bureaucratic managerialism.

Western liberalism seems on shaky ground. It was rocked in 2016 by a series of electoral upsets, first Brexit, then the election of Donald Trump. The ideology of open borders, free trade and liberal multiculturalism is being resisted by simpler and more emotional narratives – Take Back Control, Make America Great Again – and the simple dichotomy of Us versus Them (Muslim terrorists, black rioters, Mexican rapists, Polish plumbers).

We're seeing the return of far-right extremism and neo-Nazism. In the US, a movement called the Alt-Right (a name invented by neo-Nazi Richard Spencer) has won a lot of attention and online support. It's a loose confederation of people, mainly angry white men, who support white nationalism and patriarchy. One of the key books in the Alt-Right is *The Way of Men* by Jack Donovan. He suggests that men, like chimpanzees, get their identity by belonging to small gangs, who defend the perimeter against Them (Muslims, Jews, zombies, whoever). They are merely an excuse for the tribal belonging of Us. Peace and prosperity are boring and emasculating, because they don't feed men's need for tribal violence, besides the mimetic substitutes of team sports or violent computer games. Donovan longs for the collapse of civilisation and rise of ethnic gang violence, because then men can be men again. The apocalypse will be an extended exercise in male bonding.[61] This is the white extremist version of the jihadi bromance, and proof, if any need it, that violent fanaticism can grow in secular nationalism as well as religion.

After 50 years of peace and prosperity, liberal multiculturalism has apparently failed to give people a sense of belonging and the common good. It's failed to provide a sense of safety and security in a rapidly changing world. But, above all, it's descended into stale technocratic managerialism, and failed to give people a transcendent vision of the future.

One reason for our lack of vision, I suggest, is that in the decades ahead we see the prospect of climate change. And that frightens us, so we look to the past. But perhaps ecstasy has a role to play in healing our connection to the planet and altering our relationship to nature. Let's find out, as we head into the Forest of Wonder.

9: The Forest of Wonder

In 2012, in the mountains of California, Mac Macartney went underground. As part of a Native American initiation ritual, he immersed himself in the pitch-black darkness of a *kiva*, a small subterranean enclosure where indigenous people practised sensory deprivation as a means to ecstasy. Mac was in there for ten days, with barely any food or water, with two other initiates: 'We sat in silence apart from the very occasional brief exchanges such as "Are you okay?"' On the last day, they emerged for the sacrificial killing and eating of a goose. Mac was a vegetarian, but he'd decided he'd also eat the goose. Then he went back into the darkness.

After a few hours, Mac felt the hairs stand up on the back of his neck and knew he was going to witness something. He began to see the body of the goose in the darkness. It became 'as clear as a photo'. Then he saw a grey form detach itself from the body and fly away. Neuroscientists would suggest this was a hallucination – sensory deprivation is one of humans' oldest and most reliable avenues to altered states. But Mac says:

> In my understanding, I had witnessed the spirit of the goose leaving the body. Someone could say, no, that was just your brain creating a fanciful story that allowed you to feel OK about the action you'd taken. That's possible. All I know is that I felt illuminated, it gave

me profound insights, and I felt very touched. I don't want someone else telling me what it was or wasn't. I think we're equipped with powers of discernment, and I don't want to give mine away. Since then, I've had countless experiences like that, and I observe I become more peaceful, compassionate and empathic.

Mac is the founder of a spiritual community in Devon called Embercombe, and a teacher in indigenous wisdom at a place called Schumacher College, also in Devon. The college was founded in the 1990s by a former Jain monk called Satish Kumar. It was in part inspired by the back-to-earth movement of the 1960s and 1970s, in which thousands of hippies dropped out of college and went to live in sustainable-farming communes in the countryside. Schumacher College took the spirit of those communes and used it to improvise a new model of higher education. The college offers residential courses in environmental science, sustainable business and activism, permaculture, indigenous wisdom, and a philosophy called 'deep ecology'.

The essence of deep ecology, Mac says, is the belief that 'as long as environmentalism is approached as a purely rational, technocratic endeavour, it will only tinker at the edges. We need to go deeper. We need a re-understanding of our world as sacred.' Deep ecologists believe that at the root of our environmental crisis lies a broken relationship with the natural world. 'We're fundamentally and dangerously disconnected from nature,' says Mac. People disagree about when the relationship with nature was broken – some blame Christianity, while others point to the seventeenth-century shift from an animist to a materialist worldview. The writer Charles Eisenstein said at a recent talk at Schumacher: 'If we hold ourselves as the only sentient, loving beings on this planet, then the attitude of instrumental utilitarianism is natural. It's absurd to love the earth if you think it's just a bunch of chemicals bouncing around.'[1]

The Enlightenment shifted our model of human nature from a porous self in an animist universe to a walled-off self in an inanimate universe. Only rationality gives us sure knowledge of this universe; ecstatic states are delusional. Western culture's reliance on instrumental rationality enabled us to control the material world but not relate to it – Descartes, pioneer of mechanistic materialism, saw all animals as emotionless machines, and even wondered if the people in the street were autom-atons. In the words of ecologist priest Thomas Berry: 'We can no longer hear the voice of the rivers, the mountains, or the sea. The trees and meadows are no longer intimate modes of spirit presence. The world about us has become an "it" rather than a "thou".'[2]

The disconnection from nature is bad for humans: we're stuck in the narrow, fearful, lonely and boring ego-shed. The civilised mind is plagued by various emotional disorders, which deep ecologists say emerge from our lost connection to nature and our clinging to the ego. Colin Campbell, another teacher at Schumacher, says: 'The industrial age has reduced our sense of who we are to a very small component compared to what it once was. There is a starvation of the soul, a malnutrition, resulting in an internal retraction in all of us. We're more and more isolated.'[3] We have lost the ecstatic sense of a love-connection to the Earth and to non-human beings. Thomas Berry wrote:

> The human venture depends absolutely on this quality of awe and reverence and joy in the Earth and all that lives and grows upon the Earth. As soon as we isolate ourselves from these currents of life and from the profound mood that these engender within us, then our basic life-satisfactions are diminished.[4]

Our broken connection to the Earth is very bad for the Earth too. Psychedelic guru Terence McKenna declared the 'suppression of shamanic gnosis, with its reliance and insistence on ecstatic dissolution of the ego, has robbed us of life's meaning and made us enemies of the planet, of ourselves, and our grandchildren'.[5] We are stuck in what McKenna called the 'ego-dominator pathology' – a pathology obsessed with control and exploitation for power, money and status. People, animals, plants and the planet itself all become fuel for ego-satisfaction. The ego-dominator mindset uses rationality to make its exploitation as efficient as possible, but it's not actually rational – it's insane. It refuses to countenance any limit to its desires, and denies the reality of ocean acidification, global warming, deforestation, declining fresh water, and the mass extinction of species. Mac says: 'Parents all love their children, yet we're behaving in a way that threatens the future of our children.'

Refinding the love-connection

Deep ecologists say the antidote to this toxic situation is a shift in consciousness from ego-centric to eco-centric. Thomas Berry wrote: 'We need to seek relationship with nature, based on nothing less than an attitude of reverence.' We need to return to the animist world-view, where we are porous selves connected to the spirits of nature, where nature is 'not a collection of objects but a communion of subjects', in Berry's words.

But how exactly do we re-find a love-connection? The hope is that it's never entirely gone away. Children naturally feel wonder and joy when they encounter animals and plants – indeed, they learn to imitate animal noises almost before they can speak. As adults in urban industrial societies, we feel less of this love-connection, partly as the only time many of us encounter animals, besides the occasional pigeon, is the meat section of our local supermarket. And yet we still feel it too, in those sudden epiphanies in nature, which we looked at in the Entrance Gate. We feel it in the wonder, bliss and awe when we encounter non-human beings – a hummingbird, a great redwood tree, a tiger, a pod of dolphins – particularly when the animal is much bigger than us, although, alas, most large mammals are either extinct or nearing extinction. We feel it on psychedelics too, especially magic mushrooms and ayahuasca, which give people a profound sense of being part of an animist eco-system.

Deep ecologists tell us that such experiences point to a genuine spiritual connection to an animate natural world. Stephan Harding, teacher in holistic science at Schumacher and the author of *The Animate Earth*, has said: 'The most important thing now is to get the sense that we're inside a great living creature. That feeling when you're camping and you look out on the stars, or the way the moonlight falls on a lake, these are genuine communications from the Earth.'[6] We can learn to integrate those rare epiphanies, so that we shift from ego-centric to eco-centric, through the use of spiritual practices and rituals. Mac says: 'We've been connecting to nature through rituals and ceremonies for hundreds of thousands of years. The trouble is, many people are alienated from Christianity, because it's disconnected from nature and the body, and it's quite authoritarian.'

So what rituals can we use? The students at Schumacher College – Schumies, as they're known – often invent their own neo-pagan rituals in what one druid calls 'adult play'. Neo-paganism *has* be to somewhat improvised, as the old pagan customs of Britain are basically forgotten. Others turn to Buddhist practices, like meditation, as a way to experience the interdependence of all things. There is a handful of Christian deep ecologists, who seek to develop forms of Earth-compassion, like Matthew Fox's 'earth mass'. But, mainly, there's a fascination with the practices and rituals of indigenous people, like Native Americans, who are seen as having retained the spiritual connection to nature that Western civilisation lost.

Schumies' favourite ecstatic ritual is the 'vision quest'. Inspired by Pueblo and Native American culture, this involves a person heading off into the wilderness for a period of solitary fasting, contemplation and communication with what Colin Campbell calls the 'messengers' of the animate Earth. A vision quest could last anything from 24 hours to several months, and may involve taking mushrooms or ayahuasca. The idea is that through this purgation and this opening to the wilderness, one will shift from ego-centric to eco-centric and receive healing wisdom from Mother Nature, in the forms of dreams, visions and animal-encounters. You may not have literal visions, although many do.

A brief history of ecstasy in nature

Schumies are attempting to get back to an enchanted model of the psyche and nature, which existed for around 200,000 years. In pre-modern hunter-gatherer societies, humans believed they lived in an enchanted cosmos filled with spiritual forces. Existence in this enchanted universe was often terrifying – humans were besieged by wild animals, illness, starvation and natural disasters, much of which they interpreted as attacks by spiritual forces. They turned to the shaman to help them placate the spirits of nature. The shaman's ecstatic powers enabled them to cross the boundary between the tribe and nature – even to become an animal – and to maintain cordial relations with the spirit-world. The shaman might have a deep knowledge of the medicinal powers of different plants, a wisdom in part gained through psychedelic communion with nature. However, their ability to control nature through ecstasy was rather unreliable, hence humans' low life expectancy in pre-modern cultures.

During the Bronze Age, around 6,000 years ago, humans developed two new technologies that helped control nature – agriculture and cities. Cities and farming make life safer and more predictable, but humans were still threatened by the demonic power of nature. External nature might destroy us, through droughts, failed harvests, plagues, fires or floods. And our inner nature might rebel against the psychological constraints of urban life – we might go mad and be killed or thrown out of the city. The Greeks developed ecstatic rituals as ways to placate the demonic gods of nature, and to allow humans the cathartic release of their suppressed wilder selves. In the cult of Dionysus, for example, the maenads go into an ecstasy in which they feel blissfully reconnected to their inner nature and the outer natural world. Many of these nature rituals used psychedelic drugs, which were a way of healing humans' relationship with nature. Ecstasy was a way of reconciling ourselves with nature (both inner and outer nature) when we felt we had become dangerously alienated from it.

Christianity and the transcendence of nature

In Christianity, there is another radical shift in the West's relationship to nature. Instead of worshipping nature-gods, Christians worship a transcendent Supreme Creator beyond nature. Humans are different from the rest of nature: we are uniquely crafted in God's image. Only humans have immortal souls, while all other animals and plants are soulless and mortal. The rest of nature is under our dominion. We must go out and work the land, which, because of the Fall, is no longer a paradise but rather a wilderness that needs to be cultivated and exorcised of demons.

Although Christianity introduced a separation between humans and the natural world, and saw the natural world as fallen and demon-infested, nature is still God's creation, and could be used as a springboard to the ecstatic contemplation of the Creator. Nature is a book filled with meanings, symbols, signs and allegories, for those with the spiritual vision to interpret them correctly. 'Someone who has purified the eyes of his soul and is trained to see beautiful things,' wrote Gregory of Nyssa, 'makes use of the visible as a springboard to rise to contempla-tion of the spiritual.'[7] Contemplating the wonders of nature gives rise to awe – medieval churches displayed natural marvels, like jewels, ostrich eggs and whale-bones, to incite wonder in the masses. Sea-creatures provoked particular fear and trembling in the Christian mind: they are the Leviathan, proof of God's awesome power.[8]

Some Christian traditions have a particularly strong reverence for nature. The Christianity of Celtic monks in the seventh to tenth centu-ries celebrates a nature brimming with God's presence. 'What is the fruit of study?' asked St Ninian, fourth-century founder of the first stone church in Britain. 'To perceive the eternal Word of God reflected in every plant and insect, every bird and animal, every man and woman.' Celtic monks sought God in the wild places – on the islands of Lindisfarne and Iona, in simple hermit dwellings. They said prayers to the sun, moon and stars, as St Francis would later. 'O sun of the living God, old eternal king,' prays an anonymous Celtic hermit in the tenth century, 'I desire a hidden hut in the wilderness, that it may be my home, a narrow little blue stream beside it, and a clear pool, a lovely wood close by on every side, to nurse birds with all sorts of voices.'[9]

The risk of this contemplation of nature, however, is that we sink into an idolatrous and pagan nature-worship, feasting our senses and forgetting the Creator who made it all. This is a risk St Augustine warned of, in a famous passage in his *Confessions* where nature itself points him to the transcendent God:

But what do I love, when I love Thee? I asked the earth, and it answered me, 'I am not He', and whatsoever are in it confessed the same . . . I asked the heavens, sun, moon, stars. 'Nor,' say they, 'are we the God who thou seekest.' And I replied unto all the things which encompass the door of my flesh: 'Ye have told me of my God, that ye are not He, tell me something of Him.' And they cried out with a loud voice, 'He made us.'

From enchanted to materialist nature

Then, from the sixteenth to the twentieth century, the West shifted from an enchanted to a materialist world-view. In the early seventeenth century, Francis Bacon developed a new approach to investigating nature: the scientific method. Unlike the shamanic trance, the scientific method required rational, sceptical investigation of natural processes through patient trial-and-error. Bacon and other pioneers of 'natural philosophy' decided nature was driven by mechanical processes, not divine interventions. God created the cosmos but then retreated to let it run like clockwork. The body is likewise a machine. The heart, formerly seen as the seat of affections, is really a mechanical pump. The brain is a machine too. Where does that leave consciousness and free will, wondered the philosopher René Descartes. It's a question we're still grappling with.

In the nineteenth century, geologists came to realise that the Earth was much older than previously thought, several million years old rather than the 6,000 suggested by the Bible. Over those millions of years, many species had been exterminated. Nature, decided the biologist Charles Darwin in *The Origin of Species*, was decidedly brutal: 'each species . . . is constantly suffering enormous destruction . . . very young animals seem generally to suffer the most'. What's the point of this endless 'battle for life'? More life. 'When we reflect on this struggle,' Darwin wrote, 'we may console ourselves with the full belief, that the war of nature is not incessant [yes, it is], that no fear is felt [yes, it is], that death is generally prompt [no, it isn't], and that the vigorous, the healthy, and the happy survive and multiply'. Scant consolation for the unhappy!

The true consolation of the mechanical materialist philosophy was that, although nature was revealed as brutally indifferent to suffering, science gave us the power to control nature, not through prayer and magic, but through medicine and mechanics. Bacon and Descartes claimed their new scientific method would radically improve human existence. And they were right: over the following three centuries, diets improved, illnesses were cured, life expectancy went up, child mortality went down, new technologies of energy, transport, communication and sanitation were invented, and the human population soared from around 600 million in 1700 to six billion today. But the cost of these material improvements to life was that Westerners found themselves in a disenchanted and inanimate cosmos in which they were apparently the only species cursed with self-consciousness and the awareness of mortality. Mechanical materialism denied humans the spiritual connection they once felt to nature, to other living beings, and to God.

Wonder as a natural replacement for ecstasy

But it's wrong to say that modern science denies us any *emotional* connection to nature. While the natural philosophers of the seventeenth century were wary of ecstasy, they were certainly prone to wonder. Descartes insisted wonder was the first of the passions. Fellows of the Royal Society collected natural marvels, wondered at them, and circulated their investigations. Robert Hooke astounded the reading public with his *Micrographia*, a microscopic investigation of insects illustrated by Christopher Wren. The seventeenth century was the golden age of *Wunderkammer*, or cabinets of wonder – gentlemanly collections of natural marvels and oddities, from stuffed crocodiles to deformed foetuses, from unicorn horns to mechanical parrots. 'The wonder they aimed at by the profusion of these heterogeneous particulars,' wrote the historians Lorraine Daston and Katharine Park, 'was neither contemplative nor inquiring, but rather dumbstruck.'[10]

Could this sort of natural wonder be a replacement for religious ecstasy? It's a suggestion often made by atheists today – we don't need religion: we can feel awe and wonder looking at photographs of space from the Hubble telescope. We may not have divine souls, but we can wonder at the fact we are made of stardust. Richard Dawkins called his autobiography *An Appetite for Wonder*; atheist astronomer Brian Cox presents *Wonders of the Universe*; TED talks organised a conference on 'The Rediscovery of Wonder'; while the motto of the atheist church, the Sunday Assembly, is 'Wonder More'. Dawkins writes:

> All the great religions have a place for awe, for ecstatic transport at the wonder and beauty of creation. And it's exactly this feeling of spine-shivering, breath-catching awe – almost worship – this flooding of the chest with ecstatic wonder, that modern science can provide.[11]

However, as his fellow New Atheist Sam Harris points out, there's a big difference between wonder and ecstasy: we may wonder at Hubble photographs, but we are unlikely to lose control of ourselves, feel our egos dissolve in a love-connection to the cosmos, and come away with a sense of deep personal transformation. In fact, seventeenth-century natural philosophers were wary of that sort of deep, almost incapacitating wonder. It would strike them as astonishment, which is 'an excess of wonder', in Descartes' phrase. Adam Smith suggested wonder is so disturbing an emotion that scientists undertake research in order to rid themselves of it. To feel excessive wonder was to allow one's reason to be overwhelmed by 'enthusiasm' and risk losing one's sanity. Wonder, like ecstasy, was something particularly felt by women, children, the ignorant, the primitive and the insane. A new paradigm was in place, mechanical materialism. The laws of the universe were regular as clock-work, so why should anything astonish?

Thomas Traherne's ecstasy in nature

From the first years of the Scientific Revolution, some Romantics have challenged the tenets of mechanical materialism and tried to re-find an ecstatic connection to nature. An early example is Thomas Traherne, an Anglican vicar who lived in relative obscurity in the mid-seventeenth century. Traherne's poetry and prose were lost until 1896 when a manuscript was discovered in a wheelbarrow outside a second-hand bookshop in London's Charing Cross Road. It included a contemplative book called *Centuries of Meditation*, which C. S. Lewis called 'almost the most beautiful book in the English language'.[12] Traherne was deeply opposed to the philosophy of Thomas Hobbes, who argued that nature is entirely material and mechanistic and life a godless war of all-against-all. Traherne thought this world-view was false, and likely to make humans feel depressed, afraid and cut off from the cosmos. His *Centuries of Meditation* is a mystical therapy to try to help us 'see aright', 'enjoy aright'. We must change our 'frame', otherwise the foundation of our reality is 'out of course' and we will be miserable.

He begins, as later Romantics would do, by insisting that our nature is basically good, and that our misery 'proceedeth ten thousand times more from the outward bondage of opinion and custom, than from any inward corruption or depravation of Nature'.[13] Like later Romantics, he loves how children spontaneously respond with rapture to animals, plants and the natural world. He remembers his own childhood in Hereford: 'The green trees when I saw them first through one of the gates transported and ravished me, their sweetness and unusual beauty made my heart to leap, and almost mad with ecstasy, they were such strange and wonderful things . . .'

In childhood, we feel at home in creation, as if the world is a playground made for us: 'The skies were mine, and so were the sun and moon and stars, and all the World was mine; and I the only spectator and enjoyer of it.' Traherne believes that children naturally intuit the true state of affairs – humans *are* specially blessed by God, the Earth *is* a paradise. But we forgot our divinity through the dismal effect of civilised opinion and education. The fall comes in early adulthood, when Traherne goes to Oxford, and becomes infected with atheist materialism. He comes to see the world as a hostile place, and himself as a fragile and insignificant being who must compete with his fellow-men to acquire status: 'An ambition to please, a desire to gratify, a great desire to delight others [is] the greatest snare in the world.' This lack of self-esteem and need for approval drive our pathological search for honour, wealth and power. We're trying to fill a hole in our soul with things:

> there is a disease in him who despiseth present mercies, which til it be cured, he can never be happy. He esteemeth nothing that he hath, but is ever gaping after more: which when he hath he despiseth in like manner . . . The works of darkness are Repining, Envy, Malice, Covetousness, Fraud, Oppression, Discontent, and Violence. All which proceed from the corruption of Men and their mistake in the choice of riches.

But Traherne manages to come back to his previous way of seeing and writes *Centuries* to help people 'see aright' and rediscover their essential blessedness and inner wealth. We must 'disrobe ourselves of all false colours, and unclothe our souls of evil habits'. We should esteem ourselves as divine beings, not mere collections of atoms. Then we can stop begging for approval, relax and enjoy the gift of existence in this world. Life is simpler than we realise: the only thing we have to do is enjoy ourselves, appreciate nature and praise its Creator: 'The world is a mirror of infinite beauty, yet no man sees it. It is a Temple of Majesty, yet no man regards it . . . We need nothing but open eyes, to be ravished like the Cherubims.' Traherne looks on every aspect of nature and sees it shimmering with transcendence. He sees 'infinite goodness expressed in a sand', an ant is a 'great miracle', our bodies are 'the greatest treasures of all'.

To 'see aright', we should remind ourselves each day of the wonder of nature, and give thanks. Every day the sun rises and sets, the stars come out, and we take it all for granted, but isn't it astonishingly beautiful?

> Your enjoyment of the world is never right, til every morning you awake in Heaven; see yourself in your Father's Palace; and look upon the skies, the earth, and the air as Celestial Joys: having such a reverend esteem of all, as if you were among the Angels . . . You never enjoy the world aright, til the Sea itself floweth in your veins,

till you are clothed with the heavens, and crowned with stars: and perceive yourself to be the sole heir of the whole world.

For Traherne, consciousness is the ultimate *Wunderkammer*, it is a 'cabinet of infinite value'. Materialism can't really explain consciousness, so it either denies it or says it doesn't do much. Not so. Consciousness is a 'miraculous abyss of infinite abysses'. Souls are 'God's jewels, every one of which is worth many worlds,' he writes. 'The consideration of one Soul is sufficient to convince all the Atheists in the whole world.' He is particularly struck by the way consciousness, this immaterial thing, can reflect on all things, store them in the memory and contemplate them – even the entire cosmos, even God Himself. The nature of consciousness is ecstatic – it stretches out beyond itself to all things, connects to them through attention and love: 'Love is deeper than at first it can be thought. It never ceaseth but in endless things. It ever multiplies . . . By Loving a Soul does propagate and beget itself. By Loving it does dilate and magnify itself. By Loving it does enlarge and delight itself . . . But above all by Loving it does attain itself.'

God's Love multiples itself in the consciousness of all beings, like a torch lighting billions of candles. This Love spreads not just through all the beings in this world, but perhaps through infinite worlds: 'What if beyond the Heavens there were Infinite Numbers of Worlds at vast unspeakable distances. And all Those worlds full of Glorious Kingdoms?' Occasionally, Traherne attains an ecstatic vision of God's plan completed, when all beings in all universes are enlightened: 'All are happy in each other. All are like Deities. Every one the end of all things, everyone supreme, every one a treasure, and the joy of all, and every one most infinitely delighted in being so.'

I find Traherne's cosmic rapture therapeutic, and wish he was more widely read. You can enjoy the *Centuries* even if you're not a Christian or theist. True, his happy philosophy does not perhaps recognise how cruel nature can be or how much suffering life can involve. But it captures something materialism often fails to appreciate: the miracle of consciousness, and its god-like capacity to reflect on existence and reach out to all beings in love.

The eighteenth-century Sublime

In the late eighteenth century, there was a new attempt to re-forge an ecstatic connection to nature through the Romantic philosophy of the Sublime. While the Enlightenment saw astonishment as vulgar, by the late eighteenth century people yearned for something to give them the body-shaking emotions of awe and terror. And they looked to wild nature to provide that. Previously, the wilderness had filled Christians with horror: it was a place of demonic warfare. If Christians felt rapture anywhere, it was more likely to be in a well-tended garden, which reminded them of Eden. But, as Western countries became more industrially farmed, an aristocratic taste for wildness arose, informing landscape gardening, painting, poetry and philosophy.

In 1757, the philosopher Edmund Burke resurrected the classical concept of the Sublime, and made it the cornerstone of an aesthetic movement. Nature and art, Burke argued, stimulate two emotions in us: first, the sense of the Sublime, which is a sort of ecstatic suspension of one's critical faculties. He wrote: 'Astonishment is that state in the soul in which all its motions are suspended with some degree of horror . . . the mind is so entirely filled with its object, that it cannot entertain any other, nor by consequence reason on that object which employs it.'[14] The Sublime is provoked in us by scenes of vastness, infinity, great height, abysmal depth, sepulchral darkness, blazing light, loudness, power, violence – in other words, mountains, cliff-tops, cataracts, volcanoes, stormy seas. We feel dwarfed, threatened, even annihilated, yet somehow the experience can be enjoyable and revitalising. But we also yearn for a sense of the Beautiful, which we acquire from scenes of quieter harmony: soft, curving hills, calm rivers, flowers, bunny rabbits.

We still feel the call of the Sublime and the Beautiful today. Walking along Bamburgh beach opposite Holy Island, I felt soothed by the waves, calmed by the sunset, expanded by the vast sky. That was an experience of the Beautiful. Last week, by contrast, I had an experience of the Burkean Sublime. I lay in bed listening to a violent thunderstorm as it approached the hills of north London. The thunder grew louder and louder, like an approaching army of orcs. The rain hammered on my windows. It was a thrill to listen to it from the safety of my bedroom. And then there was the most almighty bang, like a bomb going off under my bed, and the room filled with light. I leaped out of bed and hopped from foot to foot. Had we just been hit? I could smell burning. I rushed to the window and looked out – I couldn't see any flames. I went down to the living room. Another crack of lightning, very close, made me leap and cower behind a door-frame. My heart was pounding, my skin was tingling, my hair was probably standing on end. It was exhilarating. The storm slowly rumbled north, and I went back to bed.

The next day, I realised my house *had* been struck by lightning – the bolt had gone through my bedroom, down into the living room, and blown out a plug, to which was attached my TV, video, Wii, Wi-Fi and free TV box, all now kaput. It was an exceptionally well-aimed lightning bolt. I didn't feel annoyed at the damage. I felt alive. I couldn't help seeing it as a message. Nature had reached into my well-protected ego-shed and given me a shake. Earlier that day, I'd been wondering whether to leave my settled life in London and go abroad for a new adventure. Wake up, the lightning seemed to say. Leave your creature comforts and hit the road (I heeded the advice and am off travelling as soon as I finish this book).

Wordsworth and neo-animist ecstasy

At the end of the eighteenth century, William Wordsworth took up Western culture's yearning for wildness and shaped it into a new religious movement. Frederic Myers, who produced a biography of him, wrote that Wordsworth showed 'that the contemplation of Nature . . . may enable us "to see into the life of things" – as far, perhaps, as beatific vision or prophetic rapture can attain'.[15] Wordsworth saw nature not just as the supplier of emotional effects, but as an animate entity that we could commune with through ecstasy.

Like Traherne, Wordsworth celebrates childhood as the moment in which humans are most spiritually attuned to the divine in nature. We emerge into the world 'trailing clouds of glory', but then the customs and institutions of fallen civilisation make us forget our inherent divinity.

His epic poem, *The Prelude*, is a hymn to a childhood spent cavorting around the Lake District. He particularly savours youthful moments of epiphany – which he calls 'spots of time' – when he feels overwhelmed by the spiritual power of nature. In one famous scene in *The Prelude*, the young Wordsworth is rowing alone one evening on a lake, when he looks up, and

> a huge cliff
> As if with voluntary power instinct,
> Uprear'd its head. I struck, and struck again,
> And, growing still in stature, the huge cliff
> Rose up between me and the stars, and still,
> With measur'd motion, like a living thing,
> Strode after me.

Nature, in *The Prelude*, brims with spiritual presences – the rivers speak to Wordsworth, the hills pursue him, the mountains throb with meaning and intention. He also feels a numinous power in certain places where sacred or dreadful things have happened. The book of nature is wiser than all the books we are forced to read in school, as he writes in 'The Tables Turned':

> One impulse from a vernal wood
> May teach you more of man,
> Of moral evil and of good,
> Than all the sages can.

Nature cultivates two emotions in us. First, moments of epiphany excite us with their sublime power. But second, through habitual communion with nature, we absorb a deep contemplative calm. While absorbed in nature, we drink from the 'quiet stream of self-forgetfulness'; we are led into 'meditations passionate from the deep/recesses in man's heart'. And these two emotions, excitement and deep calm, when habitually experienced, fill a reservoir of spiritual gladness in our psyche, which we can draw on throughout life. Where the monk had contemplated in the cloister, the Romantic contemplates while tramping around the hills and dales – Thomas De Quincey estimated Wordsworth had walked around 180,000 miles by the time he was 65.[16] The rhythmic activity of strenuous walking (or riding, or fell-running, or wild swimming) lulls our mind and takes us into a state of reverie, in which we can commune with external nature and also with the inner nature of the subliminal mind.

There is a risk that nature-contemplation degenerates into sensation-seeking: we climb a mountain to get the View, buy a painting of the View, take photos of the View. But Wordsworth insists our 'communion with the invisible world' is not just a passive aesthetic sensation. Rather, it's a marriage between the spiritual power of nature and that of humans' creative imagination. Like the Christian mystics who preceded him, Wordsworth ultimately sees creation as a 'springboard to rise to the contemplation of the spiritual'. Natural epiphanies point the soul towards an infinite divinity within nature but also beyond it. As he writes in *The Prelude:*

> Our destiny, our nature, and our home
> Is with infinitude . . .

Like Traherne, Wordsworth thinks the greatest wonder of the natural world is human consciousness, which is 'of substance and of fabric more divine'.

The artist has a crucial role in the communion of humans with nature and God. The artist is a shaman – Wordsworth describes how the spirits of the Earth chose him, tracked him down, seized him and made him their intermediary. He sees himself in a continuous tradition of indigenous prophets stretching back through Milton and Shakespeare to the human-sacrificing druids of old. It falls to the shaman-artist to reconnect industrial civilisation to nature, because we have become so deadened that we have forgotten the 'witchery of the soft blue sky'. The artist can shape our aesthetic, emotional and spiritual response, help us to see anew, so we remember our divinity, and see the divinity shimmering through nature. And this pantheistic worship of nature and man will also lead, Wordsworth insists, to a love of humanity. His poetry celebrates common folk – tramps, beggars, wayfarers. The less civilised they are, the more authentic they seem to him. This is a classic attitude of Romanticism, which celebrates the 'noble savage'. But Wordsworth, like many Romantics, is much more suspicious of the urban proletariat, which he tends to describe as a 'swarm', a 'senseless mass', or an 'abject multitude'. He happens to be in France in 1790, and is initially exhilarated by the French Revolution, which seems like a festival of redeemed humanity. But he later becomes appalled by the violence of the Terror, and disillusioned with radical politics. *The Prelude* ends with him finding a personal redemption on a hike up Scafell Pike. The Romantic loses faith in popular collective ecstasy – it leads to mob violence – but takes comfort from a personal ecstasy in nature and the arts.

Ecstatic environmentalism from Muir to Monbiot

Romanticism shaped a new attitude to wild nature, seeing it as the source of personal epiphanies. In the nineteenth century it fed into the nascent environmental movement – an early example is the Scottish-American environmentalist and mountaineer John Muir. Muir grew up in the mid-nineteenth century in a severe Presbyterian sect, under a domineering father, but escaped after university to work as a shepherd in the High Sierra of California. He took only a blanket, a compass, the Bible and the poetry of Milton and Robert Burns. The three months he spent there, sleeping rough and fending off the occasional bear, were among the happiest of his life. They were something like a conversion experience for the 30-year-old – he felt redeemed from the iron cage of his father's Presbyterianism, and found himself back in a sinless, God-soaked Eden, where he and every other creature were at 'endless Godful play'.

His journal, which he published near the end of his life as *My First Summer in the Sierra*, is an ecstatic hymn to Nature. The Sierra becomes his church, the stones give sermons, the mountain pines seem 'definite symbols, divine hieroglyphics written with sunbeams'. The cricket is 'a crisp, electric spark of joy enlivening the massy sublimity of the mountains like the laugh of a child'; the butterflies 'numbered and known and loved only by the Lord, are waltzing together high overhead, seemingly in pure play and hilarious enjoyment of their little sparks of life'; the calypso trees are 'superior beings who loved me and beckoned me to come. I sat down beside them and wept for joy'; the rocks are 'dear friends, and have warm blood gushing through their granite flesh; and I love them with a love intensified by a long and close companionship'. He sees a nature brimming with consciousness, and this consciousness manifests as ecstatic play: 'Surely all God's people, however serious or savage, great or small, like to play. Whales and elephants, dancing, humming gnats, and invisibly small mischievous microbes – all are warm with divine radium and must have lots of fun in them.'

Muir is too enraptured to see any evil in himself or in nature. He looks on the fierce belligerence of ants and admits that 'much remains to be done ere the world is brought under the rule of universal peace and love', but even the excruciating agony of an ant-bite produces a sort of ecstasy in him: 'A quick electric flame of pain flashes along the outraged nerves, and you discover for the first time how great is the capacity for sensation you are possessed of.' If he sees evil anywhere, it is in industry, which rapes his beloved creation, and puts a price on every sacred tree and mountainside. In the last decades of his life, he started the Sierra Club, which campaigned to create the great national parks of America and to preserve them as cathedrals for humanity. The Sierrans were, in the words of environmental historian Jedediah Purdy, 'a political movement dedicated to the aesthetic and spiritual experience of the solitary wanderer'. They organised 'pilgrimages' to the parks, following routes described in Muir's guidebooks as if they were Stations of the Cross. They would then send in accounts of their epiphanies to the *Sierra Club Bulletin:* 'We were acolytes in the grand temple of the eternal,' reads one letter.[17]

This attitude – where wild nature is revered as a source of healing and epiphany – is an increasingly strong strain in modern environmentalism. Jay Griffiths's 2006 book, *Wild: An Elemental Journey*, is a classic example. Griffiths is depressed and alienated while living in Hackney, and hears the animist call of the wild: 'I felt its urgent demand in the blood. I could hear its call. Its whistling disturbed me by day and its howl woke me in the night.' She sets off on a grand tour of various indigenous people, from whom she learns 'that going out into the wilds is a necessary initiation and that, for young people, lost in the wastelands of the psyche, the only medicine is the land'. Griffiths is not alone in blaming urban civilisation for making us mentally ill. There is a small but growing body of psychological research that suggests the more time we spend in nature the better we feel, the lower our stress levels, the healthier our immune systems. The psychologist Richard Louv suggests Western children are suffering from 'nature deficit disorder', that they're over-protected, over-saturated with the internet, anxious, distracted, and incapable of losing themselves in Wordsworth's 'quiet stream of self-forgetfulness'. He blames this, as many Romantics have before him, on a lack of outdoor play.[18] The environmentalist George Monbiot has also called for a re-wilding of nature and humanity. 'We've privileged safety over experience,' he says. We need to re-connect with our feral inner child, rediscover 'wonder and enchantment and delight in a world which often seems crushingly bleak'.[19] One way we could do that, he suggests, is by bringing back megafauna, such as lions and elephants, to Europe. Like Wordsworth and Muir, Monbiot worships wild nature as a source of epiphanies. He savours a moment when he is kayaking in Cardigan Bay, and is surrounded by a pod of cavorting dolphins. He writes:

> [ecstasy] is an accurate description of how I felt. Everything that weighs on my mind, that tethers me to the world of thought and work and care sloughed off. Experiences like this are among the defining moments of my life, that I will remember even if I forget all else.

The fruits and risks of ecstatic environmentalism

Ecstatic environmentalism seems to me to get a great deal right. It insists on the relationship between moments of ecstasy and nature – such moments are often a bursting out of the ego-shed and reconciliation with outer nature and our repressed inner nature. That can be enormously healing and cathartic to our bodies and souls. Deep ecologists also emphasise the power of ritual and practice to shift our consciousness from the ego-centric to the eco-centric. They rightly warn us of a lost connection to the natural world, and of its devastating effects for us and our planet. We still long for encounters with wild nature, yet we feed this yearning through YouTube clips of pandas or computer-generated simulacra like *Jurassic Park*. Psychotherapists are remembering how emotionally healing encounters with nature and non-humans can be: they take us out of our self-absorbed, wounded egos and back into a state of childlike wonder, absorption and play. A short walk in nature has been found to reduce rumination, which can cause depression.[20] Several studies have found that having a pet improves owners' mood and health, lowering blood pressure and releasing oxytocin, which increases feelings of bonding and belonging.[21] Nature is particularly healing for those suffering from trauma – both the British and US armies support charities that connect traumatised veterans with nature, by getting them to train dogs, go riding or surfing, or even swim with sharks.[22] I find my mood greatly improved by the presence of dogs – their affection is so spontaneous, so physical, in marked contrast to English society (that's why the English love dogs – they break through our icy reserve). It's strange, as Jonathan Safran Foer has noted, that we extend so much affection and care to dogs, and so little to the rest of the natural world. If we ever do shift from ego-centric to eco-centric, we may look back on this time as an era of massive cruelty to animals, not least through industrial livestock farming.[23] Deep ecologists have led the drive to grant animals and even parks and rivers the legal status and rights of persons. If a corporation can be a legal 'person', why not a park?

But, as with previous varieties we've encountered, there are risks to this particular strain of ecstasy. First, animist spirituality can be so focused on the local that it can lose a sense of higher transcendence, a sense of the spiritual power in the multiverse, perhaps a transcendent power *beyond* creation – Brahma, God or the Tao breathing creation out and breathing it back in. Second, it easily leads to what Keats called the 'egotistic sublime'. In an ecstatic state, we can see every rainbow as a sign meant just for us. Werner Herzog warns of the risks of a sentimental anthropomorphic attitude to nature in his documentary *Grizzly Man*, where the hero Timothy Treadwell feels a spiritual connection to grizzly bears, but the feeling is, alas, not mutual – a bear eats him. Herzog remarks: 'In all the faces of all the bears that Treadwell ever filmed, I discover no kinship, no understanding, no mercy. I see only the over-whelming indifference of nature.' Herzog still feels ecstasy in nature, he just doesn't infer any benevolence from it. In fact, its life-threatening savagery is precisely what excites him.

Third, as Mac warned, New Age nature-spirituality easily becomes over-attached to ecstatic experiences. This can lead to a bipolar schism, where occasional peaks are interspersed with long valleys of boredom and depression. The Romantic focus on personal spiritual growth can lead to a lack of realistic political programmes for change. One friend says of Schumacher College: 'There were some people there who only seemed up for endless sharing circles, even in the run-up to the climate negotiations in Paris. It got too therapeutic for my liking.'

The fetishism of personal epiphanies is easily packaged into consumer tourism. By the end of the eighteenth century, the Lake District was crawling with Romantic pilgrims. By the end of the nineteenth century, Yosemite was likewise stuffed with nature-worshippers, all trying desper-ately to be alone. We become obsessed with the search for the Perfect View – Muir was so obsessed with the View, he insisted on getting all Native Americans ejected from national parks because they were 'dirty' and they spoiled the View (300 Native Americans were killed in one day when they refused to leave Yellowstone).[24]

Fourth, like all forms of ecstatic ideology, ecstatic environmentalism is prone to demonisation and simplistic 'Us versus Them' dichotomies. 'There are two sides,' writes Griffiths in *Wild*, 'the agents of waste and the lovers of the wild. Either for life or against it. And each of us has to choose.' Romantic environmentalism tends to be virulently anti-cities, anti-proletariat and anti-business. Griffiths insists that the forest is 'wildly beautiful' and the town is a 'hideous wasteland' – it actually makes her sick. This attitude immediately demonises the 80 per cent of Western populations who live in cities. Peter Kareiva, director of the UCLA

Institute of the Environment and Sustainability, insists we need to avoid naive dichotomies between 'nature' and cities, instead fostering the idea of environmentalism *within* cities as well as outside them.[25] You can commune with nature in cities too: Keats heard his nightingale on Hampstead Heath; Blake saw angels in Peckham Rye.

Rejecting urban civilisation as evil, ecstatic environmentalists can fall prey to the romanticism of exotic indigenous wisdom. I'm sure we have a lot to learn from indigenous tribes, but they tend to be highly conservative and patriarchal, and have higher child mortality and lower life expectancy. Romantics might have seen Papua New Guinea as an Eden, but modern research suggests it's a rapist's paradise: a 2015 *Lancet* study found 80 per cent of married men there admitted they'd raped their partners, and 14 per cent of men had taken part in gang rapes.[26] Indigenous cultures, like Puebloans, Native Americans or our own druids, resorted to blood-sacrifices as ignorant ways to placate nature. Who now really believes that if we were all just more primitive, everything would be better? And, for Westerners, exotic indigenous cultures are not *our* cultures, not our songs. I have a great respect for Mac Macartney, but feel uncomfortable when he calls the Lakota tribe 'my people'. It can end up a sort of *Avatar*-fantasy – if only we can shed our evil whiteness and magically transform into an animist native. Mac recognises the risk of exoticism, and wants to revive the indigenous spirituality of the British druids (didn't they practise human sacrifice?). I think it's more promising to try to mobilise the five billion who follow the major religions. Pope Francis's encyclical recently tried to revive our love of creation, quoting St Francis, who sang: 'Praise be to you, my Lord, through our Sister, Mother Earth, who sustains and governs us.' However, there's a lot of work to be done. Christians in the US are less likely to worry about the environment or to want environmental legislation than atheists or New Agers, with evangelicals among the least bothered.[27]

Taken to an extreme, ecstatic environmentalism can end up being anti-humanity. The classic Romantic is the recluse living in the 'wild' – Thoreau retreating from humanity to live in Emerson's garden. There can be a longing to escape the stain of humanity and the burden of human consciousness, to become an animal – not temporarily, like a shaman, but permanently. I think of the great English nature-writer J. A. Baker, who tracked peregrine falcons, felt 'possessed' by them, and clearly yearned to become one. He writes: 'I have always longed . . . to be out there at the edge of things, to let the human taint wash away in emptiness and silence as the fox sloughs off his smell . . .'[28] It reminds one of Swift's *Gulliver's Travels*, where the narrator is so disgusted with humans he tries to become a horse. This hatred of humanity culminates, often enough, in an exuberant apocalypticism: vengeful Gaia will wipe away the stain of humanity once and for all.

Above all, ecstatic environmentalism can be fatally anti-science and anti-technology – anti-genetically-modified plants, anti-nuclear power, both of which we will need to survive the coming climate crisis. The more scientific Schumies, like Stephan Harding, recognise we may even need to try geo-engineering to cope with climate change. Nature itself, as Bacon suggested, is constantly innovating and trying out new technologies. It must be possible to combine the scientific method with a sacred reverence for nature. Bacon had a vision of how 'the souls of the living leap about and dance with infinite variety'. I think of the great naturalist, Alexander von Humboldt, who climbed to the top of the Chimborazo volcano in Ecuador, and had an epiphany of nature as 'a living whole [not] a dead aggregate'. Nature, he insisted, was 'a wonderful web of organic life', 'a natural whole animated and moved by inward forces',[29] and we need both the scientific method *and* our poetic imagination to perceive this web. His inspiring vision of the Earth as an interdependent network of animate beings turned out not to be fanciful. It turned out to be true.

It's almost time to call it a night. But let's check out one more party at the festival – follow me to the flashing strobe of Futureland, where we'll meet the transhumanists, who see ecstasy not as a return to wild nature but as an expression of humans' urge to transcend nature and become God-like through technology.

10: Futureland

A young man stands next to a cliff, facing the camera. As cinematic strings music starts to swell, he launches into his flow: 'How do we mess with our perceptual apparatus, to render life more meaningful, those are the moments that would make final cut, only in these moments do we experience the hardly bearable ecstasy of direct energy exploding on our nerve-endings . . .'

As he talks, the video bursts into a rapid-cut montage of images – children running through a field, a neural system pulsating with electricity, a woman weeping, a man diving off a cliff, a goldfish, the Big Bang. The strings stir to an epic climax as he raps and gesticulates in a cross between a Pentecostal sermon and a TED talk: 'This is the rhapsodic, ecstatic bursting forth of awe that expands our perceptual parameters beyond all previous limits and we literally have to reconfigure our mental models of the world in order to assimilate the beauty of that download, that is what it means be *inspired* – the word means to breathe in. We have a responsibility to awe.' Awe, do we?

The young man is Jason Silva, a 35-year-old 'performance philosopher', 'ideas DJ', and presenter of a viral YouTube series called Shots of Awe, which gives its millions of viewers three-minute 'nuggets of techno-rapture'.[1] Silva thinks that 'as we become increasingly sophisticated, the religious impulse is less relevant', but atheists still want awe and ecstasy. New technology, like LSD, virtual reality or the internet, can help us engineer epiphanies. Shots of Awe is a daily fix for 'wonder junkies' and 'epiphany addicts', who need a 'philosophical espresso' while they're sitting at their desks on a Monday morning. The videos are 'a neuro-storm of intense intellectual pleasure' that make grown men weep and women swoon. His rhapsodies are unscripted free-flows, inspired by hash-fuelled bull sessions at a 'salon' he ran when he was at college. What does it all amount to? Never mind, here comes another hyper-caffeinated blast:

> Technologies of ecstasy points to the fact there is something that happens in that ecstatic place of ego-death that resets the self that gives us temporary access that makes us privy to a whole host of new wild visions that transform the way we see the world and I think that today these modern digital shamans, these doctors of the word, are scientists making us question our current belief systems and de-conditioning our thinking . . . or something like that.

Transhumanist ecstasy

Jason is a 'transhumanist'. Transhumanism is a philosophy that insists technology will soon enable humans to transcend their humanity and become god-like immortals. This may sound like something dreamed up by a teenage boy with a bong and a pile of superhero comics, but it's becoming a mainstream view – the historian Yuval Noah Harari recently declared transhumanism to be the religion of the future.[2]

The roots of transhumanism are in the Californian counter-culture of the 1960s. Aldous Huxley moved to California in 1937, and spent the 1950s experimenting with ways to open the 'doors of perception', including meditation, self-hypnosis and mescaline. He suggested that, rather than following any particular religion, people could hack the ecstatic techniques of different religions and philosophies, test them with empirical science, and use this 'neurotheology' to realise man's untapped potential. He was inspired by Frederic Myers, who believed that geniuses were outliers in human evolution, emissaries from a future when all humans will develop the latent powers in their subliminal minds, including telepathy and clairvoyance. Aldous's brother Julian, the evolutionary biologist and first director-general of UNESCO, came up with a name for this optimism in man's spiritual evolution: 'The human species can, if it wishes, transcend itself – not just sporadically . . . but in its entirety, as humanity. We need a name for this new belief. Perhaps transhumanism will serve.'[3]

'We are beginning to realise,' wrote Julian, 'that even the most fortunate people are living far below capacity, and that most human beings develop not more than a small fraction of their potential mental and spiritual efficiency.' Aldous popularised the idea that humans use only 10 per cent of their brains (an idea now debunked by neuroscience but kept alive by transhumanist films like *Limitless* and *Lucy*). What if we used all 100 per cent of our brains, not just the conscious ego but the entire greater Mind with all its subliminal power? We'd be gods!

The Huxleys' evolutionary mysticism was a profound influence on the founders of Esalen, the north Californian spiritual commune. Esalen rose to prominence in the late 1960s as the centre of the Human Potential Movement. Faced with the student movement's failure to stop the Vietnam War, some hippies turned away from politics and towards spiritual exploration. Before society could be liberated, individuals must liberate themselves from 'the policemen in their head'; they must realise their essential divinity, and this realisation would ripple through society. As religious scholar Jeffrey Kripal notes, the ethos of Esalen was very close to the X-Men comics – the initiates of Esalen were the mutants, the super-powered vanguard of man's spiritual evolution.[4] But would they be Professor X, helping the masses, or Magneto, contemptuously leaving the inferior species behind? It would be a question later transhumanists returned to.

Esalen created a 'religion of no religion', in which people could learn ecstatic techniques from many different spiritual traditions, not to worship God but to discover their own divinity. Esalen's favourite technique was the encounter session, where participants expressed their inner turmoil and acted out their psychic dramas to peel away the conventional layers of their ego and find their authentic self. It also offered workshops in tantra, Reiki, lucid dreaming, 5Rhythms, and many

other techniques. And, unlike some hippie commun
new technologies, high-tech ways of finding ecstasy.
Education in Ecstasy, George Leonard, one of the le
sketched out the education of the future. Young people sh
how to access their ecstatic potential, using not just meditat   new
techniques, like LSD, transcranial magnetic stimulation, brainwave-reading
biofeedback devices and, above all, the personal computer.

Cybernetic happenings

One of the leaders of the Californian commune movement that included
Esalen was a visionary author and 'network entrepreneur' called Stewart
Brand. A Stanford graduate and former lieutenant in the army, Brand
joined the New York avant-garde in the 1950s and became inspired by
a philosophy called cybernetics, a form of systems-thinking developed
by Norbert Wiener, Buckminster Fuller, Marshall McLuhan and others.
According to cybernetics, all phenomena, organic and inorganic, could
be understood as computer-like systems of information-exchange. All
systems strive to find order, not through top-down instructions but
through positive and negative feedback. Human societies could become
better organised if they surrender control, decentralise authority and
trust in the power of information feedback to guide the system to
better outcomes. The perfect system wouldn't be entirely decentralised,
however: there was still a role for what Fuller called the 'Comprehensive
Designer' – a visionary artist-scientist who could read and channel the
information circulating in the system, then create new tools that would
steer the system and create new emergent orders.

In the 1960s, Brand and other cultural innovators, like John Cage,
used the cybernetic approach to create 'happenings', information-systems
in which artists, audience and technology would co-create in spontaneous ways to produce unexpected moments of harmony and ecstasy.
In 1963, Brand joined an artistic collective in San Francisco called
USCO, which organised happenings in an abandoned church hall, using
looping tape-decks, slide shows, strobe lighting and LSD. In effect, they
invented the rave. In 1965, Brand collaborated with Ken Kesey and the

Merry Pranksters to create the first Trips Festival in San Francisco. The audience were invited 'to wear ecstatic dress and to bring their own gadgets (A.C. outlets will be provided'). The Grateful Dead, who provided the music, were the first cybernetic pop band, not merely banging out four-minute pop songs but rather jamming, picking up the mood of the audience and steering it in new directions. This was a new religious movement, recalls journalist Tom Wolfe: 'Kesey got on the microphone and said, "Will everyone who is God please come up on stage," and twelve people came up! It was really extraordinary.'[5] Brand himself was the Comprehensive Designer of the happening, tweaking the technology, seeing what new states spontaneously emerged.

In 1968, Brand set up the *Whole Earth Catalog*, a homemade magazine of useful tools for the growing network of Californian communes to use in their quest for the good life. It included everything from *The I Ching* and compost toilets to geodomes and the latest Hewlett-Packard calculator. It was also full of articles disseminating the latest research on altered states of consciousness. The catalogue was collaborative – readers would send in their own reviews of new tools, new books, new drugs and new spiritual techniques – and would be cited as a key inspiration by the pioneers of the internet. It was 'sort of like Google in paperback form, thirty-five years before Google came along', Steve Jobs would later say. Brand drove in a van from commune to commune, selling the catalogue and some of the tools featured in it. While some communes embraced a down-to-earth primitivism, not unlike Schumacher College, Brand was more of a transhumanist. 'We are as gods,' he wrote in the first edition, 'so we might as well get good at it.'

The PC as tool of consciousness-liberation

As Fred Turner recounts in his masterful history *From Counterculture to Cyberculture*, Brand's 'killer app' was his ability to connect different networks of people. In the late 1960s, he started to plug into the world of Stanford computer-research laboratories, located near the *Whole Earth Catalog* office in the Bay Area outside San Francisco. Brand was particularly fascinated by two Stanford institutes: the Augmentation Research

Center (ARC), run by Douglas Englebart, and the Artificial Intelligence Laboratory (AIL), run by John McCarthy. Both the ARC and the AIL were filled with hippies, freaks and potheads. Indeed, the first-ever e-commerce transaction was between members of the ARC buying weed online from their friends at MIT.[6]

Brand was impressed by what he saw at the Stanford research labs. The pothead engineers had a vision of a brave new world in which computers would be like LSD – a tool for the mass liberation of consciousness. Computers gave humans access to another dimension, a virtual world, in which they could create, connect and play. He was amazed when he saw Stanford hackers playing Spacewar, an early computer game developed at MIT. He later told *The Guardian*: 'They were out of their bodies in this game that they'd created out of nothing. They were having an out-of-body experience, and up until that time the only out-of-body experiences I'd seen were drugs.'[7] He filmed the first public demonstration of the personal computer by Douglas Englebart in 1968, the so-called 'mother of all demos'. Previously, the popular conception of computers was as massive mainframes used by giant bureaucracies, like IBM or the Pentagon, to control the masses. Englebart offered a different vision: a personal computer easily controlled by a mouse, a keyboard and a Graphic User Interface, with which ordinary people could create, play, and connect to friends via email and video-teleconferencing. We take these things for granted now, but in 1968 this was nothing short of magic. It looked, one observer recalled, as if Englebart was a wizard, 'dealing lightning' from his hands.

Brand connected the tech world of the Stanford research labs to the spiritual world of the Californian communes. The computer geeks took onboard the methods of the Human Potential Movement as a tool to improve communication and innovation within their labs. Englebart introduced Esalen-style encounter sessions in his lab, as well as LSD-fuelled 'bootcamps' where engineers would dream up new programmes while high. The commune hippies, meanwhile, were struck by the potential of the technologies they saw at Stanford. 'This is the new LSD,' Ken Kesey quipped when he visited the ARC lab. The hippies had sought to escape the shackles of conformist society by moving west and setting up communes. Computing offered them a new 'electronic frontier' in cyberspace. Brand wrote: 'The real legacy of the sixties generation is the computer revolution.'[8]

The World Wide Web as spiritual community

In the 1980s, the market for personal computers took off, thanks to companies like Atari, IBM and Apple, which was run by an LSD-taking former commune-member called Steve Jobs (the name 'Apple' came from a commune where he had worked in the orchard). People started to communicate online through dial-up subscription services. One of the first was the Whole Earth 'Lectronic Link (WELL), set up in 1985 by Brand and his colleague Kevin Kelly. The WELL took the world of Californian communes online – on one popular WELL forum, people shared their reminiscences of life in various communes; on another, they swapped Grateful Dead trivia. In the 1990s, as the number of people online doubled each year, the hippie dream of a liberated, connected, playful humanity seemed to be dawning. Timothy Leary celebrated the rise of a 'neo-ecstatic society': 'The rapid spread of this ecstatic spirit is due to the recent availability of brain-change neuro-transmitters and electronic communication appliances accessible to individuals . . . Ecstatic youth plus electronics.'[9]

The personal computer and the internet would liberate us from evil corporations and enable us to work independently. We wouldn't work for money. Rather, in the spirit of a hippie commune, we would work for free, sharing our software, blogs or podcasts, and collaborating on massive projects, like Wikipedia. Hackers called the new communal spirit 'dot.communism' or 'digital socialism'. The Net would also free us from governments and religions, which had tried to assert a monopoly on ecstasy. One transhumanist, R. U. Sirius, who edited a technology magazine called *Mondo 2000*, called for 'Individual control over mental and emotional states for enhancing functionalities and ecstasies'.[10]

The Web has indeed been disruptive for religions, challenging their monopoly over religious ecstasy and creating a more democratic, non-hierarchical, networked model of spirituality. Instead of relying on the expertise of priests or psychiatrists, people can share their spiritual experiences online and compare notes, in what sociologist Joanna Kempner termed 'collective self-experimentalism'. On the websites Shroomery and Erowid, for example, psychonauts compare experiences on different home-made chemicals. Voice-hearers can compare notes on the Hearing Voices Network. Lucid dreamers compare dream-experiences on World of Lucid Dreaming Forum and LD4All. Contemplatives compare meditation experiences on sites like reddit.com/r/Meditation. No one is in charge, everyone is an authority.

Cyberspace as out-of-body experience

But the Net is more than just a means of self-education and mass communication for transhumanists. Cyberspace is itself a mystical place where you can leave your identities and even your bodies behind. As Erik Davis noted in his book *Tech-Gnosis*, there is a distinctly Gnostic flavour to transhumanist pronouncements – an urge to transcend matter and become pure information. George Gilder, techno-utopian and founder of the Discovery Institute, declared in 1994: 'The central event of the twentieth century is the overthrow of matter . . . The powers of mind are everywhere ascendant over the brute force of things.'[11] Identity in cyberspace is multiple, fluid, networked, ecstatic. We can change name, body shape, skin colour, gender or species, not just in the sense of having a photo of a cat as our profile picture but in the deeper sense of shifting our body-awareness through virtual reality. Jaron Lanier, one of the pioneers of virtual reality, recalls an early VR experiment:

> It turned out that people could quickly learn to inhabit strange and different bodies and still interact with the virtual world . . . The most curious experiment involved a virtual lobster . . . A lobster has a trio of little midriff arms on each side of its body . . . I assume it will not come as a surprise to the reader that the human body does not include these little arms, so the question arose of how to control them. The answer was to extract a little influence from each of many parts of the physical body and merge these

data streams into a single control signal for a given joint in the extra lobster limbs.[12]

The philosopher Thomas Nagel famously asked what it was like to be a bat. We may never know, but through VR we can begin to know what it's like to inhabit the body of a lobster. We can escape from the cage of our own flesh and the prison of our everyday world. Reality is broken, as game psychologist Jane McGonigal put it, but we can build virtual worlds and virtual identities that are satisfying and fulfilling in a way the real world isn't. We can join together in the collective play of the Net. As futurist Kevin Kelly notes, to surf the Net is to dissolve into a 'trancelike state', a dream-world: 'Perhaps we are tapping into our collective unconscious as we roam the web.'[13] We may start by watching foxes bouncing on trampolines, then float into an orgy, then find ourselves in a furious argument about Beyoncé, and then watch a man getting his head cut off. Everything blends into everything else.

The geek rapture

One of the greatest dreams of transhumanists is the Singularity, a day, not far away, when humans will create an artificial intelligence (AI) that becomes conscious and overtakes humans in intelligence. Sci-fi author William Gibson called it 'the geek rapture'.[14] 'We are creating our own successors,' declared the futurist Ray Kurzweil. 'Man will become to the machine what the horse and the dog are to man.'[15] Conscious machines sound far-fetched, but one has only to look at the prediction made by Gordon Moore, co-founder of Intel, in 1965, that the number of transistors per square inch would double every year. He was proved right. Transhumanists predicted this trend would continue into an exponential spike in computer processing power. It is only a matter of time, they insist, before neural nets and other inventions make the dream of AI a reality. We will create conscious machines, and they will have spiritual experiences, just like us. Kevin Kelly, a born-again Christian, looks forward to the day when a computer will say, 'I am a child of God,' and churches will need to find space on their pews for androids. Others foresee a future where AI would itself become God, and would watch over us as 'machines of loving-grace' (in the words of one transhumanist poem).[16] Kurzweil's vision for the Singularity is reminiscent of the early twentieth-century Christian mystic Pierre Teilhard de Chardin, who imagined the material universe becoming progressively more animated by spiritual ecstasy. Kurzweil likewise declares:

> In the aftermath of the Singularity, intelligence, derived from its biological origins in human brains and its technological origins in human ingenuity, will begin to saturate the matter and energy in its midst . . . the universe will become sublimely intelligent and will wake up.

The dot.commune

Beyond these futuristic fantasies, the digital revolution has already created a new model of business, in which work is seen as the principal route to ecstasy and self-actualisation. This is a strange shift from the mid-twentieth century. Back in the fifties and sixties, beatniks and student protesters criticised corporations as soulless bureaucracies that produced what the philosopher Herbert Marcuse called 'one-dimensional men'. They felt there was no room for authenticity, creativity or ecstasy in such companies – the only solution was to drop out and form your own commune. But, in the 1970s, a new corporate model appeared in Bay Area tech start-ups like Apple and Intel: the dot.commune. As in the Stanford research labs, the start-ups would be open-plan, non-hierarchical and informal. Out with suits and ties, in with flip-flops and tie-dye T-shirts. Every worker would be free to chip in and challenge ideas, and the organisation would naturally steer itself. As in a commune, the start-up would encourage personal transparency – everyone could ruthlessly criticise everyone else's ideas and personalities at 'corporate retreats'.

The dot.commune would demand total commitment: start-up workers would sleep at the office when necessary, play at the office, only hang out with other commune-members, and get into a state of Coke-fuelled flow where they could code for many days and nights in a row. 'Working 90 hours a week and loving it!' read T-shirts at Apple's offices in the 1980s.[17] The commune members' reward would be the ecstasy of making something 'insanely great' together. 'It's a wonderful, ecstatic feeling to create,' Steve Jobs declared.[18] The head of the dot.commune would be a guiding Comprehensive Designer (or tyrannical cult-leader, depending on your perspective), wandering barefoot while they dreamed up how to put a dent in the universe. Their product demos would be the corporate equivalent of the Sermon on the Mount. The prototype was Douglas Englebart's famous demo of the personal computer, but Steve Jobs really mastered the product-demo-as-spiritual-experience, orchestrating the audience into a frenzy as if the Holy Spirit were upon them. He also mastered the art of using sixties idealist rhetoric to promote his products. It's not about money, your start-up is leading a revolution, making the world a better place, and so on. Hippie communes had turned away from corporate capitalism in a search for the authentic self. But companies like Apple suggested the real way to authenticity was through consumer capitalism. 'Think different,' ran the advert for the iMac. And we all did.

Corporate ecstasy

The dot.commune model spread from Silicon Valley to other sectors in the 1990s, as terrified old-economy CEOs scrambled to create a culture of innovation before they became obsolete. They forked out thousands to go on spiritual retreats, drink ayahuasca with innovation-shamans, or hang out with Peter Gabriel at Stewart Brand's Global Business Network. They hired management consultants and business coaches to try to bring more 'flow' or 'peak experiences' to their company cultures, so their employees would be as cultishly committed as Silicon Valley hackers. 'People with high flow never miss a day. They never get sick. They never wreck their cars. Their lives just work better,' declared Jim Clifton, CEO of the Gallup Organisation.[19] Consultants

222

made companies open-office, introduced bean-bags, table-football and meditation pods, and sent employees on weekend-long Esalen-type courses, so they re-emerged as the self-transcending managers of the future. I've taught on courses like this and was astonished by the ecstatic outpourings of bobos (business bohemians) searching for career break-throughs. They cry, they laugh, they dance, they discover their inner child, they get on stage to share their breakthroughs. It's a secular version of the Alpha course. Like Don Draper meditating at Esalen in the final scene of *Mad Men*, the transcendence they reach is not a connection to God, but the realisation of a new corporate strategy.

The pioneer of corporate ecstasy, of course, is Anthony Robbins, the multi-millionaire life-coach described as 'the king of the Human Potential Movement'. What do Steve Jobs, Mahatma Gandhi, Mother Teresa and Colonel Sanders all have in common? They all knew the techniques to unleash their inner power, and Robbins can teach them to us. 'You can become ecstatic,' he writes in *Unlimited Power*, 'by imme-diately adopting the point of view that creates that emotion . . . You can adopt the specific postures and breathing patterns that create that state in your body, and *voilà*! You will experience ecstasy.' He teaches people how to reach 'peak states' by techniques like neuro-linguistic programming and fire-walking. Like William James, he insists the best way to change our minds is often through our bodies – he prepares for his seminars by immersing himself in an ice-pool, then bouncing on a trampoline. For the last three decades, Robbins has run seminars for thousands of people, each paying anything from $3,000 to $6,000 for a tent-revival experience. Attendees jump up and down to pumping house music and look to their Leader to guide them to personal break-throughs.

Although Robbins believes in a Higher Power, he preaches our power to make ourselves: 'I constructed this fucking Tony Robbins guy!'[20] He has such unshakeable faith in himself that you can't help believing change is possible for you. Today will be the day you finally shed your baggage and be reborn as a New You. He conducts dramatic therapy interventions with individuals in front of the entire audience, where he challenges their ego-patterns over the course of an hour. By the end of each intervention, as the technicians dim the lights and raise the volume on the background music, everyone in the audience is crying and applauding, crowding round the liberated person to hug them. Robbins is an absolute master at engineering mass ecstatic experiences – that's why he's worth half a billion dollars. Does it really lead to long-lasting personal change? I don't know – probably sometimes. But it doesn't lead to any structural change in the economics of the system: it's all down to you and your personal breakthroughs.

The dark side of tech-ecstasy

We are no longer quite as ecstatic about the New Economy as transhumanists were in the 1990s. We have seen the future, and it doesn't always work. The original wave of tech-optimism led to a massive stock-market bubble, which burst in 1998. Then the rise of high-tech financial trading led to an even bigger speculative bubble, which burst in 2008. Bankers got lost in the virtual worlds of their financial models, until reality knocked them down. Stock-market bubbles seem to me a sort of secular variation on the millenarian ecstasy of the Middle Ages – a new paradigm is upon us! We'll all be rich! A handful of start-ups really do change the world, but most of them just sell hype. The CEO launches their company in a blast of evangelical fervour, the investors pile in despite the lack of any corporate profits, the founders get rich, and then the stock price tanks.[21]

The personal computer and internet were supposed to liberate the individual from the conformist corporation. But the dot.commune can be just as conformist. It can lead to enforced euphoria, enforced corporate retreats, enforced adherence to the dot.commune's cult-like mantras and mission statements. The workers can be forced to devote their entire lives to the dot.commune. The cult of personal transparency and accountability can lead to workers' performance being ceaselessly monitored – nothing is private any more. And there's a major problem with diversity at many Silicon Valley firms. The reason some start-ups feel so emotionally bonded is that engineers mainly employ people like them – white and Asian men in their twenties.

In some ways I love the new economy – as a freelance blogger, the internet enabled me to be creative outside the shackles of the traditional corporation, and gave me the confidence not to be limited by academia's rigid power hierarchies. I, like you, have known the blissful hours when I am utterly absorbed in my work – nothing gives me more flow than writing. The tech journalist Nicholas Carr writes: 'Labour, whether of the body or the mind, is more than a way of getting things done. It's a form of contemplation.'[22]

But for many people, the networked economy has liberated them only from job security, leaving them on precarious short-term contracts. Like Woody in *Toy Story*, we are all on the run from obsolescence. The Bank of England estimates that robot automation threatens up to 50 per cent of jobs in the UK.[23] In the future, when everyone works less, will we use our new leisure to write sonnets and learn languages, or just take opiate painkillers, as 44 per cent of unemployed men do in the US?[24] The old business model, working with the same group of people for several years, seems like another form of community we have lost. Now, in a networked economy, we must ceaselessly market ourselves, online and offline. The individual has become like a hypertext page – you're only as important as your connections. The PC, internet and smartphone were meant to liberate our consciousness, and in some ways they have. But they have also become weapons of mass distraction – we can't concentrate for more than a few minutes without reaching for our phone to see if someone has liked us. The networked economy is surprisingly lonely. We often use the internet not to connect but to retreat from the awkward intimacy of face-to-face encounters. We have become highly dependent and even enslaved by the appliances designed to liberate us. And the 'trance-like' dream of the Net is often a nightmare, where humans get stuck in automatic feedback loops of fear, disgust and loathing. Cybernetic theorist Marshall McLuhan predicted this in 1967. He declared: 'Speedup of information-movement has the effect of putting the whole human Unconscious outside us as an environment – and thereby creating what appears in every way to be a crazy world.'[25]

Tech-hippies as the new elite

Steve Jobs liked to paint Apple as the rebel hero opposing the Big Brother of the old-style corporation (IBM). But rather than *1984*, a better parallel might be *Animal Farm*: the tech-hippies have become the new ruling elite. Apple has become one of the biggest corporations in the world. Rather than distributing wealth, the New Economy led to the greatest concentration of wealth in a small elite since the Robber Barons. Some believe in the transhumanist idea that technology will make us gods, but maybe only the tech-elite will get the upgrade. Historian Yuval Noah Harari writes in his book *Homo Deus*: 'The gap between those who know how to engineer bodies and brains and those who do not will be wider . . . than the gap between Sapiens and Neanderthals.'

Transhumanists' worship of technology reminds me of Romantics' worship of nature or neo-liberals' worship of the invisible hand of the market. All three worship a non-human force and attribute benevolent intentionality to it. Technology will set us free, if we surrender to it. But just as Werner Herzog looked on nature and saw only indifference, so tech-sceptic Nicholas Carr looks on technology and sees only amorality. 'It doesn't care whether it brings us to a higher consciousness or a diminished one,' Carr writes. 'It doesn't give a rat's ass about us.'[26] We can't leave the machines to run everything and expect a harmonious order to emerge. We need democratic deliberation – despite all its messiness and slowness – because otherwise the masses end up being controlled by machines, or by the people who control the machines.

The religion of Big Data or AI or the coming Singularity could be seen as a massive con, a way to dazzle the masses while enriching the new tech-priesthood. Technologist Jaron Lanier told the Edge Foundation:

> There's an anticipation of a threshold, an end of days . . . In the history of organised religion, it's often been the case that people have been disempowered precisely to serve what were perceived to be the needs of some deity or another, where in fact what they were doing was supporting an elite class that was the priesthood

for that deity . . . The new elite might say, 'It's not us, they're helping the AI.' It reminds me of somebody saying, 'Oh, build these pyramids, it's in the service of this deity,' but, on the ground, it's in the service of an elite.[27]

Thus the founders of Google hope to build a supermind through programs like Google Books and Google News. But, really, their algorithms are scooping up content created by human beings – writers, translators, journalists, musicians – and centralising the profit in the one per cent who control the algorithms. Apple, Facebook, Twitter, Spotify, YouTube, Oculus Rift and others promise to liberate our consciousness and improve our lives through their products, and they often do. But they control the platforms where we congregate and confess, and they monetise our communion. As in a cult, we all work for free, sharing our epiphanies online, while the controllers of the cult get rich. And we go along with this because we're terrified of being thrown out of the commune. What could be worse than being disconnected from the Net?

The ecstasy of escape

Transhumanism can lead to what Erik Davis calls 'the theology of the ejector seat':[28] the planet may be heading for eco-devastation, but the one per cent dream of escape to Huxley-esque island-utopias. They can sail away to the floating islands being engineered by libertarian tech-investor Peter Thiel, which he suggests will give the tech-elite an 'escape from politics in all its forms'.[29] Or they can beam themselves up to the space colonies being designed by billionaire-entrepreneur Elon Musk. Transhumanism can lead to a superhero fantasy of flying beyond nature, beyond Earth, beyond matter. It is unearthed ecstasy, literally – it misses the importance of humility. It's a fantasy of being in perfect control of one's mind and body. It's not really *trans*humanist, because there is nothing beyond the human to surrender to – not God, or spirit, just the reflective mirror of technology into which we leer and flex our muscles. The more we strive to become gods, by engineering a perfect human in ourselves or our children, the less we will be able to accept our imperfections, vulnerabilities and shadow selves. The dream of the perfectly engineered superman, when embraced in the past, led to the eugenicist elimination of those deemed unfit.

The ultimate transhumanist fantasy is escaping death. Ray Kurzweil is sure that we're about to reach a threshold where technology will fix the mortality bug. He takes 250 supplements a day and receives a half-dozen intravenous therapies each week, in a desperate bid to stave off death until death is hacked. Other transhumanists cryogenically freeze themselves so they can be thawed in the future, or dream of uploading their consciousness to a hard-drive. This transhumanist fixation was predicted and satirised by Aldous Huxley, in his novel *After Many a Summer,* about a Californian tycoon who tries to conquer death through technology. I think transhumanists misunderstand death, because they misunderstand consciousness. They think it is the same as intelligence or information – we can upload information to a computer, so why not our consciousness? Machines can learn, so why can't they become self-conscious? As we strive to become tech-augmented gods, we may realise that the thing that really makes us god-like – consciousness – cannot be engineered, and cannot be destroyed either. I think of Steve Jobs's last words in his hospital room as he gazed into the distance: 'Oh, wow! Oh, wow! Oh, wow!' I know this is a minority view among academics, but I think when we die we encounter a consciousness far superior to us. And we are connected to it through love. I believe this because of my own near-death experience, but also because of evidence from other people's NDEs and mystical experiences on psychedelics (which reliably reduce people's fear of death), and from the authority of mystics from the Buddha to Plato to Jesus. Consciousness, Thomas Traherne suggested, is deeply connected to love. Let me quote him again, just because it's such a beautiful and genuinely transhumanist passage:

> Love is deeper than at first it can be thought. It never ceaseth but in endless things. It ever multiplies ... By Loving a Soul does propagate and beget itself. By Loving it does dilate and magnify

itself. By Loving it does enlarge and delight itself . . . But above all by Loving it does attain itself.

Love is what's missing from the cybernetic model of consciousness and of society. Love is not a technology, it's not an information-processing algorithm, it's a relationship. Look at a small child – in some ways they are 'learning machines', but how they really learn and grow, how they really connect to their parents and to the world, is not just through information but through love. Their consciousness expands and flowers through love. A 'transhumanism' worthy of the name would recognise the importance of love, empathy and relationships in self-transcendence, not merely mechanistic techniques and life-hacks.

Fare forward, voyagers

It's time we headed to the campsite and called it a night. I've lost my phone, I have gold glitter in my beard, and I seem to be wearing a tutu. You should see what you look like. Let's get the hell out of here. But what should we take with us?

As we entered the festival, I talked about balancing two different paths to healing – the Socratic, and the Dionysiac. My first book looked at how we can heal our psyches using Greek philosophy, while this book has explored an alternative path to flourishing, through altered states of consciousness and the body. These two approaches are complementary – a healthy philosophy of life integrates both. Without Dionysus, the Socratic path risks becoming arid, over-cerebral rationalism. Without Socratic ethical reflection and practice, Dionysiac ecstasy is just a rush. Both Socrates and Dionysus are useful allies in our journey beyond the ego towards self-transcendence. Today, finally, there is a consensus emerging among psychologists and psychiatrists that ecstatic experiences are not pathological, that they're one of the most valuable experiences humans can have. There are certainly risks to ego-loss – we have examined them at length – but we can learn to mitigate the risks. And simply banning ecstasy is not an option, as King Pentheus learned. The fruits of ecstasy are that it's healing, it's creatively inspiring, it's socially connecting, and it gives people a sense of meaning and hope in the face of death.

Aldous Huxley, to my mind, was more or less the only person in our culture who properly grappled with the question of how to reorder our society to balance the Socratic and the Dionysiac. He came up with an answer of sorts in his last novel, *Island*, although it was a plan for a small utopia, rather than a large multicultural democracy. What would a politics of ecstasy look like for a whole society? We already see promising initiatives – we need more academic and independent centres of research into wisdom. These centres should be interdisciplinary, blending the sciences and the humanities, as Huxley and James did so successfully. And they should combine cutting-edge research with practical courses for ordinary people. We need a lot more research to understand how the arts alter our consciousness and our bodies, and how this can be healing. We need to expand our concept of education beyond the cognitive-rational, to explore what Huxley called 'non-verbal education', finding more of a place for the arts, sports, nature and contemplation in our schools and universities.

We need a new infrastructure of contemplation, neo-monasteries, including institutions that research and teach contemplative techniques from various different traditions, not just secular Buddhism. And we need a more convivial conversation between different religions and philosophies, recognising that we all seek transcendence, humbly comparing notes, and helping each other along the way. We in Europe should explore and preserve our inherited religion, the garden our ancestors grew for us, even if we don't literally believe all of it. But we should also be prepared to improvise new scripts, as the transhumanists are doing. Will Christianity revive in the West, or Islam take over, or some new cult of nature or technology arise? I honestly don't know, but I suspect the religion of the future needs to be scientifically literate and eco-friendly. Personally, I've struggled with religious community over the last four years – in some ways, I'm just as much of an individualist as I ever was – but one of the best communities I've found is a group of friends who check in with each other every month or so over dinner. It includes a chaplain who runs the Alpha course, and a comedian who runs the humanist group, Sunday Assembly. We can create communities of friendship even if we have different metaphysics.

As for me, I'm still learning to lose control. I'm sure many of you have explored a lot further beyond the ego than I have, and learned a lot more than me. Keep exploring. The internet lets us share our experiences and learn from each other. I covered a lot but I left a lot out – I didn't discuss light, or time, or laughter, or food, or mediums, or properly explore the relationship between ecstasy and the feminine. It's effing difficult to talk about the ineffable. I'll be content if this book serves to bring this conversation more into the mainstream of our culture. In some ways, writing a book about losing control is an oxymoron: you retreat to your attic, stay in control, and tinker with the festival in your head. That's not the same as the surrender of love: that surrender lies out there, beyond these pages. I went searching for the white light that I encountered on the mountain in Norway, and spent five years chasing it, like Alice chasing the White Rabbit. But I didn't find it again, not in such a direct form. It's frustrating to know that deeper states of mind are available *right here and now*, yet so rarely feel them. I have a sense of the cosmos as a vast ecosystem brimming with higher intelligences, and yet I wonder, why aren't they more chatty? Perhaps I could have got further if I'd been more self-disciplined. I've always believed in reincarnation, which in practical terms means I'm a bit of a slob – I don't mind if my journey to enlightenment happens at a very leisurely pace. But I hope that, when I die, I will encounter the white light once again. We'll stand face to face, look deeply into each other, and say in unison, 'What took you so long?'

Notes

Introduction: Welcome to the Festival

1. Huxley, Aldous. *The Devils of Loudun*. London: Vintage Classics, 2005.
2. Maslow, Abraham. *Religions, Values and Peak Experiences*. Columbus: Ohio State University Press, 1964.
3. Csíkszentmihályi, Mihály. *Flow: The Psychology of Optimal Experience*. New York: Harper Perennial, 1991.
4. Murdoch, Iris. *The Sovereignty of Good*. London: Routledge, 2001.
5. Gordon Wasson, R. *The Road to Eleusis: Unveiling the Secret of the Mysteries*. Berkeley: North Atlantic Books, 1978.
6. The obesity figure comes from the NHS's obesity statistics for 2014; the alcohol-dependency figure comes from Alcohol Concern's online alcohol statistics; the US National Institute on Drug Abuse estimated 2.1 million Americans were addicted to opiate painkillers in 2012 and almost half a million addicted to heroin, in evidence given to the US Senate Caucus on International Narcotics Control.
7. Sontag, Susan. 'The Pornographic Imagination', *The Susan Sontag Reader*. New York: Farrar, Strauss and Giroux, 1982.
8. Bourguignon, Erika. *Religion, Altered States of Consciousness, and Social Change*. Columbus: Ohio University Press, 1973.
9. Taylor, Charles. *A Secular Age*. Harvard: Harvard University Press, 2007.
10. Heyd, Michael. *"Be Sober and Reasonable": The Critique of Enthusiasm in the Seventeenth and Early Eighteenth Centuries*. London: Brill, 1995.
11. Pocock, J.G.A. 'Enthusiasm: The Anti-Self of Enlightenment', *Huntington Library Quarterly*, Vol. 60, No. 1/2.

12. Smith, Adam. *The Wealth of Nations*. New York: Modern Library, 2000.

13. See, for example, Tylor, Edward Burnett, *Primitive Culture*. Cambridge: Cambridge University Press, 2010.

14. Ehrenreich, Barbara. *Dancing in the Streets: A History of Collective Joy*. New York: Metropolitan Books, 2006.

15. There are several books on the history of hysteria, but my favourite is Taves, Ann, *Fits, Trances and Visions: Experiencing Religion and Explaining Experience from Wesley to James*. Princeton: Princeton University Press, 1999.

16. As recently as 1950 the Catholic theologian Ronald Knox sniffed: 'The history of enthusiasm is largely the history of female emancipation . . . and it is not a reassuring one.' Knox, Ronald. *Enthusiasm: A Chapter in the History of Religion*. Notre Dame: University of Notre Dame Press, 1994.

17. Huxley, Aldous. 'Visionary Spectacle'. In *Moksha: Aldous Huxley's Classic Writings on Psychedelics and the Visionary Experience*. Rochester: Park Street Press, 1977.

18. Berger, Peter. *A Rumour of Angels: Modern Society and the Rediscovery of the Supernatural*. New York: Doubleday, 1969.

19. Robinson, Marilynne. *The Givenness of Things*. New York: Macmillan, 2015.

20. For Hitchens' quote on ecstasy, see here: http://www.philosophyforlife.org/hitchens-on-ecstasy.

21. Cardena, Etzel, and Carlos Alvarado. 'Altered Consciousness From the Age of Enlightenment Through Mid-20th-Century'. In *Altering Consciousness: Multidisciplinary Perspectives*. Santa Barbara: Praeger, 2011.

22. See Newberg, Andrew, *Principles of Neurotheology*. Farnham: Ashgate, 2010. The psychologist Julian Jaynes put forward a theory in his *The Origin of Consciousness in the Breakdown of the Bicameral Mind* (New York: Mariner Books, 1976) that ecstatic experiences are the right hemisphere of the brain suddenly communicating with the left. The theory was recently refined by Iain McGilchrist in *The Divided Brain and the Search for Meaning* (New Haven: Yale University Press, 2009). I haven't explored this theory in this book – although future research may uncover more on this interesting possibility.

23. Durkheim, Émile. *The Elementary Forms of Religious Life*. Oxford: Oxford World Classics, 2008; Lewis, I. M. *Ecstatic Religion: A Study of Shamanism and Spirit-Possession*. London: Routledge, 2002; Turner, Victor. *The Ritual Process: Structure and Anti-Structure*. New York: Transaction Books, 2011; Haidt, Jonathan. *The Righteous Mind: Why Good People are Divided by Politics and Religion*. London: Penguin, 2012.

24. Luhrmann, Tanya. *When God Talks Back: Understanding the American Evangelical Relationship with God*. New York: Viking Press, 2012.

25. James, William. 'What is an emotion?', *Mind*, Vol. 9, No. 34. See also Damasio, Antonio. *Descartes' Error*. New York: Putnam's, 1994; Porges, Stephen. *The Polyvagal Theory: Neurophysiological Foundations of Emotions, Attachment, Communication and Self-regulation*. New York: W. W. Norton and Company, 2011.

26. Aristotle. *Politics*, Book VIII. Penguin, 1981.

27. Howden, L. M., and J. A. Meyer. 'Loneliness Among Older Adults: A National Survey of Adults 45+'. AARP, September 2010; Age and Sex Composition in the United States: 2010 Census Brief. See also Age UK's 'Loneliness and Isolation Evidence Review'; and Undy, Helen, et al. 'The Way We Are Now: 2015', Relate, 1 September 2015.

28. Quoted in Pytell, Timothy, 'Transcending the Angel beast: Viktor Frankl and humanistic psychology', *Psychoanalytic Psychology*, Vol. 23, No. 3 (2006).

29. Armstrong, Karen. 'Ecstasy gone awry', *The Guardian*, 23 May 2003.

30. Kornfield, Jack. *After the Ecstasy, the Laundry: How the Heart Grows Wise on the Spiritual Journey*. New York: Random House, 2001.

1: The Entrance Gate

1. Ehrenreich, Barbara. *Living with a Wild God: A Nonbeliever's Search for the Truth about Everything*. New York: Hachette, 2014.

2. Chotiner, Isaac. 'Barbara Ehrenreich: I'm an atheist, but don't rule out mystical experiences'. *New Republic*, 21 April 2014.

3. Quoted in Rankin, Marilynne, *An Introduction to Religious and Spiritual Experience*. London: Bloomsbury, 2009.

4. Hardy, Alister. *The Spiritual Nature of Man*. London: Clarendon Press, 1979.

5. You can see the full results here: http://www.philosophyforlife.org/the-spiritual-experiences-survey.

6. Hay, David. *Religious Experience Today: Studying the Facts*. London: Mowbray, 1990.

7. All entries in the RERC database are available online at http://www.uwtsd.ac.uk/library/alister-hardy-religious-experience-research-centre/online-archive.

8. Russell, Bertrand. *The Autobiography of Bertrand Russell*. London: Routledge, 2014.

9. Quoted in Alcoholics Anonymous, *Pass It On: The Story of Bill Wilson and How the AA Message Reached the World*. New York: Alcoholics Anonymous, 1984.

10. Books by NDE researchers include Lommel, Pim van, *Consciousness Beyond Life*. London: Harper Collins, 2010; Fenwick, Peter, and Elizabeth Fenwick, *The Truth in the Light*. Hove: White Crow Books, 2012. For a sceptical take, see Blackmore, Susan, *Dying to Live: Near-Death Experiences*. New York: Prometheus Books, 1993.

11. Shushan, Gregory. *Conceptions of the Afterlife in Early Civilizations*. London: Bloomsbury, 2011.

12. Roach, David. 'Heaven tourism books pulled from nearly 200 Christian bookstores'. *Baptist Press*, 15 March 2015.

13. See Sommer, Andreas, *Psychical Research and the Formation of Modern Psychology*, due to be published in 2017, Stanford University Press.

14. Longden, Eleanor. 'Making Sense of Voices: A personal story of recovery', *Psychosis*, Vol. 2, No. 3 (October 2010).

15. Cardena, Etzel, Steven J. Lynn and Stanley Krippner. *Varieties of Anomalous Experience*. New York: American Psychological Association, 2013.

16. See the work of Anil Seth at University College, London. For example, 'The hard problem of consciousness is a distraction from the real one', *Aeon*, 2 November 2016.

17. Myers, Frederic. *Human Personality and its Survival after Bodily Death*. New York: Dover Publications, 2005.

18. Grof, Stanislav, and Christina Grof. *Spiritual Emergency: When Personal Transformation Becomes a Crisis*. New York: Hachette, 1989.

19. Heriot-Maitland, Charles, Matthew Knight and Emmanuelle Peters. 'A qualitative comparison of psychotic-like phenomena in clinical and non-clinical populations'. *British Journal of Clinical Psychology*, Vol. 51, No. 37–53 (2012)

20. Quoted in Fernyhough, Charles, *The Voices Within: the History and Science of How We Talk to Ourselves*. London: Profile Books, 2016.

21. See the Pew Research Centre's report 'Americans may be getting less religious, but feelings of spirituality are on the rise': http://www.pewresearch.org/fact-tank/2016/01/21/americans-spirituality.

2: The Revival Tent

1. Wiseman's comment was made at a Conway Hall event in 2016. Church attendance figures from the Church of England's annual attendance survey, Statistics for Mission, the non-religious outnumbered the religious in the UK in 2013, according to the NatCen British Social Attitudes survey.

2. Micklethwait, John, and Adrian Wooldridge. *God Is Back: How the Global Rise of Faith Is Changing the World*. London: Allen Lane, 2009. For Schama's remarks on Alpha, see Brownie, Marie, 'Britain is becoming a more religious place, says historian', *Christian Today*, 26 June 2014.

3. You can watch all the Alpha talks here: https://www.youtube.com/user/thealphacourse.

4. Chaeyoon, Lim, and Robert Putnam. 'Religion, Social Networks, and Life Satisfaction', *American Sociological Review*, Vol. 75 (December 2010): http://asr.sagepub.com/content/75/6/914.abstract.

5. Roberts, Emyr, and R. Geraint Gruffydd. *Revival and its Fruit*. Bryntirion: Bryntirion Press, 1981.

6. For a marvellously snooty denunciation of revivalism, see Knox, Ronald, *Enthusiasm: A Chapter in the History of Religion*. Notre Dame: University of Notre Dame Press, 1994.

7. Ostling, Richard. 'Laughing for the Lord', *Time*, 15 August 1994.

8. To be specific, I was told that as a Christian I must accept the teachings of St Paul as 'God-breathed'. Some Christians, including the Bishop of London, have since told me I don't need to accept everything St Paul says. HTB doesn't specifically teach the inerrancy of the Bible.

9. On the search for the historical Jesus, see Ehrman, Bart, *Jesus, Interrupted: Revealing the Hidden Contradictions in the Bible*. New York: Harper Collins, 2009. For a debate on the nature of Jesus, see Borg, Marcus, and N. T. Wright, *The Meaning of Jesus: Two Visions*. New York: Harper Collins, 1999. On the Church's exclusion of non-canonical gospels, see Pagels, Elaine, *The Gnostic Gospels*. New York: Random House, 1979.

10. Dein's comment was made at a seminar on cultural psychiatry at Queen Mary University of London in 2016. For a meta-analysis of prayer and healing, see Hodge, David R., 'A Systematic Review of the Empirical Literature on Intercessory Prayer'. *Research on Social Work Practice*, Vol. 17, No. 2 (March 2007).

11. Luhrmann, Tanya. *When God Talks Back: Understanding the American Evangelical Relationship with God*. New York: Viking Press, 2012.

12. See Will Allen's documentary *Holy Hell* (WRA productions, 2016) about a Californian cult that worshipped a man as the living embodiment of God. He was actually a porn actor and serial abuser, but was still capable of sending his followers into altered states of consciousness, simply through the powers they attributed to him.

13. Charcot, Jean-Martin. 'The Faith Cure': http://trove.nla.gov.au/newspaper/article/3556990.

14. You can watch the clip of the Pentecostal preachers defending their use of

private jets here: https://www.youtube.com/watch?v=AdH2DGSXjss&feature=youtu.be.

15. It's a comparison he often makes, for example in Ford, David. *The Future of Christian Theology*. London: Wiley, 2011.

16. Quoted in Dyer, Geoff, *But Beautiful*. Edinburgh: Canongate Books, 2012.

3: The Ecstatic Cinema

1. In a survey I did in 2016, most respondents said they sometimes had 'big dreams' which were unusually vivid and memorable, but such dreams didn't happen very often. They mainly happened during life-crisis, and people found them helpful in adapting to those crises. You can read more about the survey here: http://www.philosophyforlife.org/the-big-dream-survey.

2. Jung, Carl. *The Essential Jung*. London: Fontana Press, 1998, particularly pages 71 and 91.

3. Jung, Carl. *Man and His Symbols*. New York: Doubleday, 1964.

4. From his John Peel lecture, which you can read here: http://downloads.bbc.co.uk/6music/johnpeellecture/brian-eno-john-peel-lecture.pdf.

5. Eliade, Mircea. *Shamanism: Archaic Techniques of Ecstasy*. Princeton: Princeton University Press, 1951.

6. See Lewis-Williams, David, *The Mind in the Cave: Consciousness and the Origins of Art*. London: Thames & Hudson, 2002.

7. See McNamer, Sarah, *Affective Meditation and the Invention of Medieval Compassion*. Philadelphia: University of Pennsylvania Press, 2010.

8. Huxley, Aldous. 'Visionary Spectacle'. In *Moksha: Aldous Huxley's Classic Writings on Psychedelics and the Visionary Experience*. Rochester: Park Street Press, 1977.

9. In conversation at the Sydney Writers' Festival in 2015, available here: https://soundcloud.com/sydneywritersfestival/john-bell-and-jonathan-bate-on-shakespeare. See also Bate, Jonathan, *The Genius of Shakespeare*. London: Pan Macmillan, 1998.

10. *In Our Time: Metamorphoses*, BBC Radio 4, 2 March 2000. Available here: http://www.bbc.co.uk/inourtimeprototype/episode/p00546p6.

11. Coleridge, Samuel. 'Progress of the Drama'. In *Coleridge on Shakespeare*. London: Routledge, 2013.

12. Laski, Marghanita. *Ecstasy: A Study of Some Secular and Religious Experiences*. West Point: Greenwood Press, 1961.

13. Rosenbaum, Ron. *The Shakespeare Wars*. New York: Random House, 2006.

14. Martz, Louis L. *The Poetry of Meditation: A Study in English Religious Literature of the Seventeenth Century.* New Haven: Yale University Press, 1976.

15. Hulme, T. E. 'Romanticism and Classicism'. In *Selected Writings*. Manchester: Fyfield Books, 2003.

16. My interview with Guite is on my website, but see also Guite, Malcolm, *Faith, Hope and Poetry: Theology and the Poetic Imagination.* Farnham: Ashgate Books, 2012.

17. In a tweet, 9 December 2014.

18. Speer, Nicole K., *et al.* 'Reading stories activates neural representations of visual and motor experiences'. *Psychological Science,* Vol. 20, No. 8 (August 2009); available here: https://www.ncbi.nlm.nih.gov/pmc/articles/PMC2819196.

19. Diderot, Denis. 'Elegy for Richardson', 1762. Available online here: http://graduate.engl.virginia.edu/enec981/dictionary/25diderotC1.html.

20. On fantasy fiction's power to create otherworlds, see Tolkien, J. R. R. 'On Fairy Stories'. In *Tree and Leaf.* London: HarperCollins, 2009.

21. There are several studies of epiphany in the novel, including Kim, Sharon, *Literary Epiphany in the Novel, 1850–1950.* London: Palgrave, 2012.

22. See Crichton Miller, Emma, 'Is art a window into another world?'. *Aeon,* 14 December 2012: https://aeon.co/essays/is-art-a-window-into-another-world.

23. Prinz, Jesse. 'Why wonder is the most human of all emotions'. *Aeon,* 21 June 2013: https://aeon.co/essays/why-wonder-is-the-most-human-of-all-emotions.

24. Nietzsche, Friedrich. *Human, All Too Human.* London: Penguin Classics, 1994.

25. Richter, Gerhard. *Writings 1961–2007.* New York: Distributed Art Publishers, 2009.

26. Tillich, Paul. *On Art and Architecture.* New York: Crossroad, 1987.

27. In Rodman, Seldman, *Conversations with Artists.* New York: Devon Adair, 1957.

28. Elkins, James. *Pictures and Tears: A History of People Who Have Cried In Front of Paintings.* London: Routledge, 2001; Winterson, Jeanette. *Art Objects: Essays on Ecstasy and Effrontery.* London: Random House, 1995.

29. Akers, Matthew, and Jeff Dupre. *The Artist is Present, HBO,* 2012.

30. See Caputo, Giovanni, 'Dissociation and hallucinations in dyads engaged through interpersonal gazing'. *Psychiatry Research,* Vol. 228, No. 3 (30 August 2015). See also Nagasawa, Miho, *et al.,* 'Oxytocin-gaze positive loop and the co-evolution of human-dog bonds', *Science,* Vol. 348, No. 6232 (17 April 2015).

31. For Eisenstein on ecstasy, see Eisenstein, Sergei, *Nonindifferent Nature.* Cambridge: Cambridge University Press, 1987. See also Werner Herzog's lecture, 'On the Absolute, the Sublime, and Ecstatic Truth'. Available here: http://www.bu.edu/arion/on-the-absolute-the-sublime-and-ecstatic-truth/.

32. Quoted in 'Surrealist Cinema', *Arena,* BBC, 1987.

33. Stanley Kubrick, in a 1965 interview by Joseph Gelmis: '*2001* . . . is basically a visual, nonverbal experience. It avoids intellectual verbalisation and reaches the viewer's subconscious in a way that is essentially poetic and philosophic.' Available here: http://www.visual-memory.co.uk/amk/doc/0069.html.

34. Recounted in Agel, Jerome, *The Making of Kubrick's* 2001. Los Angeles: New American Library, 1970.

35. For more on the links between animism and animation, see my essay 'Everything is Full of Gods', http://www.philosophyforlife.org/everything-is-full-of-gods.

36. Kelly, Kevin. *The Inevitable: Understanding the 12 Technological Forces That Will Shape Our Future.* London: Viking Press, 2016.

37. See Myers, Frederic, *Human Personality and its Survival after Bodily Death.* New York: Dover Publications, 2005. See also the chapter on genius in Kelly, Edward, and Emily Williams Kelly, *Irreducible Mind: Towards a Psychology for the 21st Century.* London: Rowman & Littlefield, 2007. For the survey on authors and hearing voices, see Fernyhough, Charles, *The Voices Within: The History and Science of How We Talk to Ourselves.* London: Profile Books, 2016.

38. Lynch, David. *Catching the Big Fish: Meditation, Consciousness and Creativity.* London: Penguin, 2006; Hughes, Ted, 'Poetry in the making'. In *Winter Pollen.* London: Faber & Faber, 1995. For explorations of poetry, creativity and ecstasy, read Hirsch, Edward, *The Demon and the Angel.* New York: Houghton Mifflin Harcourt, 2002; and Moores, D. J., *The Ecstatic Poetic Tradition.* Jefferson: McFarland Press, 2014.

39. Quoted in Freud, Sigmund, *The Interpretation of Dreams.* London: Basic Books, 2000.

40. This and preceding quotes from Hirsch, *The Demon and the Angel.*

41. Iyer, Pico. *The Man Within My Head.* London: Vintage Books, 2012.

42. Listen to my interview with Roger Scruton here: https://www.youtube.com/watch?v=_OJ17FFDOxE.

4: Rock and Roll Main Stage

1. On music and courtship, see Miller, Geoffrey, 'Evolution of human music through sexual selection'. In *The Origins of Music.* Cambridge: MIT Press, 2001. On music and bonding, see Pearce, Eiluned, *et al.*, 'The ice-breaker effect: singing mediates fast social bonding'. *Royal Society Open Science*, Vol. 2. No. 10 (October 2015).

2. Hobbs, Dawn R., and Gordon G. Gallup. 'Songs as a Medium for Embedded Reproductive Messages'. *Evolutionary Psychology*, Vol. 9, No. 3 (July 2011).

3. Quoted in Lewis, I. M., *Ecstatic Religion: A Study of Shamanism and Spirit-Possession*. London: Routledge, 2002.

4. Al-Ghazzali. *Al-Ghazzali On Listening to Music*. Lahore: Kazi Publications, 2003.

5. Lewis, *Ecstatic Religion*.

6. For music as a trance-inducing ritual, see Becker, Judith, *Deep Listeners: Music, Emotion and Trancing*. Bloomington: Indiana University Press, 2004.

7. See Ehrenreich, Barbara, *Dancing in the Streets: A History of Collective Joy*. New York: Metropolitan Books, 2006.

8. Guralnick, Peter. *Sweet Soul Music: Rhythm and Blues and the Southern Dream of Freedom*. Edinburgh: Canongate Books, 2002.

9. See Mosher, Craig, 'Ecstatic Sounds: The Influence of Pentecostalism on Rock & Roll'. *Popular Music and Society*. Vol. 31, No. 1 (2008).

10. In a speech at South by Southwest festival, available here: http://www.rollingstone.com/music/news/dave-grohls-sxsw-keynote-speech-the-complete-text-20130315.

11. For example, in Bloom, Allan, *Closing of the American Mind*. New York: Simon & Schuster, 1988; and Scruton, Roger, *Modern Culture*. London: Continuum Books, 1998.

12. Interview with Dalton, David, *Rolling Stone*, 28 May 1970: http://www.rollingstone.com/music/features/little-richard-child-of-god-19700528.

13. See Levitin, Daniel, *This Is Your Brain On Music*. Boston: Dutton, 2006; Jourdain, Robert. *Music, the Brain and Ecstasy*. London: Harper Collins, 1997.

14. Moore, Kimberly, 'A systematic review of the neural effects of music on emotional regulation'. *Journal of Musical Therapy*, Vol. 50, No. 3.

15. Ellis, Robert J., and Julian F. Thayer. 'Music and Autonomic Nervous System (Dys)function'. *Music Perception*, Vol. 27, No. 4. See also Porges, Stephen W., *The Polyvagal Theory: Neuro-Physiological Foundations of Emotions, Attachment, Communications and Self-Regulation*. New York: W.W. Norton, 2011.

16. See Becker, *Deep Listeners*.

17. Vickhoff, Bjorn, *et al.* 'Music structure determines heart rate variability of singers'. *Frontiers of Psychology*, 9 July 2013

18. Haidt, Jonathan. *The Righteous Mind: Why Good People are Divided by Politics and Religion*. New York: Pantheon, 2012.

19. Kennaway, James. *Bad Vibrations: The History of the Idea of Music as a Cause of Disease*. Farnham: Ashgate, 2012.

20. Interview with Beyoncé, *Marie Claire*, 16 September 2008: http://www.marieclaire.co.uk/news/celebrity-news/beyonce-interview-182533.

21. Maconie, Stuart. 'Ziggy Stardust changed our lives', *Daily Mirror*, 7 June 2012.

22. Collin, Matthew. *Altered State: The Story of Ecstasy Culture and Acid House*. London: Profile Books, 1997.

23. Quoted in Collin, *Altered State*.

24. Lachman, Gary. *Aleister Crowley: Magick, Rock and Roll, and the Wickedest Man in the World*. London: Penguin, 2014.

25. *Cracked Actor*, BBC documentary, 1975.

5: Psychedelic Wonderland

1. Johnson, Matthew, *et al.* 'Pilot study of the 5-HT2AR agonist psilocybin in the treatment of tobacco addiction'. *Journal of Psychopharmacology*, 11 September 2014.

2. Krebs, Teri, and Pai-Orian Johnasen. 'Lysergic acid diethylamide (LSD) for alcoholism: Meta-analysis of randomized controlled trials'. *Journal of Psychopharmacology*, Vol. 26, No. 7 (July 2012). See also Sessa, Ben, 'Can psychedelics have a role in psychiatry once again?' *British Journal of Psychiatry*, Vol. 186 (2005).

3. Carhart-Harris, Robin, *et al.* 'Psilocybin with psychological support for treatment-resistant depression: an open-label feasibility study'. *Lancet Psychiatry*, 17 May 2016.

4. Catlow, B. J., *et al.* 'Effects of psilocybin on hippocampal neurogenesis and extinction of trace fear conditioning'. *Experimental Brain Research*, Vol. 228, No. 4 (August 2013).

5. Grob, Charles, *et al.* 'Pilot Study of Psilocybin Treatment for Anxiety in Patients With Advanced-Stage Cancer'. *Archive of General Psychiatry*, Vol. 68, No. 1 (2011). The two most recent studies of psilocybin as palliative treatment for the terminally ill are Ross, Stephen, *et al.*, and Griffiths, Roland, *et al.*, both in a special issue of the *Journal of Psychopharmacology*, No. 30 (December 2016).

6. Marsa, Linda. 'How psychedelics are helping cancer patients fend off despair'. *Aeon*, 28 March 2014.

7. Griffiths, Roland. 'Psilocybin can occasion mystical-type experiences having substantial and sustained personal meaning and spiritual significance'. *Psychopharmacology*, 26 May 2006.

8. Grof, Stanislav. *LSD Psychotherapy*. Alameda: Hunter House, 1994.

9. Lewis-Williams, David. *The Mind in the Cave: Consciousness and the Origins of Art*. London: Thames & Hudson, 2002.

10. Gordon Wasson, R. *Soma: Divine Mushroom of Immortality*. San Diego: Harcourt, 1968.

11. Gordon Wasson, R. *The Road to Eleusis: Unveiling the Secret of the Mysteries*. Berkeley: North Atlantic Books, 1978.

12. Quoted in Gasser, Peter, *et al*., 'LSD-assisted psychotherapy for anxiety associated with a life-threatening disease: A quantitative study of acute and sustained subjective effects'. *Journal of Psychopharmacology*, Vol. 1, No. 12 (2014).

13. Huxley, Aldous. *Moksha: Aldous Huxley's Classic Writings on Psychedelics and the Visionary Experience*. Rochester: Park Street Press, 1977.

14. You can read Wasson's Life article here: http://www.imaginaria.org/wasson/life.htm.

15. Hoffman, Albert. *LSD, My Problem Child*. Santa Cruz: MAPS, 2005.

16. James Fadiman interview on the Tim Ferriss podcast, available here: http://fourhourworkweek.com/2015/03/21/james-fadiman/.

17. Carhart-Harris, Robin, *et al*. 'The entropic brain: a theory of conscious states informed by neuroimaging research with psychedelic drugs'. *Frontiers in Human Neuroscience*, 3 February 2014.

18. Hill, Scott J. *Confrontation with the Unconscious: Jungian Depth Psychology and Psychedelic Experience*. London: Muswell Hill Press, 2013.

19. Quoted in *Psychedelic Science*, BBC Radio 4, 7 April 2016.

20. In Forte, Robert (ed.), *Entheogens and the Future of Religion*. New York: Inner Traditions Books, 2012.

21. Carbonaro, T., *et al*. 'Survey study of challenging experiences after ingesting psilocybin mushrooms'. *Journal of Psychopharmacology*, 30 August 2016.

22. See Szabo, Attila, 'Psychedelics and immunomodulation: novel approaches and therapeutic opportunities'. *Frontiers in Immunology*, 14 July 2015.

23. Sacks, Oliver. *Hallucinations*. London: Pan Macmillan, 2012.

24. Sting, *Broken Music: A Memoir*. London: Random House, 2005.

25. You can watch Freimoser and Fountoglou's presentation from Breaking Convention here: https://vimeo.com/141606158.

26. Strassman, Rick. *DMT: The Spirit-Molecule*. New York: Inner Traditions, 2000.

27. See Doblin, Rick, 'Pahnke's 'Good Friday Experiment': A Long-Term Follow-Up and Methodological Critique'. Available here: http://www.neurosoup.com/pdf/doblin_goodfriday_followup.pdf.

28. Quoted in Smith, Huston, 'Do drugs have religious import?' *Journal of Philosophy*, Vol. LXI, No. 18 (17 September 1964).

6: The Contemplation Zone

1. MacCulloch, Diarmaid. *Silence: A Christian History*. London: Penguin, 2013.

2. The best history of Western mysticism is Bernard McGinn's *Presence of God* (New York: Crossroad, 1994, 1998, 2005, 2013, 2017), the first four volumes of which have been published. Professor McGinn is now working on the fifth volume, exploring the impact of the Reformation and the Counter-Reformation. I haven't come across any books specifically about the decline of Christian contemplation in the West and the cultural attack on mysticism, which seems a worthwhile topic.

3. Breuer, Joseph, and Sigmund Freud. *Studies in Hysteria*. London: Hogarth Press, 1955.

4. Kerouac, Jack. *The Dharma Bums*. London: Penguin, 2011.

5. Kabat-Zinn, Jon. 'Some reflections on the origins of MBSR, skilful means, and the trouble with maps'. In Kabat-Zinn, Jon, and Mark Williams (eds), *Mindfulness: Diverse Perspectives on its Meaning, Origins and Applications*. London: Routledge, 2013.

6. Flanagan, Owen. *The Bodhisattva's Brain: Buddhism Naturalized*. Cambridge: MIT Press, 2011.

7. See, for example, Antoine Lutz *et al.*, 'Long-term meditators self-induce high-amplitude gamma synchrony during mental practice'. *Proceedings of the National Academy of Sciences*, Vol. 101, No. 46.

8. Black, D. A. 'Mindfulness research publications by year, 1980–2013'. American Mindfulness Research Association website: https://goamra.org/resources/find-program.

9. Figures from the American Mindfulness Research Association: https://goamra.org/resources/find-program.

10. Busch, Volker, *et al.* 'The effect of deep and slow breathing on pain perception, autonomic activity, and mood processing – an experimental study'. *Pain Medicine*, Vol. 13, No. 2 (February 2012).

11. Benson, Herbert. *The Relaxation Response*. London: Avon Books, 2000.

12. Lutz, Antoine, *et al.* 'Regulation of the Neural Circuitry of Emotion by Compassion Meditation: Effects of Meditative Expertise'. *PLOS One*, 26 March 2008.

13. Williams, Mark, and Danny Penman. *Mindfulness: A Practical Guide to Finding Peace in a Frantic World*. London: Piatkus, 2011.

14. Kornfield, Jack. 'Intensive Insight Meditation: A Phenomenological Study'. *Journal of Transpersonal Psychology*, Vol. 11, No. 1 (1979).

15. Goleman, Daniel. *The Meditative Mind*. New York: G. P. Putnam, 1988.

16. Quoted in McGinn, Bernard, *Essential Writings of Christian Mysticism*. London: Modern Library, 2006.

17. Williams, Mark. Introduction to Stead, Tim, *Mindfulness and Christian Spirituality: Making Space for God*. London: SPCK, 2016.

18. Maupin, Edward. 'On Meditation'. In Tart, Charles (ed.), *Altered States of Consciousness*. New York: Harper Collins, 1990.

19. Leigh Fermor, Patrick. *A Time to Keep Silence*. London: John Murray, 1957.

20. Huxley, Aldous. *The Perennial Philosophy*. London: Harper Perennial, 2009.

21. Weber, Max. 'Science as a Vocation'. *The Vocation Lectures*. London: Hackett, 2004.

7: The Tantric Love Temple

1. Urban, Hugh. *Zorba the Buddha: Sex, Spirituality, and Capitalism in the Global Osho Movement*. Oakland: University of California Press, 2016.

2. This and all further quotes on Osho from Urban, *Zorba*.

3. Scruton, Roger. *Modern Culture*. London: Continuum Books, 1998.

4. May, Simon. *Love: A History*. London: Yale University Press, 2011.

5. Sontag, Susan. 'The Pornographic Imagination'. *The Susan Sontag Reader*. New York: Farrar, Strauss and Giroux, 1982.

6. See Skinner, Marilyn, *Sexuality in Greek and Roman Culture*. London: Wiley-Blackwell, 2013.

7. See Dodds, E. R., 'The Greek shamans and the origins of Puritanism', *The Greeks and the Irrational*. Oakland: University of California Press, 2004.

8. Zaehner, Robert Charles. *Mysticism, Sacred and Profane: An Inquiry into Some Varieties of Praeternatural Experience*. Oxford: Oxford University Press, 1957.

9. Kripal, Jeffrey. *Roads of Excess, Palaces of Wisdom: Eroticism and Reflexivity in the Study of Mysticism*. Chicago: University of Chicago Press, 2001.

10. Berkowitz, Eric. *Sex and Punishment: Four Thousand Years of Judging Desire*. New York: Counterpoint, 2012.

11. Porter, Roy. 'Mixed feelings: The Enlightenment and sexuality in eighteenth-century Britain'. In Boucé, Paul-Gabriel (ed.), *Sexuality in Eighteenth-century Britain*. Manchester: Manchester University Press, 1982.

12. Dabhoiwala, Faramerz. *The Origins of Sex: A History of the First Sexual Revolution*. Oxford: Oxford University Press, 2012.

13. Podmore, Colin. *The Moravian Church in England, 1728–1760*. London: Clarendon Press, 1998.

14. On the sexual spirituality of the Moravians, Blake and Swedenborg, I am indebted to Schuchard, Marsha Keith, *Why Mrs Blake Cried: William Blake and the Erotic Imagination*. London: Century, 2006.

15. Woolf, Virginia. *Moments of Being: Autobiographical Writings*. London: Pimlico, 2002.

16. Urban, Hugh. *Magia Sexualis: Sex, Magic and Liberation in Modern Western Esotericism*. Oakland: University of California Press, 2006.

17. Kripal, Jeffrey. *Authors of the Impossible: The Paranormal and the Sacred*. Chicago: University of Chicago Press, 2010.

18. Turner, Chris. *Adventures in the Orgasmatron: How the Sexual Revolution Came to America*. New York: Farrar, Strauss and Giroux, 2011.

19. Lawrence, D. H. *Studies in Classic American Literature*. London: Penguin, 1990.

20. Quoted in Allyn, David, *Make Love, Not War: The Sexual Revolution, an Unfettered History*. London: Taylor & Francis, 2001.

21. Allyn, *Make Love, Not War*

22. Quoted in Miller, James, *The Passion of Michel Foucault*. Harvard: Harvard University Press, 2001.

23. Sade, Marquis de. 'Philosophy in the bedroom'. In *Justine, Philosophy in the Bedroom, and Other Writings*. New York: Grove Press, 2007.

24. Bataille, Georges. *Eroticism, Death and Sensuality*. San Francisco: City Lights, 1986.

25. Urban, *Magia Sexualis*.

26. Eno, Brian, and Grayson Perry. 'Brian Eno and Grayson Perry on how the internet taught us we are all perverts', *New Statesman*, 7 November 2013.

27. Quoted in Glucklich, Ariel, *Sacred Pain: Hurting the Body for the Sake of the Soul*. Oxford: Oxford University Press, 2001.

28. Quoted in Miller, *The Passion of Michel Foucault*.

29. Sagarin, Brad, *et al.* 'Consensual BDSM Facilitates Role-Specific Altered States of Consciousness: A Preliminary Study'. *Psychology of Consciousness*, 22 September 2016.

30. Scarry, Elaine. *The Body in Pain: The Making and Unmaking of the World*. Oxford: Oxford University Press, 1985.

31. Sosis, Richard, and Eric Bressler. 'Cooperation and Commune Longevity: A Test of the Costly Signaling Theory of Religion'. *Cross-Cultural Research*, Vol. 37, No. 2 (May 2003).

32. Kornfield, Jack. 'Sex Lives of the Gurus'. *Yoga Journal*, July/August 1985.

33. Wismeijer, A. A., and M. A. van Assen. 'Psychological characteristics of BDSM practitioners'. *Journal of Sexual Medicine*, Vol. 10, No. 8 (August 2013).

34. Miller, *The Passion of Michel Foucault*.

35. Wade, Jenny. *Transcendent Sex: When Love-Making Opens the Veil*. New York: Gallery Books, 2004.

36. Dawson, Lesel. *Lovesickness and Gender in Early Modern English Literature*. Oxford: Oxford University Press, 2004.

8: The Mosh-Pit

1. 'Young, British and Radicalised', *Newsbeat*, BBC Radio 1, 17 November 2015.

2. Ehrenreich, Barbara. *Blood Rites: Origins and History of the Passions of War*. New York: Henry Holt, 1997.

3. Quoted in Harari, Yuval Noah, *The Ultimate Experience: Battlefield Revelations and the Making of Modern War Culture, 1450–2000*. London: Palgrave Macmillan, 2008.

4. Broyles, William. 'Why Men Love War', *Esquire*, November 1984.

5. Gray, John. *Straw Dogs: Thoughts on Humans and Other Animals*. London: Granta Books, 2002.

6. Hedges, Chris. *War Is a Force that Gives Us Meaning*. New York: PublicAffairs, 2002.

7. Buford, Bill. *Among the Thugs: The Experience, and the Seduction, of Crowd Violence*. London: Harvill Secker, 1990.

8. Churchill, Winston. *The Story of the Malakand Field Force: An Episode of Frontier War*. London: Dover Books, 1897.

9. Harari, *The Ultimate Experience*.

10. 'Young, British and Radicalised', *Newsbeat*, 2015.

11. Quoted in Elias, Norbert, *The Civilizing Process*. Oxford: Blackwell, 1994.

12. Jeffrey, James. 'Iraq Is Always With You', *The Guardian*, 18 March 2013.

13. Quoted in Ehrenreich, *Blood Rites*.

14. Junger, Sebastian. *Tribe: On Homecoming and Belonging*. London: Hachette, 2016.

15. Ath-Thaghri, Abul Harith. 'And as for the blessing of your Lord then mention it', *Dabiq*, Issue 11.

16. Popper, Karl. *The Open Society and its Enemies*. Princeton: Princeton University Press, 2013.

17. Quoted in Creswell, Robyn, and Bernard Haykel, 'Battle Lines', *New Yorker*, 8 and 15 June 2015.

18. Atran, Scott. 'Why ISIS has the potential to be a world-altering revolution', *Aeon,* 15 December 2015.

19. LeShan, Lawrence. *The Psychology of War: Comprehending its Mystique and its Madness*. New York: Helios Press, 2002.

20. Quoted in Nabeelah Jaffer, 'The secret world of ISIS brides', *The Guardian*, 24 June 2015.

21. Quoted in 'Young, British and Radicalised', *Newsbeat*, 2015.

22. Cohn, Norman. *The Pursuit of the Millennium: Revolutionary Millenarians and Mystical Anarchists of the Middle Ages*. Oxford: Oxford University Press, 1983.

23. Pew Research Centre. 'The World's Muslims: Unity and Diversity', 9 August, 2012.

24. Pew Research Centre. 'Jesus Christ's Return to Earth', 14 July 2010.

25. Burkert, Walter. *Greek Religion: Archaic and Classical*. Harvard: Harvard University Press, 1985.

26. See Girard, René. *Violence and the Sacred*. Baltimore: Johns Hopkins University Press, 1977.

27. Quoted in Cohn, *The Pursuit of the Millennium*.

28. 'The preachings of Abu Hamza', Press Association, 7 February 2006.

29. Wood, Graham. 'What ISIS really want', *The Atlantic*, March 2015.

30. Witnesses at the gay club say Mateen was a regular, and his ex-wife said he had 'gay tendencies'.

31. Jung, Carl. *The Essential Jung*. London: Fontana Press, 1998.

32. See Cavanaugh, William, *The Myth of Religious Violence: Secular Ideology and the Roots of Modern Conflict*. Oxford: Oxford University Press, 2009.

33. Elias, *The Civilizing Process*.

34. 'Homicidal thoughts are common for teens', *Monitor on Psychology*, APA, June 2000.

35. Pinker, Steven. *The Better Angels of our Nature: Why Violence Has Declined*. London: Viking Books, 2011.

36. Cavanaugh, *The Myth of Religious Violence*. See also Wilson, Peter H., *Europe's Tragedy: A New History of the Thirty Years War*. London: Penguin, 2010.

37. Tocqueville, Alexis de. 'The origins of the French Revolution'. In *Alexis de Tocqueville on Democracy, Revolution and Society*. Chicago: University of Chicago Press, 1982.

38. Quoted in Schama, Simon, *Citizens: A Chronicle of the French Revolution*. London: Random House, 1989.

39. See McNeill, William. *Keeping Together in Time: Dance and Drill in Human History*. Harvard: Harvard University Press, 1995.

40. Quoted in Schama, *Citizens*.

41. Tolstoy, Leo. *War and Peace*. London: Penguin Classics, 2006.

42. Carlyle, Thomas. *On Heroes, Hero-Worship, and the Heroic in History*. London: James Fraser, 1841.

43.	Quoted in Kershaw, Ian, *The 'Hitler Myth': Image and Reality in the Third Reich*. Oxford: Oxford University Press, 2001.

44.	Both quotes in this paragraph are from Ehrenreich, *Blood Rites*.

45.	See the *Atlantic's* video of a 2016 post-election alt-right conference, available online here: https://www.youtube.com/watch?v=1o6-bi3jlxk.

46.	Elias, *The Civilizing Process*.

47.	Elias, Norbert, and Eric Dunning. *The Quest for Excitement: Sport and Leisure in the Civilizing Process*. Dublin: University College Dublin Press, 2008.

48.	Csíkszentmihályi, Mihály. *Applications of Flow in Human Development and Education*. London: Springer, 2014.

49.	Quoted in Elias and Dunning, *The Quest for Excitement*.

50.	See Taylor, Jacob, and Emma Cohen, 'Moving in sync allows the body to do things it couldn't do alone', *Aeon*, 18 July 2016.

51.	Dietrich, A. 'Functional neuroanatomy of altered states of consciousness: the transient hypofrontality hypothesis'. *Conscious Cognition*, Vol. 12, No. 2 (June 2003).

52.	Quoted in Kotler, Steven, *The Rise of Superman: Decoding the Science of Ultimate Human Performance*. New York: Houghton Mifflin Harcourt, 2014.

53.	Quoted in Peralta, Stacy, *Riding Giants*. StudioCanal, 2005.

54.	Foster Wallace, David. 'Roger Federer as Religious Experience', *New York Times*, 20 August 2006.

55.	Quoted in 'The greatest try ever scored', BBC Sport, 26 January 2013.

56.	Dyer, Geoff. *White Sands: Experiences from the Outside World*. London: Penguin, 2016.

57.	Barnes, Simon. 'Murray ends 77-year wait for British win', *The Times*, 8 July 2013.

58.	In Peralta, *Riding Giants*.

59.	Dean, Will. 'A reason to feel sorry for Premier League footballers?' *The Independent*, 4 May 2013.

60.	See Kuper, Simon. *Football Against the Enemy*. London: Orion, 2011.

61.	See Donovan, Jack. *The Way of Men*. New York: Dissonant Hum, 2012. See also Evans, Jules, 'How the alt-right emerged from men's self-help', *Philosophy for Life*, available here: http://www.philosophyforlife.org/how-the-alt-right-emerged-from-mens-self-help.

9: The Forest of Wonder

1.	Eisenstein, Charles. 'The Earth Talks', Schumacher College, 22 September 2015.

Available online: https://www.youtube.com/watch?v=losz7_A14Cw

2. Berry, Thomas. *The Great Work: Our Way Into the Future*. New York: Harmony/ Bell Tower, 1999.

3. Campbell, Colin. 'Ritual, Omens and Divination', Schumacher College, 2 July 2014. Available online: https://www.youtube.com/watch?v=kqUKS1G8tTA.

4. Berry, *The Great Work*.

5. McKenna, Terence. *Food of the Gods: The Search for the Original Tree of Knowledge*. London: Rider Books, 1992.

6. Harding, Stephan. 'Gaia theory and deep ecology: an interview'. Available online: https://www.youtube.com/watch?v=523bXlK5t34.

7. Quoted in Clément, Olivier, *The Roots of Christian Mysticism*. New York: New City Press, 1996.

8. Quoted in Daston, Lorraine, and Katherine Park, *Wonders and the Order of Nature, 1150–1750*. London: Zone Books, 1998.

9. Quoted in Waal, Esther de, *Every Earthly Blessing: Rediscovering the Celtic Tradition*. New York: Morehouse Books, 1999.

10. Daston and Park, *Wonders and the Order of Nature*.

11. Dawkins, Richard. 'Is Science a Religion?', *Humanist*, January/February 1997.

12. Lewis, C. S. *The Letters of C. S. Lewis to Arthur Greeves*. London: William Collins, 1979.

13. There is no widely available edition of Traherne's *Centuries of Meditation*, if you can believe it. I very much hope a mainstream publisher will bring one out. You can get versions of it on ebook, such as the 2009 Christian Classics Ethereal Library edition, or selections in Inge, Denise, *Happiness and Holiness: Thomas Traherne and His Writings*. Canterbury: Canterbury Press, 2010.

14. Burke, Edmund. *A Philosophical Enquiry into the Origin of our Ideas of the Sublime and Beautiful*. Oxford: Oxford World's Classics, 2008.

15. Myers, Frederic. *Wordsworth*. New York: Harper & Brothers, 1887.

16. De Quincey, Thomas. *Recollections of the Lake Poets*. London: Penguin, 1970.

17. Quoted in Purdy, Jedediah, *After Nature: A Politics for the Arthropocene*. Harvard: Harvard University Press, 2015.

18. Loud, Richard. *Last Child in the Woods: Saving our Children from Nature-Deficit Disorder*. New York: Workman Publishing, 2005.

19. Monbiot, George. 'Falling in Love Again', *The Guardian*, 17 July 2015.

20. Bratman, Gregory, *et al.* 'Nature experience reduces rumination and subgenual prefrontal cortex activation', *Proceedings of the National Academy of Sciences*, Vol. 112, No. 28.

21. Vormbrock, J. K., and J. M. Grossberg. 'Cardiovascular effects of human-pet dog interaction'. *Journal of Behavioural Medicine*, Vol. 11, No. 5 (October 1988). See also Nagasawa, Miho, *et al.* 'Oxytocin-gaze positive loop and the co-evolution of human-dog bonds', *Science*, Vol. 348, Issue 6232 (17 April 2015).

22. See for example http://warriorcanineconnection.org. See also Rogers *et al.*, 'High-intensity sports for post-traumatic stress disorder and depression: feasibility study of ocean therapy'. *American Journal of Occupational Therapy* (July 2014). For a general overview, see Phillips, Dave, 'Scuba, parrots, yoga: veterans embrace alternative therapies for PTSD', *New York Times*, 17 September 2015.

23. Safran Foer, Jonathan. *Eating Animals*. New York: Hachette, 2009.

24. See Kaireva, Peter, 'Failed metaphors and a New Environmentalism for the 21st Century', *Distinctive Voices*. Available here: https://www.youtube.com/watch?v=4BOEQkvCook.

25. Kaireva, 'Failed metaphors'.

26. Jewkes Rachel, *et al.* 'Prevalence of and factors associated with non-partner rape perpetration: findings from the UN Multi-country Cross-Sectional Study of Men and Violence in Asia and the Pacific'. *Lancet Global Health*, Vol. 1, Issue 4.

27. See Rosenau, Josh. 'Evolution, the Environment, and Religion'. Available here: https://ncse.com/blog/2015/05/evolution-environment-religion-0016359.

28. Baker, J. A. *The Peregrine*. London: Collins, 2011.

29. Quoted in Wulf, Andrea, *The Invention of Nature: The Adventures of Alexander von Humboldt*. New York: Alfred A. Knopf, 2015.

10: Futureland

1. You can watch Jason Silva's Shots of Awe here: https://www.youtube.com/user/ShotsOfAwe.

2. Harari, Yuval Noah. *Homo Deus: A Brief History of Tomorrow*. London: Vintage, 2016.

3. Huxley, Julian. *New Bottles for New Wine*. New York: Harper & Brothers, 1957).

4. Kripal, Jeffrey. *Mutants and Mystics: Science Fiction, Superheroes, and the Paranormal*. Chicago: University of Chicago Press, 2011.

5. Tom Wolfe, quoted in Brown, Mick, 'I never took LSD, it was far too dangerous', *Daily Telegraph*, 4 November 2016.

6.   Markoff, John. *What the Dormouse Said: How the Sixties Counterculture Shaped the Personal Computer Industry*. London: Penguin, 2005.

7.   Cadwalladr, Carole. 'Stewart Brand's *Whole Earth Catalog*, the book that changed the world', *The Observer*, 5 May 2013.

8.   Quoted in Turner, Fred, *From Counterculture to Cyberculture: Stewart Brand, the Whole Earth Catalog, and the Rise of Digital Utopianism*. Chicago: University of Chicago Press, 2006.

9.   Leary, Timothy. Introduction to *The Politics of Ecstasy*. Berkeley: Ronin Publishing, 1998.

10. Sirius, R. U. *Transcendence: The Disinformation Encyclopaedia of Transhumanism and the Singularity*. New York: Disinformation Books, 2015.

11. Davis, Erik. *Tech-Gnosis: Myth, Magic and Mysticism in the Age of Information*. New York: Harmony Press, 1998.

12. Lanier, Jaron. *You Are Not A Gadget: A Manifesto*. London: Penguin, 2010.

13. Kelly, Kevin. *The Inevitable: Understanding the 12 Technological Forces That Will Shape Our Future*. London: Viking Press, 2016.

14. MacIver, Malcolm. 'The Geek Rapture and Other Musings of William Gibson'. *Discover* blog, 17 October 2011.

15. Kurzweil, Ray. *The Singularity Is Near: When Humans Transcend Biology*. London: Viking Press, 2006.

16. Brautigan, Richard. *All Watched Over By Machines of Loving Grace*. San Francisco: Communication Company, 1967.

17. Isaacson, Walter. *Steve Jobs*. New York: Simon & Schuster, 2011.

18. Isaacson, *Steve Jobs*.

19. Quoted in Sam Binkley, *Happiness as Enterprise: An Essay on Neoliberal Life*. New York: SUNY Press, 2014.

20. Berlinger, Joe. 'I am not your guru', Netflix, 14 March 2016.

21. See Lyons, Daniel, *Disrupted: My Misadventures in the Start-up Bubble*. New York: Hachette, 2016.

22. Carr, Nicholas. *Utopia Is Creepy: And Other Provocations*. New York: W. W. Norton, 2016.

23. Elliott, Larry. 'Robots threaten 15m UK jobs, says Bank of England's chief economist', *The Guardian*, 12 November 2015.

24. Krueger, Alan. 'Where have all the workers gone?' Paper presented at Boston Federal Reserve Bank's Economic Conference, 14 October 2016.

25. McLuhan, Marshall. 'Love', *Saturday Night Magazine*, February 1967.

26. Carr, *Utopia Is Creepy*.

27. Lanier, Jaron. 'The Myth of AI: A Conversation With Jaron Lanier', *Edge*, 14 November 2014.

28. Davis, *Tech-Gnosis*.

29. Thiel, Peter. 'The education of a libertarian', *Cato Unbound*, 13 April 2009.

Acknowledgements

There's a fair amount of material that didn't make it into the book, including my experience learning how to lucid dream, and a visit to a spiritualist medium. You can find the bonus material here: www.philosophyforlife.org/lose-control.

At that link you can also read the full interviews with several of the people in the book, check out the full results of the surveys I referred to, and see my list for recommended further reading. And you can sign up for my newsletter, find out where I'm doing talks, and follow what I'm researching now - the journey continues!

A big thank-you to Professor Thomas Dixon at the Centre for the History of Emotions, and the Wellcome Trust for funding my research. Thanks to the brilliant Will Francis – an agent who genuinely loves books. Thanks to Jenny Lord, for all her help in making this project happen, to Simon Thorogood for wise, patient editing advice, to Hazel Orme for expert sub-editing, and to all the brilliant people at Canongate, as well as my other publishers abroad (particularly Regine Dugardyn). Thanks to the BBC and AHRC for their support over the years, including through the New Generation Thinker scheme. Thanks to Vanessa Chamberlin, Sebastian Ling and Oliver Robinson for reading drafts of chapters. A huge thanks to all my interviewees. Thanks to the various communities who let me in, particularly HTB and Saracens. If I've offended anyone, I apologise – this is such a personal, emotionally charged topic, and I'm sure I've got many things wrong. Thanks to friends and blog readers for feedback, suggestions and survey responses. Thanks to my substitute church group. Thanks to my family for their love and support. And thanks to God (there, I said it!).

Index

257

THE
RUNAWAY
SPECIES

HOW HUMAN CREATIVITY
REMAKES THE WORLD

ANTHONY BRANDT
& DAVID EAGLEMAN

THE INTERNATIONALLY BESTSELLING AUTHOR
OF *THE BRAIN*, *INCOGNITO* AND *SUM*

'The unaccountable, jaw-dropping quality of genius'
Geoff Dyer, *Observer*

CANON‖GATE

GEOFF DYER

WHITE SANDS

From the author of YOGA FOR PEOPLE WHO CAN'T BE BOTHERED TO DO IT

Experiences from the Outside World

'Brilliant . . . Dyer's eyes miss nothing'
Peter Conrad, *Observer*

'A national treasure' Zadie Smith

CANON ❚❚ GATE

INSANELY GIFTED

TURN YOUR DEMONS INTO CREATIVE ROCKET FUEL

JAMIE CATTO

'A friendly warning: prolonged exposure to Jamie Catto
could blow your mind' *DAILY TELEGRAPH*

'Crucially, tangibly useful' *Sunday Times*

CANON ▌▌GATE